The English fi

A history of the development of the chimney, chimney-piece and firegrate with their accessories, from the earliest times to the beginning of the XIXth century

L. A. Shuffrey

Alpha Editions

This edition published in 2019

ISBN : 9789389525175

Design and Setting By
Alpha Editions
email - alphaedis@gmail.com

THE · ENGLISH FIREPLACE

A HISTORY OF THE DEVELOPMENT OF THE CHIMNEY, CHIMNEY-PIECE AND FIREGRATE WITH THEIR ACCESSORIES
From the Earliest Times to the Beginning of the XIXth Century

By

L. A. SHUFFREY

ILLUSTRATED BY 130 COLLOTYPE PLATES
FROM PHOTOGRAPHS CHIEFLY BY
W. GALSWORTHY DAVIE
WITH MANY OTHER ILLUSTRATIONS

LONDON

B. T. BATSFORD, 94 HIGH HOLBORN

Preface

SOME years ago my friend Mr. W. Galsworthy Davie, whose photographs of architectural work are known to many, turned his attention to photographing the fine examples of old chimney-pieces which he met with in his various photographic tours, and asked me to co-operate with him in the production of a book on the subject of the Fireplace and its accessories. I accepted the task light-heartedly, thinking that some thirty years' association with grates and chimney-pieces would have made it an easy one for me, but in this I was mistaken, as I soon found that the subject required much personal research and a further study of old examples, as well as the making of numerous sketches and measured drawings for the elucidation of its history. It became necessary also to get Mr. Davie to photograph many important examples in historic houses, and so, by filling in the gaps, produce a representative collection.

The fireplace, as the spot around which family life has centred, must always retain its interest, and the open form has remained popular in England to a greater extent probably than in any other country. Constructed at first on lines of the severest utility, it grew in importance during the Gothic period, and still more during the Elizabethan Renaissance, when the chimney-piece became the most important feature of the room and both thought and skill were lavished upon it. From that time it has reflected the changes of style in architecture, so that to give an account of its treatment at the hands of architects, carvers and sculptors up to the end of the eighteenth century is to review the phases of decorative art of each period. Built of plain stone or brick at first, we afterwards find it embellished with elaborate wood carving during the Tudor and Stuart periods, and settling down in the last half of the eighteenth century to works in marble of modesty and refinement.

I desire, on behalf of both Mr. Davie, my publisher and myself, to thank the numerous owners of the buildings containing the examples given for kindly allowing them to be photographed or drawn, and as their number is great I hope that they will accept this general acknowledgment of their kindness.

In addition to the plates and illustrations supplied by Mr. Davie other photographers have been good enough to contribute examples of one kind or another; particulars of whose work will be found set forth in the note of acknowledgment, as well as details of my indebtedness to draughtsmen and others for illustrations that they have kindly supplied.

I cannot conclude without expressing my thanks to my publishers, Mr. Herbert Batsford and Mr. Harry Batsford, for the assistance which they have given me, and particularly to the latter for his help in superintending the production of the book which has been unduly prolonged by me.

L. A. SHUFFREY.

38, Welbeck Street,
Cavendish Square,
July, 1912.

Note of Acknowledgment

MY thanks are firstly due to Mr. W. Galsworthy Davie, whose journeyings have brought to light many interesting examples and whose photographs, as mentioned in the preface, form the greater part of both plates and photographic text illustrations. The following are the illustrations which have been supplied from other sources :—

Mr. Harold Baker, Birmingham, Plate xx; Mr. Herbert Bell, Ambleside, Plate xxi; Mr. J. A. Cossins, Birmingham, Figs. 147 and 148; Mrs. Delves Broughton, Figs. 11 and 150, Plates lxxxiv, xci; Mr. Horace Dan, Rochester, Figs. 186–8, Plates xvii, xcix, cxxviii; Mr. G. Fryer, Brentford, Plate lxii; Mr. J. Henry Hogg, Kendal, Figs. 99 and 100; Mr. Jarman, Bury St. Edmunds, Plate xc; Mr. Kevis, Petworth, Plate v; Messrs. Bedford Lemere & Co., London, Plates xxii–iii, ciii, cviii, cix; Mr. Thomas Lewis, Birmingham, Plates lxxii, lxxiii, civ* and civ**; Mr. E. Milner, London, Plate cxxviii; Messrs. H. P. Robinson & Son, Reigate, Plate xiii; Messrs. R. Wilkinson & Co., Trowbridge, Fig. 98.

Mr. Arthur Bulleid has kindly permitted the reproduction of Fig. 2; the executors of the late Dan Gibson of Fig. 149, drawn by him; Figs. 10, 79 and 166 are redrawn by permission from *Country Life*, and Figs. 143 and 145 are from *The Connoisseur*. My publisher has lent me various illustrations from his works on English Architecture, while I have to thank Mr. T. A. Williams for his sketches of the Conway Castle fireplaces; Mr. W. T. Walker for his drawing of the fireplace in the Abbey Ruins, Reading; the Authorities of the British Museum for permission to reproduce the Holbein drawing forming the frontispiece (the photograph by Artists Illustrators, Ltd.); and Mr. Walter Spiers for permission to photograph designs by the Adam Brothers in the Soane Museum. Drawings not otherwise specified are by me.

L. A. S.

CONTENTS

The plates are placed as near as possible to their references, except in the sections on The Elizabethan Renaissance and Later Renaissance Chimneypieces. There the plates are so numerous that to have placed them according to their positions in the text would have greatly impeded ready reference; they are, therefore, grouped at the end of each division; see particulars overleaf.

BRIEF SUBJECT LIST OF EXAMPLES ILLUSTRATED

Note.—Ordinary numbers refer to the figures of the Text Illustrations, and Roman numerals denote Plates. Illustrations are not referred to under their pages in this list.

References such as *p. xi.* are to Illustrations in the Introduction.

It is obviously impossible to index the book fully as regards minor subjects or accessories, examples of which occur on almost every plate. Plates or text illustrations devoted exclusively to such subjects have been indexed under their respective heads, and the more prominent examples occurring on the general plates have also been included. Under CHIMNEYPIECE and FIREPLACE the main divisions alone could be indicated; more detailed references will be found under the headings of the various styles.

TOPOGRAPHICAL LIST OF SUBJECTS ILLUSTRATED

(PLATES & TEXT ILLUSTRATIONS)

Note.—In the third column ordinary figures refer to the figure numbers (not the pages) of text illustrations, and Roman numerals to plates. In the description column, F denotes that the subject illustrated is a Fireplace.

All references to metropolitan examples are collected under the word LONDON, which thus forms a small sub-index.

Subject names of Accessories, etc. (e.g. Grates, Andirons, etc.), will be found in the separate Subject List of Illustrations which precedes the present one.

Roman figure *page* references (in italics) are to the Illustrations of the Introduction.

Subject.	Description.	Plate or Fig. No.	Page where referred to.
ABINGDON ABBEY ..	Chimney	19 ..	20
„ „ ..	Dormitory F	21 ..	22
„ „ ..	Upper Room F	18 ..	20
ADAM BROTHERS ..	Designs in the Soane Museum	181–2 ..	202, 204
„ GRATES	„ „ „	186–7 ..	208
„ MANTEL	In the V. & A. Museum ..	184 ..	206
ANCIENT MANUSCRIPT	Illustration of Hooded Fire ..	78 ..	71
ASTON HALL, Warwicks.	The Long Gallery F ..	XX ..	104
„ „ „	Hob Fireplace	147 ..	152
„ „ „	Tiled Fireplace	148 ..	154
AUDLEY END, Essex ..	Drawing room F	XXXII ..	111
„ „ „ ..	Great Hall F	XXXIII ..	111
AYDON CASTLE	Chimney	22 ..	23
BAMPTON CASTLE, Oxon	Upper Room F	29 ..	29
BANBURY, Oxon, REIN-DEER HOTEL	Globe Room F	LII ..	118
BARNSTAPLE, CROSS ST.	Plaster Overmantel	LX ..	121
„	Oak Chimney-piece	XLI ..	115
BARRINGTON COURT ..	Stone Chimney	58*a* ..	49
BASKET GRATE	With Standards	149 ..	154
BELTON HOUSE, Grantham	Dining-room F	156 ..	166
„ „ „	Chapel Gallery F	..	*p. xxxvii*
BLENHEIM PALACE ..	Marble Chimney-piece ..	165 ..	179

Subject.	Description.	Plate or Fig. No.	Page where referred to.
CHRISTCHURCH, Hants	Norman Chimney	17	.. 18
CLEEVE ABBEY, Somerset	Refectory Fireplace	40	.. 40
COBHAM HALL, Kent ..	Long Gallery F	XIV	.. 101
,, ,, ,, ..	Music room F	CXXIV	..
COBHAM, Kent	Hall of Almshouses	32	.. 29
CONINGSBURGH CASTLE	Interior of Keep	15	.. 17
,, ,,	Upper F	16	.. 17
CONWAY, PLAS MAWR	F	VIII	.. 87
,, ,, ,,	Withdrawing room F ..	88	.. 87
CONWAY CASTLE ..	Banqueting Hall F	30	.. 28
,, - ,, ..	Round Tower F	31	.. 29
COTE HOUSE, Oxon ..	Stone Chimney Stack ..	116	.. 127
COVENTRY, ST. MARY'S GUILDHALL	Kitchen Fireplaces	64	.. 58
DARTMOUTH BUTTER WALK	Overmantel	L	.. 118
DODINGTON HALL, Som.	Hall Fireplace	97	.. 97
DUNSFOLD, Sussex ..	Chimney Corner	86	.. 77
EAST BARSHAM, Norfolk	Brick Chimney	58	.. 49
EASTON NESTON, Nthants.	Dining-room F	166	.. 180
ELHAM, Kent	Stone Fireplace Lintel and Overmantel	LIV	.. 119
ENFIELD	F in Old Palace	XVII	.. 102
ENMORE, TYRLANDS FARM, Somerset	Fireplace and Chimney ..	74	.. 67
EWHURST, Surrey ..	Chimney Corner	87	.. 79
GIBBS, JAMES ARCHBL.	Design for Chimney-piece ..	167	.. 181
GILLING CASTLE, Yorks.	Great Chamber F	100	.. 109
GLASTONBURY, Somerset	Plan of Kitchen	60	.. *p. xxx*, 53
,, ,,	Section of ditto	62	.. 54
,, ,,	Kitchen F	61	.. 54
,, ,,	Ditto, exterior	63	.. 56
,, MARSH VILLAGE	Plan of British Hut	2	.. 2
GLINTON, Northants ..	Stone Chimney	110	.. 126
GODALMING, UNSTEAD FARM	Brick Chimney Stack ..	115	.. 127
GOMSHALL, Surrey ..	Chimney Stack	88	.. 79
GRANTHAM, CHURCH *See also* Belton House	Library F	50	.. 44
GREAT CHALFIELD, Wilts	Chimney	55	.. 48
GREENWICH, KING'S PALACE	Design by Inigo Jones ..	150*a*	.. 159

Subject.	Description.	Plate or Fig. No.	Page where referred to.
GRETTON, Northants ..	Plaster Overpiece	105	.. 121
GROOMBRIDGE PLACE	Cast-iron Fireback	LXV	.. 137
GUILDFORD CASTLE ..	Gatehouse F	XXIII	.. 104
„ GUILDHALL	Mayor's Parlour F	LI	.. —
HADDON HALL, Derbysh.	Dining-room F	52	.. 53
„ „ „	State Bedroom F	LIX	.. 120
„ „ „	Brass Firedogs and Grate ..	138	.. 143
„ „ „	Brass Rosette Firedogs ..	140	... 145
HALIFAX, OLD COCK INN	Cast Firedogs	141	.. 146
HALL STOVE	Eighteenth century example ..	196	.. 215
HALTON HOUSE, HASTINGS	Marble Chimney-piece ..	CXXV	.. —
HAM HOUSE, PETERSHAM	Silver-mounted Fire-pan, Fire-iron and Bellows	144	.. 148
„ „	Fireirons		.. *p. xxxv*
„ „	Tapestry Room F	LXXXIX	.. 171
HAMPTON COURT PALACE	Brick Chimney	56	.. 49
„ „ „	Wolsey's Kitchen	IV	.. 59
„ „ „	Silver-gilt Andirons	145	.. 147
„ „ „	King's Drawing-room F ..	LXXIX	.. 161
„ „ „	King's Private Dressing-room F	LXXX	.. 162
„ „ „	King's Dressing-room F ..	LXXXI	.. 163
„ „ „	King's Gallery F	153	.. 165
„ „ „	Queen's Gallery F	LXXXII	.. 165
HARDWICK HALL, Derby	The Great Hall F	XIX	.. 103
HARRINGWORTH, Nthants.	Turret Chimney	35	.. 32
HIGHGATE, Kent ..	Cast-iron Fireback	67	.. 138
HIGH WYCOMBE, Bucks	Wood Mantel in London & County Bank	168	.. 183
„ „ „	Fireplace in the Adam style ..	184	.. 206
HOB GRATE	In the Adam style		.. *p. xlii*
HOLBEIN, HANS ..	Design for Chimney-piece ..	*Frontispiece*	.. 82
HOLKHAM HALL, Norfolk	Inigo Jones' Design with drapery	170	.. 185
„ „ „	The Sculpture Gallery ..	171	.. 186
„ „ „	The Drawing-room	172	.. 187
HOLLAND HOUSE, *see under* LONDON.			
HORHAM HALL, Essex ..	Enamelled Andirons now in the V. & A. Museum ..	146	.. 147
HORSHAM PARK, Sussex	Dining-room F	XCVII	.. 182
„ „ „	Drawing-room F	CII	.. 184
HORTON HALL, Northants	Marble Chimney-piece ..	175	.. 193

Subject.	Description.	Plate or Fig. No.	Page where referred to.
LONDON—			
3, TENTERDEN ST.	Drawing-room F	CVI	190
,, ,,	Back Drawing-room F	CVII	191
70, WIMPOLE STREET	Drawing-room F	CXXII	206
LOSELEY, Surrey	Great Chamber F	IX	95
,, ,,	Dining-room F	X	95
LOWER LYPIATT, Glos.	Stone Chimney-piece	LXXXVII	170
LUDLOW CASTLE	Upper Room F	28, 49	27, 44
LYDDINGTON BEDE HOUSE	Upper Chamber F	43	38
MAIDENHEAD	"St. Ives," F at	CI	184
MANTEL-BEAMS	Kelvedon, Essex	84	74
,, ,,	V. & A. Museum	82	74
,, ,,	Taunton Museum	81	75
,, ,,	The Cedars, Hillingdon	83	75
,, ,,	Faversham, Kent	85	75
MANUSCRIPT, MEDIEVAL	Illustration of Andirons	117	129
MEARE, Somerset	Stone Hooded Fireplace	27	27
MICKLETON, Glos.	Cotswold Stone Chimney	113	126
MINSTER LOVELL, Oxon	Ground-floor Fireplace	41	37
MONTACUTE, Somerset	Renaissance Chimney of Stone	108	123
MORETON, LITTLE, HALL, Cheshire	Retiring Room F	XI	96
MOYNS PARK, Essex	Brick Chimney-stack	106	123
,, ,, ,,	Bronze Firedogs	139	144
MUCHELNEY, Somerset	Priest's House F	75	69
NETLEY ABBEY, Hants	Stone Hooded Fireplace	20	22
NORTHBOROUGH, Nthants.	Turret Chimney	33	31
NORTHLEIGH, Oxon	Roman Villa Hypocaust	3	3
NORTON HALL, BURY ST. EDMUNDS	Drawing-room F	XC	182
NORWICH	Stone Chimney-pieces from, in V. & A. Museum	LV, LVI	120
OCKWELLS MANOR	F	VI	82
,, ,,	Billiard-room F	XXV	105
OXFORD, LINCOLN COLLEGE	Louver	4	6
,, BREWER ST.	Stone F	90	82
PENSHURST PLACE, Kent	Smoke Louver	5	10
,, ,, ,,	Central Hearth with Coupled Andirons	9	9

Introduction

IN the following pages an endeavour has been made to trace the development of the domestic fireplace in this country from its primitive form as a fire of wood or peat kindled on the earth or on a slab of stone in the centre of the Early British hut to that which it reached at the end of the eighteenth century, when it consisted of a highly finished steel grate for burning coal set in a richly carved marble chimney-piece. To follow the subject through the first half of the nineteenth century would exhibit both grate and mantel in their most degraded form, and to trace its vagarious course through the second half forms no part of the scope of this work.

A sufficient number of fireplaces still remain to illustrate the progress of our subject and to show the application of the succeeding styles of architecture to this useful part of a dwelling : from the Romanesque introduced by the Normans onward through the Gothic periods. That this is so is due to the fact that the fireplace then formed an integral part of the structure, and it is in ruined buildings where the floors have fallen away and laid bare their construction that these can be best studied, as at Colchester, Coningsburgh and Ludlow Castles.

The one apartment which stands out most prominently in the history of domestic habitations, from Saxon times and throughout the mediaeval period, is the common hall, the central chamber to which additions were made at each end as the house plan developed, the banqueting hall of the palace or manor-house, the dining hall of the college, hospital or bede-house, the house-place of the yeoman and the single living room of the cottage. This was sometimes referred to in old documents as the fire-house when it was the only apartment in which a fire was made.[1] The hall, placed usually on the ground floor, but sometimes over a basement, was invariably open to the roof, and its means of heating, which was singular to this apartment, was by a fire of logs on a central hearth. The smoke escaped in various ways, as through a hole in the roof or through the joints of its unplastered tiles, under the eaves or through an open door or window. In a large hall with a high roof, such as at

[1] *The Evolution of the English House*, by S.O. Addy, p. 59.

Stokesay Castle, it is imaginable that there may have been no great inconvenience in this arrangement, which utilised to the full extent the radiant heat from the fire; but in smaller halls, although the smoke from wood is less objectionable than that from coal, the discomfort attending the use of a central fire must have been considerable when we bear in mind that it often had to serve for both cooking by day and to sleep round by night. Chaucer in the *Nonne Preestes* tale says: "Full sooty was her bower and eek hir halle, in which she eet ful many a sclendre meal." Yet we learn from old writers that it was as late as the sixteenth century when chimneys first came into general use in the less important houses, and examples of the former plan may still be found in the crofters' homes of the Shetland Isles. Although recessed fireplaces with chimneys were constructed in the walls of other chambers in the twelfth century, they were not generally adopted for the hall until the fifteenth. The desire to get rid of the smoke from the central fire without admitting wind or rain led to the introduction of the smoke turret or louver. This was in use in Henry the Third's reign, several being mentioned in the Liberate Rolls, but none of so early a date remain. Constructed at first as an exit for the smoke only, it was later made to serve as a lantern also, and in the sixteenth century became an elaborate feature on the roof of the hall[1] (page 7).

As at this period, when windows in the walls were made exceptionally large, its use for giving light could not have been of great importance, it is probable that the dominant motive was to produce external effect.

One of the few central hearths that remain is in the fourteenth century hall of Penshurst Place, Kent, and on it stand the coupled andirons in their original position, although of later date than the building (Fig. 8). The ancient Yule-tide revels in these great halls must have presented a striking picture, when the ascending flames from this log-fire lighted up the gaily dressed company seen in contrast to the blackened timbers of the lofty oaken roof.

An alternative to the log-fire for this central position was the brazier; an iron pan standing on spreading legs in which charcoal or

[1] See drawing by S. H. Grimm of the louver over the great hall of Cowdray Castle, Midhurst, in *Domestic Architecture of England during the Tudor Period*, by Garner & Stratton (Fig. 97).

peat was burned. A simple one remains at Chastleton House, Oxon, but that these were sometimes more elaborate is shown by an item from the Bursar's Accounts given in *Willis's History of Cambridge*, by Jno. Willis Clarke, of £12 paid for a brazier for the hall of Trinity College, in 1702. It was in the halls of the colleges at Oxford and Cambridge that these remained latest in use. When gas-coke was substituted for charcoal the fumes were found to be so offensive that the central hearths were gradually abandoned in favour of fireplaces with chimneys which were inserted in the walls.

To find the origin of our present day fireplace we have to go back to the time when the Normans, in whose strongholds, built of two or more storeys, the central position was impracticable, placed the fire in a shallow recess under an arch in the side wall of the chamber. The back of the recess sloped in its ascent and finished with a hole for the escape of the smoke carried through the outside wall (Fig. 14). This may be seen at Colchester Castle, erected about 1080, and the same means of exit is found as late as Henry I's keep at Oxford.[1] This means of escape for the smoke does not appear to have been successful, as we find a flue carried up in the wall and finished with a tall cylindrical chimney at Christchurch, Hants, and Boothby Pagnell, Lincolnshire, both being Norman buildings. In the latter no recess is made for the fire, but a hood is constructed over the hearth to collect the smoke (see Illustration). Hoods may also be seen in two stages of development in the Coningsburgh Keep (Figs. 15 and 16).

FIREPLACE, BOOTHBY PAGNELL.

Fireplace hoods of stone sloping back to the wall continued to be built during the thirteenth and fourteenth centuries, the earlier having engaged jamb-shafts for support and the latter a series of projecting corbels. As fireplaces increased in numbers the tendency was towards a deeper hearth recess, when the hoods became unnecessary and ceased to be used.

The flat four-centred arch which came into use about the

[1] Ella S. Armitage, *Early Norman Castles of the British Isles.*

beginning of the fifteenth century was largely used for fireplaces, for which it is particularly suitable. These were either built flush with the wall or with a slight projection.

The deep lintel supplied an unrivalled position for the exercise of the art of the stone carver, of which he frequently availed himself, many being enriched with tracery, containing shields and badges and with foliage in the spandrels of the arches. These fireplaces were erected in days when no distinction was made by the craftsman between ecclesiastical and domestic work, and they consequently resemble closely the recessed wall tombs of the period. Some of the finest examples are those which have recently been so unfortunately ruined by being removed from their setting in the walls of Tattershall Castle, Lincolnshire (Plates I and II).[1] Whatever commercial value these may now have, their artistic worth is sadly diminished, as this depended so largely upon their fitness for the positions which they occupied, their broad and simple lines being in scale with the building, and their interesting detail shown to its fullest advantage in contrast to the plain brick walls.[2]

This was the period when the Gothic fireplace in England reached its highest development. In point of size and elaboration it never attained the importance given to many Continental examples; as those, for instance, in the Town Halls of Courtrai and Oudenarde. The hood was much sooner abandoned in this country than in France, and we have nothing to equal the examples of it at Langeais, Blois and other châteaux in the valley of the Loire. An exception may be made, certainly in point of size, in favour of the large triple fireplace in the Parliament Hall of Linlithgow Palace (see illustration), where a stone hood is carried on groups of clustered shafts over an opening 20 feet wide. This magnificent fireplace was erected by James IV of Scotland, and was probably built under French influence.

For the linings of fireplace recesses we find a continuous use of brick or tile in some form since the Norman period; those at Colchester Castle are of the large flat shape made by the Romans, at Abingdon Abbey they measure 9 inches by ¾ inch on the face,

[1] Since going to press we are pleased to see an announcement in the daily papers that these chimney pieces are re-instated in their original positions in the building.

[2] Measured drawings of the Castle in which two fireplaces are shown and their heraldry described will be found in a monograph of the Castle, by Fred R. Reed, 1872.

while at Bodiam Castle a large kitchen fireplace is lined with what appear to be ordinary roofing tiles, as also the oven. At Tattershall Castle and in Tudor fireplaces, when brick had become the ordinary building material, the average size was 9 inches by 2 inches.

Bricks were also used occasionally for the flat arched openings

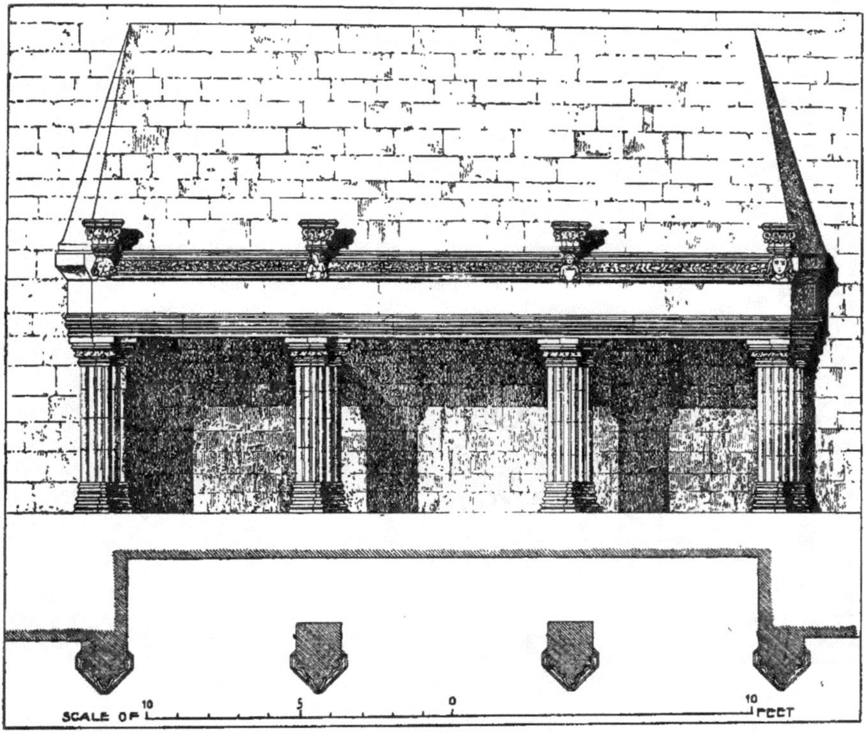

THE PARLIAMENT HALL, LINLITHGOW PALACE.

with plain chamfer or ovolo mould on the angle, and less frequently with a double order as at Darenth, Kent.[1]

It was in connexion with the late Gothic and Tudor fireplaces that the elaborate brick chimneys were introduced which became such an important feature in the buildings of the sixteenth century and James I's reign (page 50).

1 *Architectural Association Sketch Book*, Old Series, vol. ii., pl. 18.

In districts where a supply of suitable stone was not available a beam of oak was used to span the wide fireplace openings, and these were sometimes richly carved, as shown on page 74. They were used as a lintel resting on jambs of brick or stone in many instances, whilst others were framed into the main timbers of the building.

The kitchen held an important place in the domestic establishment of the Middle Ages; those which remain show by their great size the extensive scale on which hospitality was dispensed by kings and nobles and the religious houses. For the Saxons the hall fire may have sufficed to cook their food, but the Normans brought with them a more elaborate menu, as we read that the monks of S. Swithin's House at Winchester rebelled when the number of courses at dinner was reduced from thirteen to ten. The Norman buildings of more than one storey presented greater difficulty in getting rid of smoke and smell than the one-storied hall open to the roof, and from the fact that their kitchens do not now remain, it is assumed that they were more or less temporary structures. Hudson Turner mentions that cooking was done in an outside court in buildings open at the top, and in the Bayeux Tapestry, where cooking operations are elaborately shown, there is no indication of any enclosure. In the twelfth century buildings of Fountains Abbey the kitchen has two fireplaces, each 16 feet wide, with lintels formed of joggle-jointed voussoirs 3 feet 8 inches deep. We see in the fine kitchen at Glastonbury Abbey (Fig. 62) that provision was made for carrying off the fumes from the cooking by means of a cupola in the centre, the four angle fireplaces having had chimneys to take away the smoke, but at Stanton Harcourt (Fig. 66), where the fire was placed against a side wall with no chimney, both smoke and steam had to find their way out through the continuous range of louvers in the upper part of the kitchen, into which the ovens also opened.

In the representations of cooking to be seen in the Bayeux Tapestry a pot is suspended by a hanger from an iron bar which rests on two forked supports, each of which is held by a man. When the fire was in the open or on a central hearth some means of supporting this long bar, which afterwards, when fireplaces were recessed, stretched from wall to wall, was necessary, and on reference to Fig. 9, which shows the coupled andirons from Voelas, we see provision made for this pot-bar to rest upon in the form of horns. Among the remains found at Welwyn which are attributed by Sir A. J. Evans to pre-Roman times in Britain was an iron grate or fire-basket with legs 3 feet 6 inches high and fire-dogs ending in ox heads,—a noticeable similarity to those at Voelas and others which have been found. The fire burns on a brandreth, an iron grate raised on legs over which the pot is suspended. At Stanton Harcourt the pot-bar rests on screen walls (Fig. 65), and when the fireplace became recessed these were built sloping, with ranges of irons projecting to take the spits, as at Hampton Court (Plate IV). At Plas Mawr, Conway, the side walls are dispensed with and sloping iron ranging bars, with crooks, take their place. From this it is probable that the name range now in use for cooking was derived. The spits were originally turned by boys, for Aubrey tells us that "the poor boys turned the spitts and lickt the dripping pan and became huge lusty knaves."

The Renaissance movement, which first began to influence our native architecture when Henry VIII and Cardinal Wolsey brought Italian artists into this country, affected but slowly fireplace design. Italian ornament crept into the spandrels of the Tudor arch and its mouldings lost their Gothic character. Two notable exceptions are the Holbein design in the British Museum, shown in the frontispiece, and the large Italian Renaissance chimney-piece (Plate VII) at the Priory, Reigate, which encloses a Tudor arched stone fireplace which existed before the chimney-piece was placed there. Both of these designs show the Renaissance style fully developed and have features which are frequently found in later examples. A similarity in the general disposition of parts to the Holbein design is found in the Loseley example (Plate IX), and we first meet with the Caryatid, which became a very favourite feature, in chimney-pieces of this and succeeding periods.

When in Queen Elizabeth's reign many Flemish and German craftsmen came to England during a time of great building activity, the chimney-piece became an object of display such as they could be conveniently employed upon, and many examples of this period remain. It ceased to be an integral part of the structure, the most ambitious examples being isolated exercises in design, in which the orders of architecture play an important part, and which often show very little relationship with their surroundings (see Plate XVI).

For the execution of these, foreign marbles were imported to supplement our native materials. Many chimney-pieces by foreigners are coarse in detail, lacking in unity of scale, and of questionable proportions. They were generally erected in buildings which in general design still followed closely the traditional style, but it is surprising how ready the native craftsman appears to have been to try his hand in the new style for the decorative part of his work; his Gothic traditions had to be abandoned, and a new grammar learned in which to express himself. His early efforts produced very crude results, which were improved as time went on.

Quite apart from these very varied and ambitious stone and marble chimney-pieces, stand those of oak, some of which remain in their original condition, whilst others are sadly mutilated. The increased use of wainscoting for walls led to their development. This began with an elaboration of the compartment which contained the fireplace, and formed one of those into which the walls were often divided by pilasters. The Tudor stone arch was abandoned in favour of a rectangular fireplace opening, to which importance was given by enriching both jambs and lintel with carving: birds, beasts and reptiles being represented. Plate LIII is from a fine example of both chimney-piece and lining, taken from the old palace of Bromley-by-Bow, and now set up with the complete room panelling in the Victoria and Albert Museum. A stone from the chimney of this room contains the date 1606, and it is to about this time that many important chimney-pieces belong. Another Middlesex example with characteristic stone lining existed until recently in Mildmay House, Mildmay Park, and at Canonbury adjoining there were several in Sir John Spencer's house, the finest now being set up in the great hall at Castle Ashby, a house of the Comptons, whose ancestor married the Canonbury heiress (see illustration). Hatfield House, Audley End and Holland House supply further examples. This was a time when much oak work was produced, generally of a very elaborate character, in chimney-pieces and hall screens. The style is characterized by intricate strapwork panels, emblematic figures in niches, caryatides and tapering pilasters, combined with a plentiful use of surface carving. The quality of the work varies very much, individual details being often crude, and the satisfaction derived from it may generally be said to be in inverse proportion to the amount of elaboration which it exhibits. Never before had wood been tortured into such strange forms. Jacobean woodwork on walls was frequently accompanied by ornamental plasterwork in ceilings, and many overmantels were made of this material, especially in Devon and Somerset. (Plates LX and LXI.)

Least affected by the change in style was the chimney corner, the hospitable place of assembly in farm-house, cottage or inn, with its low wide-spreading man-tel-tree, where were beguiled the long and dimly lighted hours by song and story; where piled-up wood ashes retained their heat through the night and were easily quickened for use the next day. The brick-lined oven with its iron door, the stock-pot suspended from the chimney bar by a hanger, the andirons and the iron crane with its many way adaptability, all showed the artistry of the village smith; where "What of the night" could be answered by a glance up the wide-mouthed chimney, when resting in its cosy seats and sheltered from the draughts by a high-backed settle. The fire of logs or peat burned on a raised hob or reredos on which the andirons stood; and placed against the back wall to protect it was a cast-iron fire-back. On a shelf bracketed out from the mantel beam rested the

THE HALL FIREPLACE, CASTLE ASHBY.

simple but artistic utensils, on the brightness of which the careful housewife set her pride; fixed to the wall above was the rack for spits or guns with its quaint shapings, and suspended from a nail, the bellows, then more used than now to rouse the slumbering fire with added fuel.

The fireplace utensils of mediæval days, beyond those previously referred to for use in the cooking of food, appear to have been limited to the pair of andirons for raising the ends of the logs above the hearth to assist combustion. Those shown in old manuscripts have the usual straddle legs, and the standards terminate with a scroll like a shepherd's crook (Fig. 117).[1] These were of wrought iron, but in the early part of the sixteenth century, on the development of iron foundries in the Weald of Sussex, the production of cast-iron fire-dogs or brand-irons and fire-backs became an important branch of manufacture and made a valuable artistic addition to the open hearth. Their ornamentation gave them an individuality, and through the durability of their material the many that remain provide a subject of considerable antiquarian interest. They came into use at a time when the Gothic style was giving way to the Renaissance and show the fusion of the two styles in their design. The material, cast iron, was thought too humble for the owners of the great houses built towards the end of the sixteenth and during the seventeenth century, when bronze, in the form of balusters, and silver figures standing on iron bases, cased with the same metal and richly embossed, came into use, and elaborate French and Italian ones were imported.

When towards the end of Elizabeth's reign wood for fuel became scarce and sea-borne coal came into domestic use, a fire-basket was devised to burn it in. In inventories made in the seventeenth century in addition to the pairs of andirons which figure in so many rooms, we meet with a " fire shovell and tongs " amongst the goods of William Jones of Chastleton, and at Hengrave Hall a " cradell of iron to burn sea-cole in " (see Plates LXVIII and XIX). The trade in coal increased, in spite of a great prejudice against its use at first, until in the reign of William and Mary it had become the staple fuel. In London the rebuilding after the great fire of 1666 increased very largely the number of fireplaces, most rooms being

[1] Chambers, O. Fr. *andier;* Mod. Fr. *laudier=l'andier.* The termination was early confused with iron, hence the spellings and-iron and hand-iron.

provided with them, and these were made of a reduced size to suit coal fires. The inconvenience from coal smoke was great, as we read in John Evelyn's Diary; also that he and others interested themselves in the subject of "smoke abatement" to the extent even in those early days of inventing a smokeless fuel, and putting forward suggestions of a more Utopian and less practical character.

FIRE-IRONS AT HAM HOUSE.

When Inigo Jones settled down to practise architecture in London after his second visit to Italy, in 1614, he introduced a more scholarly rendering of classical architecture than that in vogue, founded on the works of the Italian Renaissance architects. There is some uncertainty whether before that time he had been responsible for any work in the bastard classical style which then prevailed, and in which important and pronounced examples of chimney-pieces are to be found of much later date than 1614, as those in the long gallery of Aston Hall about 1630 (Plate XX), Boston House, Brentford, 1623 (Plate LXII), and the large oak chimney-pieces in the drawing and dining rooms at Blickling Hall, the latter being dated 1627.

He effected a complete revolution in the treatment of interiors, by the adoption of a larger scale for the panelling of the walls, proportioning his cornices to the whole height of the rooms, and substituting paint and gilding for the oak which had previously been used and left in its natural state. In this treatment of the walls, the chimney-piece had to be reconsidered, and we have in the south wing of Wilton House a splendid series of examples by him, shown in Plates LXXIII–LXXVII. These chimney-pieces of statuary marble are said by Campbell to have been made in Italy, presumably from drawings sent out by Inigo Jones, as they had to fit their positions in the various rooms. The overpieces are of wood, and both these and the mantels show the influence of published designs by contemporary French architects. Some original drawings by Inigo Jones and his pupil and successor John Webb still exist. It is not clear to what extent the designs are to be attributed to the master or his pupil, nor is it very important that a distinction should be made. The chimney-pieces of Inigo Jones were much appreciated by his successors, who published them in books as his designs and made use of them to a great extent during the early part of the eighteenth century.

The chimney-piece in the hands of Sir Christopher Wren assumed a form which differed from any that preceded it. It became again, in a sense, structural, in that it was incorporated in the general scheme of design of the room, and although isolated chimney-pieces of marble are found in Wren's work at Hampton Court, those most characteristic of him are in the suite of oak-panelled rooms along the south side of the building. In these rooms Wren initiated two features which have been closely connected with fireplaces since, the mirror in the overmantel and the shelves for the display of china. The stone or marble surround to the fireplace opening took the form of a heavy bolection moulding, as seen in Plates LXXIX–LXXXI, and the overpiece was an elaboration of the broad oak wall panelling of the apartment. It is over Wren's fireplaces that the most elaborate examples of Grinling Gibbon's carving are to be found, hanging in festoons down the sides and connected at the top over a mirror or picture frame. This richly gifted carver, who was brought into prominence by John Evelyn, as described by Horace Walpole, "gave to wood the loose and airy lightness of flowers and chained together

CARVING OVER THE FIREPLACE IN THE CHAPEL GALLERY, BELTON HOUSE.

The modern statuary and carving which now occupies the centre of this panel has been omitted.

the various productions of the elements with a free disorder natural to each species." We may infer from the number of important mansions where the work of Gibbon and his school still remains, as at Belton House, Holme Lacy, Petworth and Cassiobury, that the prevailing fashion in his day was to provide over the chimney-piece a field for his operations. Of the splendid series at Chatsworth, although carried out by other executants, the carving was doubtless inspired by Grinling Gibbon and the chimney-pieces by Sir Christopher Wren. Gibbon, who in his letters to Evelyn spells his name without the final *s*, died in 1721, an dhis style died with him, so far as that particular quality of lightness described by Horace Walpole is concerned. This is very singular seeing how many carvers must have worked under him in S. Paul's Cathedral and the City churches, which were all carried out during his lifetime, in addition to the work in many country mansions.

This wealth of carving in London alone, more effective then, when fresh from the chisel, than now when choked with numerous coats of varnish, might have been expected to provide a model for generations of carvers to come, yet such is the desire for change and the power of fashion that we find it, before the middle of the eighteenth century, supplanted by an indifferent copy of the style of French Louis XIV (Plate XCVIII), which culminated in the unrestrained extravagancies of the Chippendale school (Figs. 176, 177). This change was probably helped on by the example of the Italian plasterers Artari and Bagutti, who were largely employed by James Gibbs the architect, and whose work in the Rococo style is an over-prominent feature in the interiors of his buildings. Plate LXXXIV shows the application of this style to a chimney-piece at Weald Hall, Brentwood.

Sir John Vanbrugh's heavy hand asserted itself in his chimney-pieces. He had followers who produced many ponderous specimens in marble, some of which may be seen in the northern state rooms of Hampton Court Palace finished after the death of Sir Christopher Wren.

The most characteristic chimney-piece of the first quarter of the eighteenth century had flat pilasters on either side of the fire-place opening finishing with consoles which supported the shelf entablature, as seen in Plates XLIII–CIII and the illustration opposite. They were made of both wood and marble, no distinction being made in the design, and when of the former were frequently continued upwards with an overpiece. It is not difficult to find its prototype in the architectural framework of a Renaissance door or window. An alternative form of support for the shelf entablature was the terminal figure or caryatid facing frontwards as at Houghton Hall (Plate civ**), sideways as in the hall at Rushbrooke, or both frontwards and in profile on either side of the chimney-piece as at Wentworth Woodhouse (Plate cv). These "termes," as they were called, were largely used in the formal halls of this period, a fireplace being placed at each end as at Up-park in Sussex; the carving of the human head became more realistic, and as it gained in natural expression it lost in decorative effect and suitability for its purpose.

THE PAINTED ROOM, WENTWORTH WOODHOUSE, YORKSHIRE.

A third type of chimney-piece had side columns, either three quarter or detached to support the entablature. Seen first in the Holbein design in couples and standing on pedestals, the column is met with in each of the succeeding periods; it is however most characteristic of the second half of the eighteenth century, when many well proportioned designs were carried out.

During the eighteenth century very many books were published containing designs for internal decoration of houses, in most of which the chimney-piece figures. These were by the leading architects, carvers and cabinet-makers. In the books by architects the designs follow classical lines, but in those by cabinet-makers, amongst some reasonable designs, we find many most fantastic productions. The highly ornamented mirror frame founded on the French style of Louis XV had come into fashion, and chimney-pieces were designed to accord with or to incorporate it, as in Fig. 176. Examples of the style in stucco remain, as in the Court Room of the Stationers' Hall (Plate cx).

A GRATE BY CHIPPENDALE.

This fashion lasted throughout the reigns of George I and II, but does not appear to have found much favour with the architects of that time, nor are the examples of chimney-pieces to be now met with numerous. Its influence may be seen in the hob grate (Fig. 179) and in the fender at the top of Plate CXIII. Side by side with this florid French work in these eighteenth century books we find designs in the revived Gothic style associated with Strawberry Hill. That many-sided designer William Kent—whose decorative work never exceeded mediocrity—was captivated by it, for we find in Jas. Vardy's "Designs by Inigo Jones and Kent," 1744, designs for screens, pulpit and chimney-piece in this style. Some examples remain, as the large chimney-piece of Hopton Wood stone which reaches from floor to ceiling in the hall of Tissington Hall, Derbyshire. Triple clustered and banded pillars run up each side of the fireplace into the overmantel and terminate with crocketed pinnacles; mechanical Gothic forms are repeated in a

THE MORNING ROOM, 43, PORTLAND PLACE, LONDON.

lifeless way over all the flat surfaces and the opening is enclosed by a cusped arch of a very debased kind.

Into this medley of styles came a leavening influence, first by the publication of Stuart and Revett's "Antiquities of Athens" in 1742, and followed in 1773 by the first volume of R. & J. Adam's *Works in Architecture*. These publications introduced a purer classical taste, founded on Greek architecture, to which nothing could be more opposed than the French Renaissance practised by the Chippendale school.

Assisted by Pergolesi, the brothers Adam gave to the treatment of marble in chimney-pieces a refinement in decorative detail which had not been previously seen in this country (Plates cxv–cxxi). Their influence was widespread. Many houses were designed by them for wealthy patrons in the country, and they were builders in London on an extensive scale. For their best chimney-pieces they used the pure white statuary marble with yellow Siena and verde-antique for inlays, and for cheaper work introduced ornament of composition laid on wood. For overmantels they used large mirrors in light gilt frames, or as an alternative, a medallion figure subject, with stucco ornamentation carrying the decoration of the room into the chimney breast.

A CAST-IRON HOB GRATE WITH ADAM ORNAMENT.

The fire-grate received their careful attention, as seen in Figs. 186, 187, from drawings by them in the Soane Museum, and the ornament then introduced was largely applied to grates of cast iron, for which it is particularly suitable—Figs. 191–194.

A similar character to that of Adam's work is found in the chimney-pieces of James Stuart at Litchfield House, No. 15, St. James's Square. That in the drawing-room has a frieze of figures below the entablature, attributed to John Flaxman, R.A. During the last quarter of the eighteenth century many marble chimney-pieces received the help of eminent sculptors as Joseph Wilton, R.A., and in the house of Richard Cosway the miniaturist, 20, Stratford Place, the chimney-pieces of which were carved by Thomas Banks, R.A. Smith in "Nollekens and His Times" says he once saw the painter in his princely mansion standing "at the fireside upon one of Madame Pompadour's rugs leaning against a chimney-piece dedicated to the sun, the ornaments of which were sculptured by Banks." The large mirror had become the fashion and had to be placed low enough for the exquisites of the day to see themselves to full advantage, and the height of the chimney-piece was reduced to a very moderate dimension.

Sir John Soane designed chimney-pieces under Greek inspiration with some success; his endeavour appears to have been to build up a chimney-piece in the Greek spirit, rather than to apply borrowed details to current designs.

Great progress was made during the eighteenth century in both design and manufacture of fire-grates, many of which have not since been surpassed in either respect.

The fire-basket with short side supports, which has been referred to at Penshurst as an early form for burning coal, continued to be made with details influenced by the style in vogue. Obelisks of pierced brass on four small pillars took the place of the short columns, and a pierced brass apron of flowing design was placed below the horizontal bowed bars; in others scrolled feet sufficed to support the basket. For less important rooms the hob grate was devised, the earlier ones showing the French influence in their ornamentation, the later the more formal style of the Adam Brothers. These were made of cast iron and the ornament adopted was modelled with great delicacy and suitability for the material used. *The Stove Grate Maker's Assistant*, by W. Glossop, published in 1771, shows many well designed grates of the basket type, and a few hob grates of less merit. The most characteristic grate of the latter half of the century, not, however, shown in Glossop's book, consisted of a fire-basket with bowed or rounded bars with side panels and pierced apron surrounded by a frame which enclosed the opening, as in Plate CXXIII. These were ornamented with studs and bosses and sometimes engraved, and had fenders to match. General proportions and details were most carefully thought out and produced a very satisfactory result. At the same time efforts were made to improve grates from the economic side and various plans were devised; an account of some of the most important is given in the Appendix, p. 221.

The chief of these experimenters was Count Rumford, who devoted himself to improving the construction of the fireplace opening and the form of the mouth of the flue, and left a series of Essays on the subject. He was the first to recommend brick in place of iron for the back and sides of the fire-place, thereby effecting a very material improvement, as brick retains the heat—which in the case of iron more readily passes through and goes up the chimney. His example and precepts do not appear to have effected any lasting improvement in the construction of fireplaces, as we find that in the early part of Queen Victoria's reign they were made mainly of black iron, and the Count's name remained attached only to a form of hob grate which is not even mentioned in his essays.

The open fireplace has always retained its popularity in this country. The closed stove for domestic use has never found that favour here which it has on the Continent and in America; nor have we produced anything like the German enclosed stoves of enamelled earthenware of the sixteenth and seventeenth centuries, examples of which may be seen in the Victoria and Albert Museum; although something of this kind must have been referred to by Harrison, a contemporary writer, who says "As for stoves, we have not hitherto used them greatly yet do they now begin to be made in divers houses of the gentry and wealthy citizens, who build them not to work and feed in as in Germany and elsewhere but now and then to sweat in as occasion and need shall require it." We are not aware that any stoves now remain to which this remark might have referred. The abundance of fuel and its comparative cheapness may have hindered that strictest economy being practised by the adoption of the close stove; and this coupled with our changeable climatic conditions and the uncertainty of duration of any spell of cold weather may have prevented that earnest grappling with the subject which has been found necessary in colder climates than ours. It is only during the last few years, since the introduction of anthracite coal for domestic use, that any great increase has taken place in the manufacture of close stoves. These have undoubted merits for use in halls and other positions, where the brightness of an open fire is not very necessary, and where, by keeping them burning continuously, a greater proportion of the heat generated can be utilised. The open fire certainly remains the most popular, as it is also the most artistic, means of heating our apartments; being unequalled not only for its cheerfulness and charm, but also as a means of ventilation in constantly changing the air of the room where it is in use.

MARBLE BAS-RELIEF IN CHIMNEY-PIECE IN FRONT DRAWING ROOM, 43, PORTLAND PLACE (*v.* PLATES CXX AND CXXI).

ERRATA

Page	62, Fig. 68,	Title—Couvre-Few,	*should*	*be*	Feu.
,,	105, 1st line	—Plate XXIII	,,	,,	XXIV.
,,	114, 29th ,,	— ,, XI	,,	,,	XL.
,,	184, 26th ,,	—Mrs. Gordon	,,	,,	Jordan
,,	191, 10th ,,	—Sienna	,,	,,	Siena

THE ENGLISH FIREPLACE

The Primitive Fireplace

IN primitive habitations the fireplace was the central hearth, the focus around which the walls were built; hence the necessity for a screen to protect this bonfire from the wind, as well as the person from the draught, may reasonably be considered to have been an important factor in the development of that round form of house which is thought to have been the earliest.[1]

In the excavated mounds of a British marsh village discovered near Glastonbury, Somerset, in 1892–3, hearths of clay were found in the middle of the circular wooden huts: these had been added to from time to time, and in one hut the two uppermost were of stone (Fig. 2). It is probable that the smoke from these hearth fires escaped through the door, or through a hole in the roof, as in the cabins of the Irish and the hovels of the Scotch, or in the modern charcoal-burner's hut.[2] This village is thought to belong to a period preceding the Roman occupation, and was

[1] Sir Walter Scott, in Note M to *Ivanhoe*, describing the castles or burghs of the Zetland Islands, says: "The tower has never, to appearance, had roofing of any sort; a fire was made in the centre of the space which it encloses, and originally the building was probably little more than a wall drawn as a sort of screen around the great council fire of the tribe."

[2] A writer in the *Encyclopædia Britannica* says: "The early Irish houses had no chimney; the fire was made in the centre of the house, and the smoke made its exit through the door or through a hole in the roof, as in the corresponding Gaulish and German houses. The introduction of chimneys probably led to the change in the form of the houses from round to oblong."

inhabited by a people who practised metal working and the crafts of the weaver and potter. Every mound appeared to contain a roughly circular fireplace, about 4 ft. in diameter. Fig. 2 is a plan of one of these huts supplied by Mr. Arthur Bulleid.

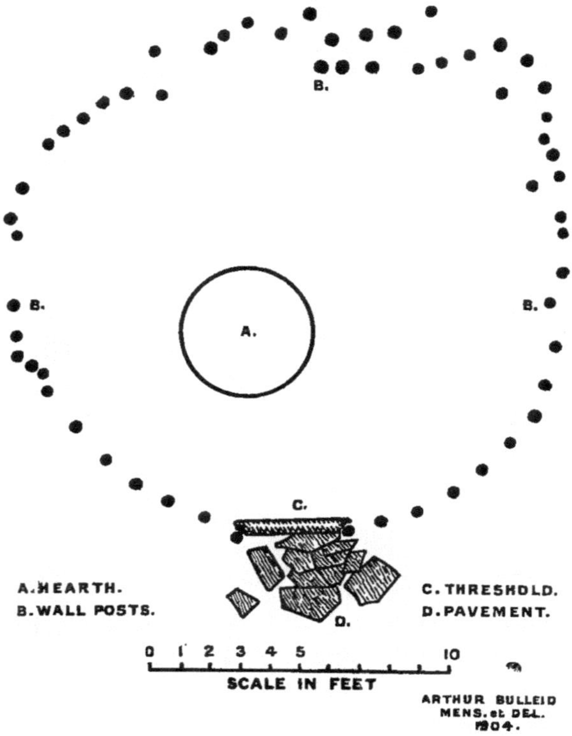

FIG. 2. PLAN OF HUT, MARSH VILLAGE, GLASTONBURY.

THE ROMAN METHOD OF HEATING

The Romans during their sojourn in Britain heated the rooms of their villas by means of hypocausts and movable braziers, in which charcoal was the fuel used. The remains of these hypocausts show them to have been constructed on an elaborate system, by which the floors and sometimes the walls of the various rooms were heated by hot air from a chamber beneath. The heat, generated in a furnace which was stoked from the outside of the building, was carried through these chambers and flues under the floors, and in some instances up rectangular earthenware tubes built on the face of the wall, to which they were secured by iron holdfasts. The tubes connected at the bottom with the hypocaust, as at Northleigh, Oxon (Fig. 3). The floor of the chamber is in this instance supported on piers, 7 in. square, built of

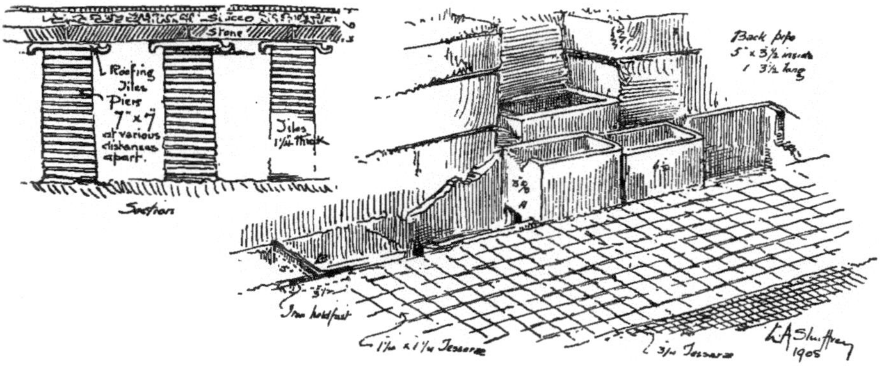

FIG. 3. HYPOCAUST, ROMAN VILLA, NORTHLEIGH, OXON.

tiles 1¼ in. thick, at distances varying from 10 in. upwards apart, and is formed of large flat stones resting upon the piers. These stones are covered with stucco which forms the bed for a mosaic pavement. As the walls above ground of these Roman villas have been destroyed there is nothing to show how the smoke from the furnaces was carried off, or whether they were provided with chimneys. The question whether the ancient Romans built chimneys is one much debated by writers on this subject, but an inspection of the remains of their villas leads to the opinion that they were well acquainted with the action of smoke and heated air. At Northleigh, behind the front row of pipes, others were found at intervals, as shown in Fig. 3, which were discoloured with smoke, from which the others were almost free; it is conjectured that these may have been open at the top for the discharge of smoke at the eaves of the building, and that the front row, being closed at the top, had no draught through them and consequently but little discoloration.

The Roman method of heating, introduced by a people of luxurious habits and accustomed to a warmer climate than the British, does not appear to have been copied by the Britons or their successors, the Saxons, for whose houses, built mainly of wood and plaster, it would have been unsuitable. No chimneys are seen in representations of Saxon houses. The fire was kindled on a hob of clay in the centre of the large dining hall open to the roof, through which the smoke found its way out by a hole or through an open door or window.[1]

THE SAXON FIREPLACE

The term hearthmen is significantly applied to those familiar retainers who sat at the same fire as their lord, and at night retired to the same dormitory. "A bed, made of rushes and covered by a coarse kind of cloth manufactured in the country, called *brychan*, is placed along the side of the room, and they all in common lie down to sleep. The fire continues to burn by night as well as by day at their feet, and they receive much comfort from the natural heat of the persons lying near them."[2] As wood and peat were the fuel used the inconvenience from smoke would not have been so great as if coal had been burned; the central position was the most efficient for diffusing heat in the apart-

[1] T. Hudson Turner, *Parker's Domestic Architecture*, vol. i. Accenso foco in medio calido effecto cænaculo, Bede l. 1. c. 3.

[2] Giraldus Cambrensis, *Itinerary through Wales*

ment, and for buildings mainly constructed of timber the safest as a preventive of fire.[1]

In the consideration of our subject it may be found more convenient to deal with the central hearth fire first, rather than to combine it chronologically with the recessed wall fireplace, although both continued in use almost to our own time.

The central position for the hearth-fire was retained for use in the hall or house place, of one storey, open to the roof, long after fireplaces were made in the walls of other apartments. The smoke originally had to find its way out through the unceiled roof, under the eaves or through unglazed windows; but when an advance was made in the direction of domestic comfort and the latter were filled with glass, shutters or other substitute, to keep out wind and rain, some better means of escape for it had to be devised. This want was met by the introduction of the smoke turret or louver.

THE SMOKE LOUVER

An aperture was formed in the roof, vertically over the hearth, generally octagonal in shape, but sometimes hexagonal or square, from which rose the turret, with openings to the outer air, formed so as to exclude the rain and let the smoke out. The French word for opening, *l'ouvert*, gave the name to these turrets and to the louver-boards which are still used for a similar purpose.

The smoke louver appears to have been an introduction of the latter half of the thirteenth century, as the hall of Stokesay

[1] Beckman says: "That there were no chimneys in the tenth, twelfth and thirteenth centuries seems to be proved by the so-called ignitegium or pyritegium, the curfew of the English and the couvre-feu of the French. This was used for covering up the fire, made in a hole or pit in the ground under an opening formed in the roof. A law was passed fixing the time for these covers to be put on, signified by the ringing of a bell, by William the Conqueror in 1068, the time being at seven in the evening, to prevent nocturnal assemblies."

Castle belonging to the earlier half is not provided with one, the unglazed circular openings in the gabled windows at the sides providing a convenient means of exit for the smoke, but in the orders given by Henry III for alterations to the buildings belonging to him frequent mention is made of this feature. They occur in a series of records in Latin called the "Liberate Rolls," translations of which, by T. Hudson Turner, are given in the first volume of *Parker's Domestic Architecture*. The louver is first referred to in the 32nd year of this reign, where the Keeper of Woodstock is ordered "to make a hearth of freestone, high and good, in the chamber above the wine cellar in the great court; and a great louver over the said hearth, and two great louvers in the Queen's Chamber, and two glass windows in the King's wardrobe"; and again the King to Godfrey de Liston orders "wainscote to be put above our dais, and a louver to be made in the hall there to carry away the smoke."

Several louvers still remain in buildings of the fifteenth and sixteenth centuries. In Fig. 4 is shown that over the hall of Lincoln College, Oxford, erected 1437, which is in its original condition and is made of oak covered with lead. This hall has been furnished during the past century with a fireplace in one of the walls, so that the louver is not now in use; but Parker, when writing on the subject, in 1853, mentions that it had been used within the recollection of some of the older fellows. The removal of the fire from the middle of the hall to the side was the subject of comment by Dr. Johnson, who, when visiting Oxford with Boswell in 1754, speaking of the form of old halls, says, "In these halls the fireplace was anciently always in the middle of the room, till the Whigs removed it to one side." The turret on the roof of Westminster Hall is stated by Parker to be an exact copy of the original. He gives an illustration of the interior of the Abbot's hall at West-

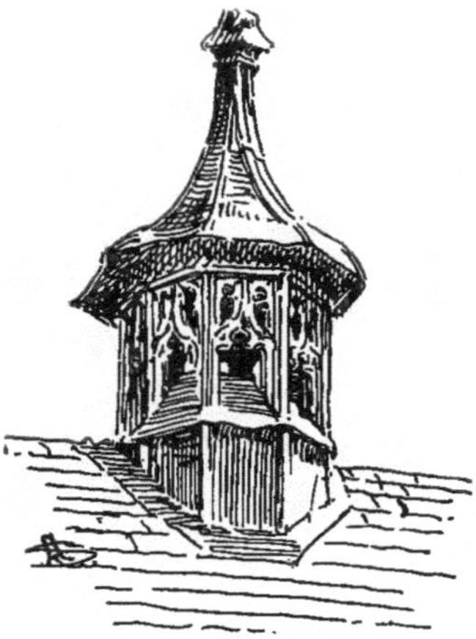

FIG. 4.

FIG. 5.

FIG. 6.

FIG. 7.

SMOKE LOUVERS, IN THE HALLS OF—

FIG. 4. LINCOLN COLLEGE, OXFORD.

„ 5. PENSHURST PLACE, KENT (NOW REMOVED).

„ 6. BARNARD'S INN, HOLBORN.

„ 7. STAPLE INN, HOLBORN.

minster School with the raised hearth, brazier and louver above, which were sketched by Jewitt before their removal in 1850. The louver of square form still remains.[1] Figs. 6 and 7 show existing louvers on the halls of Barnard's and Staple Inns, Holborn, the latter belonging to the sixteenth century, shows that they continued to be built up to that time.

The "femerell" or "louver" originally over the Great Hall at Hampton Court, as described in Mr. Ernest Law's Guide to the palace, from existing old accounts, must have been an object of some magnificence. It was of three stages with openings alternately glazed and trellised. "Inside there were four pendants of oak and a carved rose crownyd standyng in the crowne vowght." This was gilded and on a blue ground. Outside there were numerous pinnacles, on which were placed heraldic "kynges beastes," four lions, four dragons and four greyhounds, all of which were elaborately painted and bore gilded vanes, while as a centrepiece was "a greate lyon crownyd, baryng a great vane, layde in oyle, servyng the top of the femerall."[2] The accounts also mention "hewing and settyng the pavyng of the herthe in the Kynge's new hall, of Reygate stone," its size being 6 ft. square.

It is probable that as wall fireplaces have been introduced into halls the necessity for retaining many louvers has ceased, and on getting dilapidated they have been removed. Others, like the elaborate one over the hall of Trinity College, Cambridge, have been entirely filled with glass to act as a lantern only. At Eltham Palace the internal construction of the louver remains, but nothing externally, the plan of it being an elongated hexagon.

This method of carrying away the smoke provided the *raison d'être* for a picturesque architectural feature, pleasantly breaking

[1] See illustration in *Parker's Domestic Architecture*, Fifteenth Century, part i, chapter iii.

[2] A similarly elaborate louver of four stages is shown in S. H. Grimm's drawing of the exterior of the hall of Cowdray Castle, Midhurst. (Garner and Stratton's *Tudor Domestic Architecture*.)

the skyline of a large hall roof, and its disuse is a loss, for which it is sometimes difficult to find a substitute.

THE REREDOS

In the liberate rolls of Henry III, referred to previously, the hearth under the great louver was ordered to be of free-stone, high

FIG. 8. CENTRAL HEARTH IN THE HALL OF PENSHURST PLACE, KENT, WITH COUPLED ANDIRONS.

and good, showing that the hearth was sometimes raised above the floor, as that is in the hall of the Hospital of St. Cross, near Winchester, where a fire of charcoal is still occasionally made. At Penshurst, Kent, the central hearth still exists (Fig. 8). This is a brick-paved octagonal space, 8 ft. across, level with the floor and surrounded by a low curb. On it stand the coupled andirons connected by a billet bar supported in the middle. These andirons are of later date than the fourteenth century hall, as they bear the pheon badge of the Sidneys, to whom the manor was given by Edward VI. The smoke turret has been removed, but is shown in a drawing of the exterior given in *Nash's Mansions*, from which the sketch (Fig. 5) is traced.

Other firedogs have been found, coupled in the same manner as those at Penshurst, which show the form to be one of great antiquity. One pair of these, described by the late J. Romilly Allen as Kelto-Roman, is shown in Fig. 9.[1] This very interesting piece of wrought ironwork was dug up on the farm of Carreg Coedog, near Bettwys-y-Coed, and is now in the possession of Colonel Wynne Finch. It is obviously for use in a central hearth and measures 2 ft. 10 in. in width and 2 ft. 5½ in. in height, the two vertical bars being 1½ in. square, and the billet bar 2¼ in. deep by 1⅛ in. wide. The loops up the sides of the uprights were probably for the purpose of resting the spit-irons in for roasting purposes. These are absent in the Penshurst dogs, as this building was provided with a kitchen adjoining the hall, in which the cooking would be done.

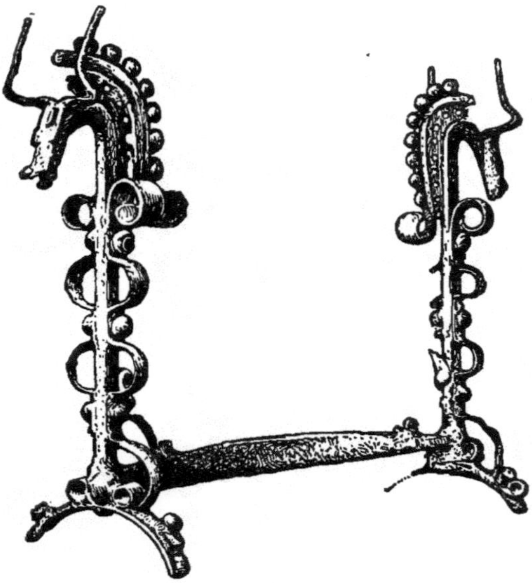

FIG. 9. KELTO-ROMAN FIREDOG AT VOELAS.

[1] *Archæologia Cambrensis*, January, 1901.

FIG. 10. "REREDOS" FROM THE SHETLAND ISLES.

FIG. 11. A CROFTER'S FIREPLACE IN THE SHETLAND ISLANDS.

We find the name "reredos" attached to the central hearth, but there is nothing in the form of those previously mentioned to suggest the origin of this name. It is probable that its form, when the name was first applied to it, and when referred to by old writers, was different, and that it then had the rere back which the word implies. Harrison, writing in the sixteenth century, says, "Each one made his fire *against* a reredos in the hall, where he dined and dressed his meat."

In the Shetlands a fire may still be seen in the middle of the house, with a back or hob against which cooking is done (Fig. 10),[1] and this may be regarded as a survival of the object to which the name reredos was applied; placed originally in the middle of the room, with a hole in the roof over for the exit of smoke, it was afterwards moved to the side wall and a hood constructed over it, as in Fig. 11.

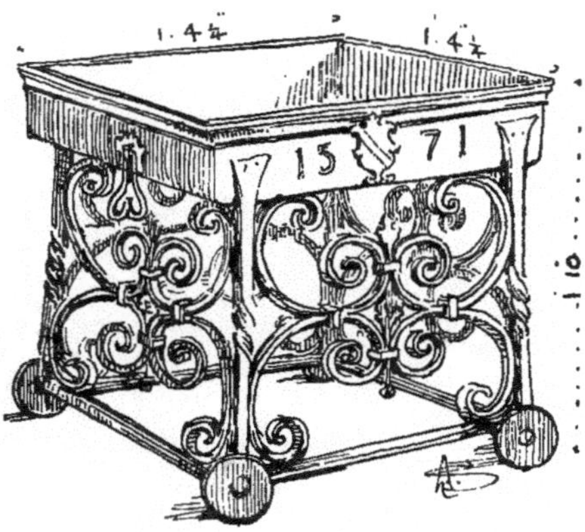

FIG. 12. SIXTEENTH-CENTURY BRAZIER.

Instead of a fire of logs, as shown in Fig. 8, at Penshurst, an iron brazier, in which charcoal was burned, sometimes stood on the central hearth, such as that shown in Fig. 12. The hall of Trinity College, Cambridge, retained till 1866 the brazier which had been in use for upwards of 160 years.[2] Coke superseded charcoal for use in these braziers.

[1] *Country Life*, March 27, 1909.
[2] *The Building of a University*, by Rev. Augustus Jessop, D.D.

The Wall Fireplace and the Evolution of the Hood and Chimney

THE inconvenience or practical impossibility of having a central fire in the hall in buildings of more than one storey, the roofs of which were required for defensive purposes, probably led to the fireplace being first placed against the side wall, and the earliest examples occur in the magnificent strongholds erected soon after the Conquest, such as at Rochester, Castle Hedingham, Colchester and Coningsburgh. Where the sleeping apartments were formed in the thickness of the walls, with openings to the great chamber and windows in the outside wall, the passage of smoke from a central fire must have been unbearable, and the plan first adopted was to form a shallow recess in the thickness of the wall, of semi-elliptical shape, lined with thin Roman-shaped

FIG. 13. ROCHESTER CASTLE.

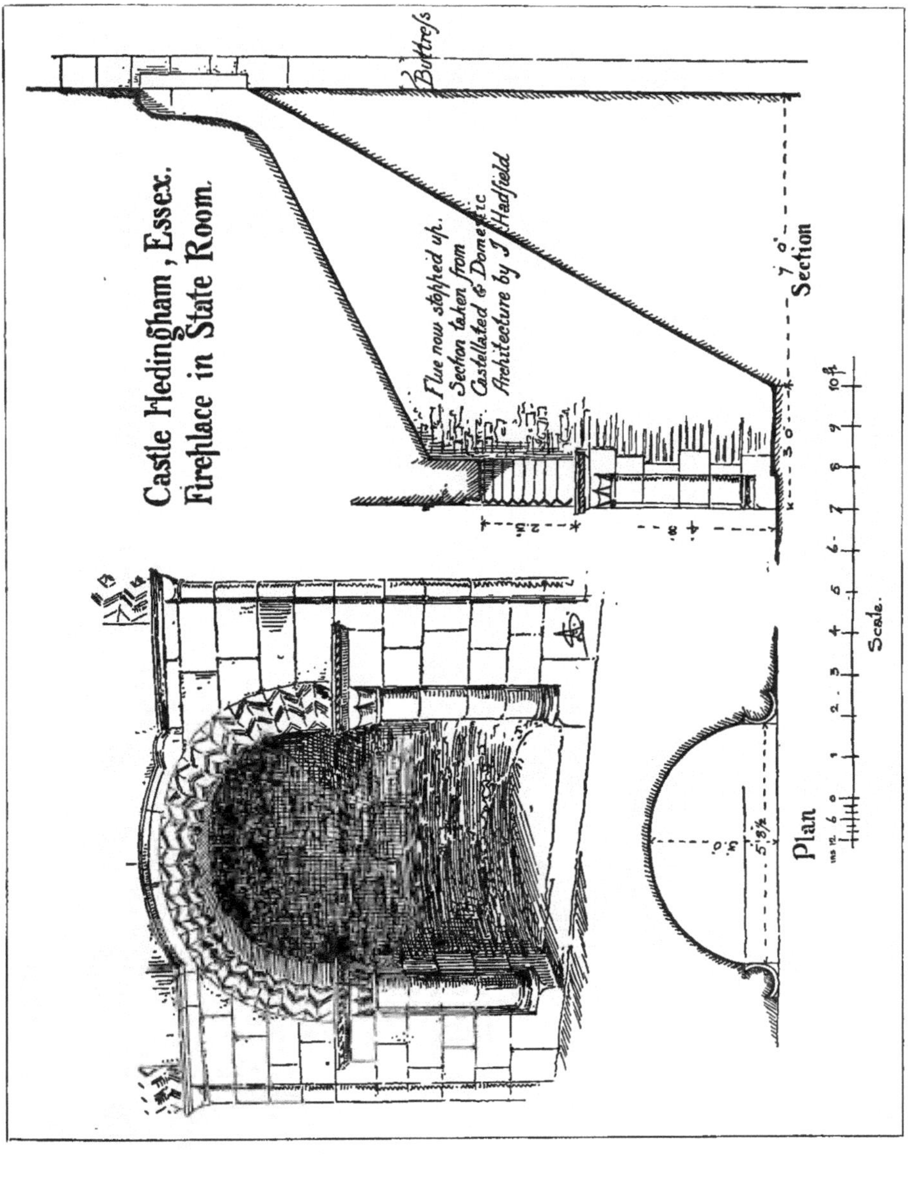
Castle Hedingham, Essex.
Fireplace in State Room.
Flue now stopped up.
Section taken from
Castellated & Domestic
Architecture by J. Hadfield
Buttress
Section
Plan
Scale.

FIG. 14.

bricks or tiles laid in either horizontal or herring-bone courses. This space, shallow at the level of the floor, or in some cases not recessed at all, was deepened in its ascent by the sloping of the back, forming a wide throat to the flue, which, rising

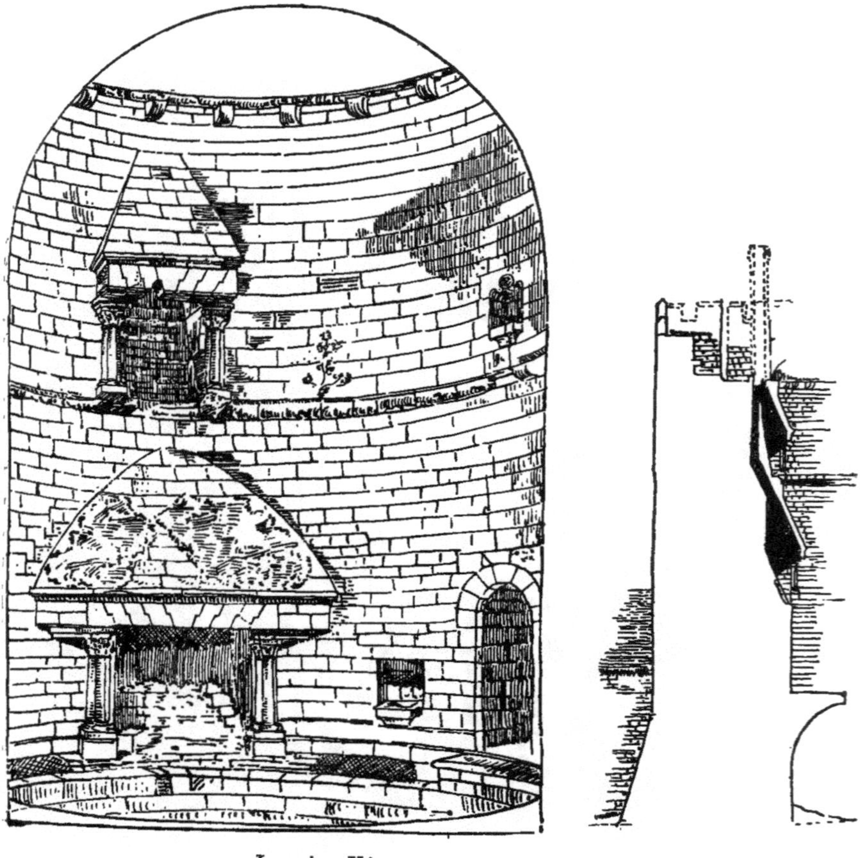

Interior View. *Section.*

FIG. 15. CONINGSBURGH KEEP.

obliquely through the back wall, divided and finished with two vertical apertures on its outside face. One external opening, no doubt, proved very inefficient for carrying away the smoke during certain conditions of the wind, and the plan adopted at Castle Hedingham was to make the flue discharge right and left on either side of a flat buttress (Fig. 14). A similar arrangement of the flues exists at Colchester Castle.

The fireplace openings at both Castle Hedingham and Rochester (Fig. 13) are treated like door or window openings, with engaged shafts in the jambs, and semicircular arches enriched with the characteristic zigzag ornaments of the Norman period, the dates assigned to these buildings being about 1130.

FIG. 16.

UPPER FIREPLACE IN CONINGSBURGH KEEP.

In the circular keep of Coningsburgh Castle fireplaces were constructed in the wall of each storey which have no recess at the floor level beyond that which is formed by the triple-clustered jamb shafts (Figs. 15 and 16). These support a corbelled-out joggle-jointed stone lintel, finished with a moulded string course, from which the hood of masonry recedes, forming a curved line against the circular wall of the chamber. The difficulty of forming a wide semicircular arch in the circular wall may have led to the adoption of the corbelled-out lintel, to complete which the receding hood was a natural sequence.

Fig. 16 shows the upper chamber fireplace, in which the sloping hood has returned sides, an advance in design beyond the lower one. The illustration, which is taken from Clark's *Military Architecture*, shows the flues, in the section, carried up in the thickness of the wall and furnished with chimney-shafts, the form of these latter being, however, conjectural only.

FIG. 17. A CHIMNEY-SHAFT AT CHRISTCHURCH, HANTS.

In the hall of a ruined late Norman house at Christchurch, Hants, is a fireplace, from the large circular tunnel of which rises the flue, terminated with its original tall cylindrical chimney-shaft (Fig. 17), and at the Jew's House, Lincoln, also in the Norman style, a fireplace on the upper floor, which is built in a singular way, on an external arched projection over the front doorway, was originally terminated with a similar cylindrical shaft, which appears to have been the earliest form of chimney; we thus see that the smoke

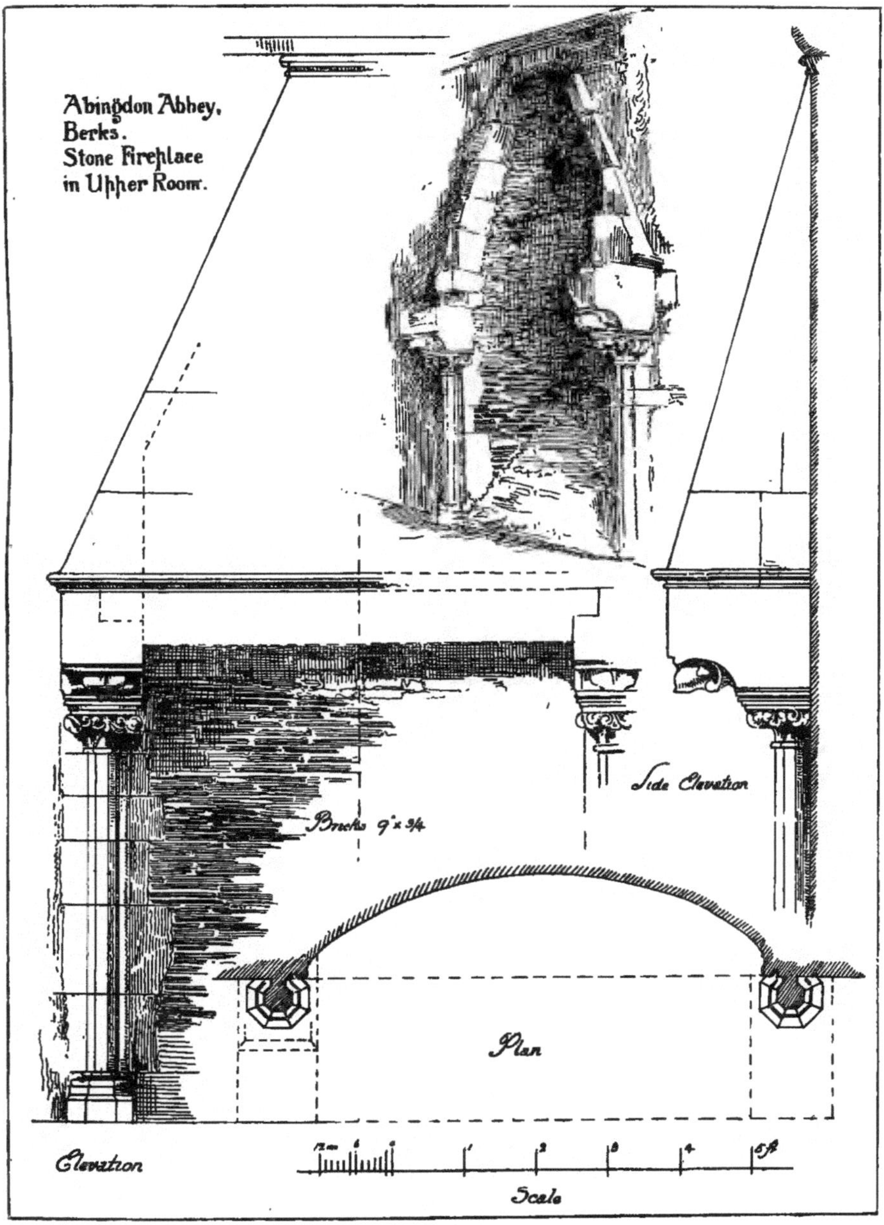
Abingdon Abbey,
Berks.
Stone Fireplace
in Upper Room.
Side Elevation
Bricks 9" x 3/4
Plan
Elevation
Scale

FIG. 18.

flue terminating with a chimney, as we now understand the term, developed during the Norman period of architecture in England.

EARLY ENGLISH FIREPLACES

Fireplaces with projecting stone hoods tapering back to the main wall continued to be built in the thirteenth century, some examples of which still remain, as shown in Figs. 18 and 20, both from monastic buildings. The fireplace shown in Fig. 18 is in an upper room of the Abbot's Buildings at Abingdon, Berks, and must have been a fine one when in its original condition. The hood was carried on stone corbels supported by engaged octagonal columns, the caps of which are well carved with the three-lobed leaves so characteristic of the Early Pointed style. The lintel has disappeared, probably through ill-treatment, and the void shows the careful way in which these hoods were constructed. The back of the fireplace is built of thin bricks nearest the fire and with rubble masonry above; the flue goes back into the main wall, from which rises the massive chimney (Fig. 19), and the smoke is carried away through gablets facing four ways, each having three lancet-shaped openings. Old drawings of this chimney show an iron finial rising from the centre.

FIG. 19. CHIMNEY AT THE ABBEY, ABINGDON.

FIG. 20. NETLEY ABBEY, HANTS.

The other fireplace referred to of the same period is at Netley Abbey, near Southampton (Fig. 20), where the shafts have moulded caps, from which project heavy stone corbels carrying the hood, as in the previous example, but at the sides is a fresh development, in the form of a moulded shelf, cut out of the main corbel stone which carries the hood. These corbels, or shelves, have reasonably been described as for the purpose of holding lights, but probably originated in the necessity for having very large stones tailing well into the wall to carry the weight of the projecting hood, as a slight movement at the sides would be likely to make the front of the hood collapse, as the illustrations show them to have done, though not necessarily by fair means. In a fireplace in the dormitory of Abingdon Abbey, belonging to a later period these corbels, or shelf stones, are seen in a simpler form (Fig. 21). Having no side abutment, various forms of joggle-jointed voussoirs were adopted to prevent their slipping, as at Coningsburgh (Fig. 15).

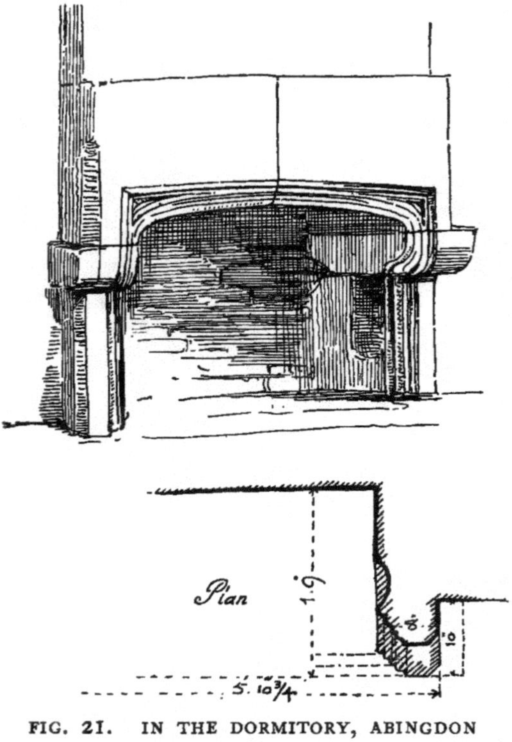

FIG. 21. IN THE DORMITORY, ABINGDON ABBEY.

At Aydon Castle, Northumberland, the chimney of the fireplace in the lower hall is finished in an unusual way (Fig. 22). The back of the fireplace projects from the wall externally, and the chimney is carried up as an engaged cylindrical shaft with vertical apertures just below the parapet for the exit of smoke and terminated by a conical cap attached to the wall. This shows an intermediate stage in chimney development, and we shall see that, although early examples remain of chimneys open at the top as previously referred to, others with vertical openings in the sides of the shaft for the exit of smoke continued to be built. That at Sherborne Abbey (Fig. 23) is another example.

FIG. 22. CHIMNEY AT AYDON CASTLE, NORTHUMBERLAND.

The following extracts from the Liberate Rolls of the time of Henry III's reign, previously referred to, show that fireplaces were becoming general in the various manor-houses belonging to the King, also that they were objects on which both the painter's and sculptor's art were to be exercised.

The word chimney, when used by old writers, was not restricted in its meaning to the shaft of the chimney, but included the fireplace.

In roll 24, Henry III, Edward Fitz-Otho, keeper of the King's works at Westminster, is ordered to "raise the chimney of the Queen's chamber, and to paint the chimney of the chamber aforesaid, and on it to cause to be portrayed a figure of Winter, which, as well by its sad countenance as by other miserable contortions of the body, may be observedly likened to winter itself."

Again, 32 Henry III, the Sheriff of Wiltshire is commanded to "pull down the mantel before the chimney in the King's chamber at Clarendon, and to make a new mantel there, on which mantel he is to cause to be painted the wheel of Fortune and Jesse." Further, 35 Henry III, the King to the Sheriffs of Wiltshire: "We command you—and rebuild the chimney in our Queen's hall, with two marble columns on each side of the chimney; and sculpture the mantel of the chimney with the twelve months of the year."

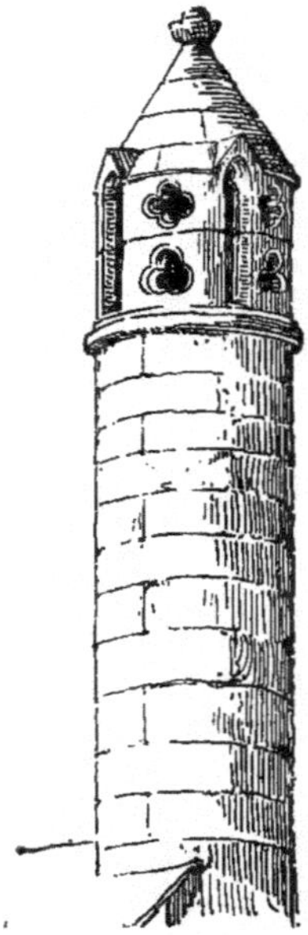

FIG. 23. CHIMNEY, SHERBORNE ABBEY, DORSET.

From the number of references to chimneys we might infer that they were a new introduction, if it were not that in one case the order is given "to raise the flue of the chimney of our chamber there (Woodstock) higher by six feet," and in others "to repair and rebuild," showing their previous existence.

The custom, which had hitherto prevailed, for the lord and lady to dine in the great hall with their servants and retainers was giving way in favour of the greater privacy of taking their meals in a separate apartment, and it is in the lord's withdrawing chamber, often called the solar, that some of the earliest fireplaces are to be found. This room, placed transversely and adjoining the dais end of the hall, was usually over the cellar and approached from the hall by a flight of steps, as at Stokesay. At Aydon Castle, Northumberland, both hall and solar are on the upper floor, with fireplace in the solar only. This change of custom is referred to by Longlande in ***Pierce the Plowman's Vision.***

FIG. 24. FIREPLACE IN NORTH TOWER, STOKESAY CASTLE, SHROPSHIRE.

"Elynge is that halle eche day in the wyke,
Ther the lorde ne the lady liketh nat to sitte.
Nowe hath eche ryche a reule to eaten by himsilve
In a privey parlour for pore mennys sake;
Or in a chamber wyth a chymney, and leve the cheef halle
That was mad for melis men to eten inne."

The lady's chamber, or bower, we have seen was also provided with a chimney in Henry III's time.

Fireplace hoods were sometimes constructed of wood and plaster. The bailiff of Kennington is ordered to make a chimney of plaster in the Queen's chamber there. It is thought that many of these may have disappeared, having become ruinous in a roofless building and fallen down, leaving no trace behind.

The fireplace in an upper room at Stokesay appears to have had a hood of wood and plaster (Fig. 24). The original moulded oak curb or frame, projecting 3 ft. from the wall, still remains. This is carried on stone corbels springing from shafts with moulded caps. Although this hood probably was of wood and plaster it was not constructed with a flue entirely on the face of the wall but has a recessed throat to the chimney, the front of which has disappeared, the flue terminating in the usual way with two short chimneys as in Fig. 25. It is not very clear why this throat, if having had a hood of lath and plaster, should have been finished with dressed stones, and the stone lintel at the top ornamented with sinkings on its face. This is the only one of the kind which we have met with.

FIG. 25.

We see from the foregoing illustrations that the typical thirteenth century fireplace was hooded and with jamb shafts on

FIG. 26. FIREPLACE IN SOUTH WING, CHARNEY, BERKS.

each side of a shallow recess, which sloped backward as it ascended. Less important examples occur where the fire hearth is deeper and recessed into the wall in the ordinary way. These may be seen in the tower of Stokesay with arched heads of segmented form as in Plate XLII, the licence to crenellate this building being obtained in 1291, and at Charney, Berks, where the head is in the form of a flattened trefoil (Fig. 26).

Stone-hooded fireplaces continued to be built during the fourteenth century with the same changes in mouldings and carving which mark the buildings of that period generally. The jamb shafts with caps and bases gave place to moulded jambs which projected from the main wall by a series of curves forming corbels to support the hood, as seen in the examples from Meare, Somerset (Fig. 27), Ludlow Castle (Fig. 28), and Bampton, Oxon (Fig. 29). The projecting side stones at the base of the hood, as in the earlier example at Netley (Fig. 20), continued to be built. At Meare these take the form of a capital

FIREPLACES OF THE "DECORATED" PERIOD

FIG. 27.

terminated at its base with foliage (Fig. 27), and at Ludlow a carved boss of foliage with head in the centre and moulding to form a shelf is seen (Fig. 28). At Bampton (Fig. 29) an ingenious arrangement of lintel is shown, the moulded course and part of the hood being worked on the same stone which rests on the corbels. This device has been successful, as it remains in good condition after five hundred years, whereas many others have fallen.[1] The hood at Meare is a fine one; the lintel forming its base, said to be all in one stone, forms on plan an obtuse angle in the centre in an unusual way. In the banqueting hall of the Edwardian Castle of Conway a fireplace belonging to the period under consideration, shows a vigorous and original treatment of the abutment stones (Fig. 30),

FIG. 28. LUDLOW CASTLE.

[1] This fireplace is in the part of the building of Aymer de Valance, who obtained his licence to crenellate his castle in 1315.

and Fig. 31 shows a less elaborate example in one of the round towers. This may be compared with the Norman fireplace at Coningsburgh (Fig. 15), both being constructed in a circular wall. The fireplace in the late fourteenth-century hall of Cobham College, Kent, is shown in Fig. 32. Although this may be grouped with the hooded fireplaces, the mouldings and form

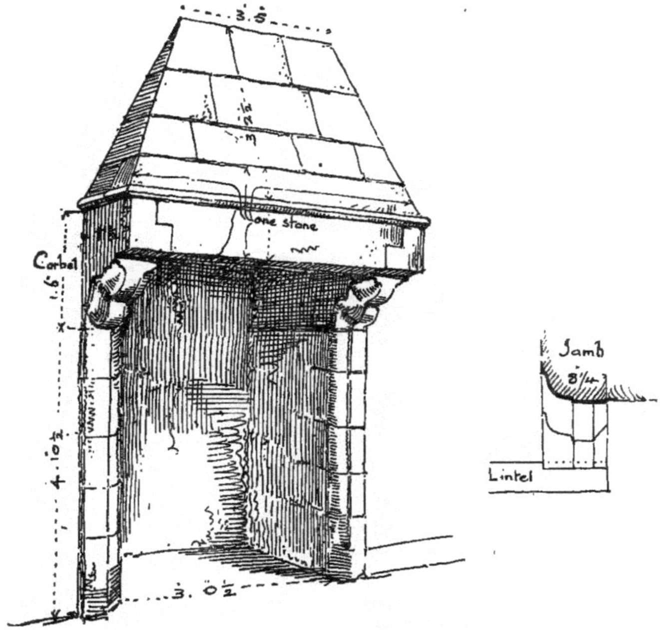

FIG. 29. STONE FIREPLACE, BAMPTON CASTLE, OXFORDSHIRE.

of arch indicate a later date, and the clumsy way in which the hood encroaches on the corbel to roof principals suggests that it is a later insertion. This chimney-piece is of clunch, carved with very small ornaments on the faces of corbels and in spandrel. As was commonly done in old fireplaces, the chimney is divided into two flues, which have separate shafts built of small red bricks.

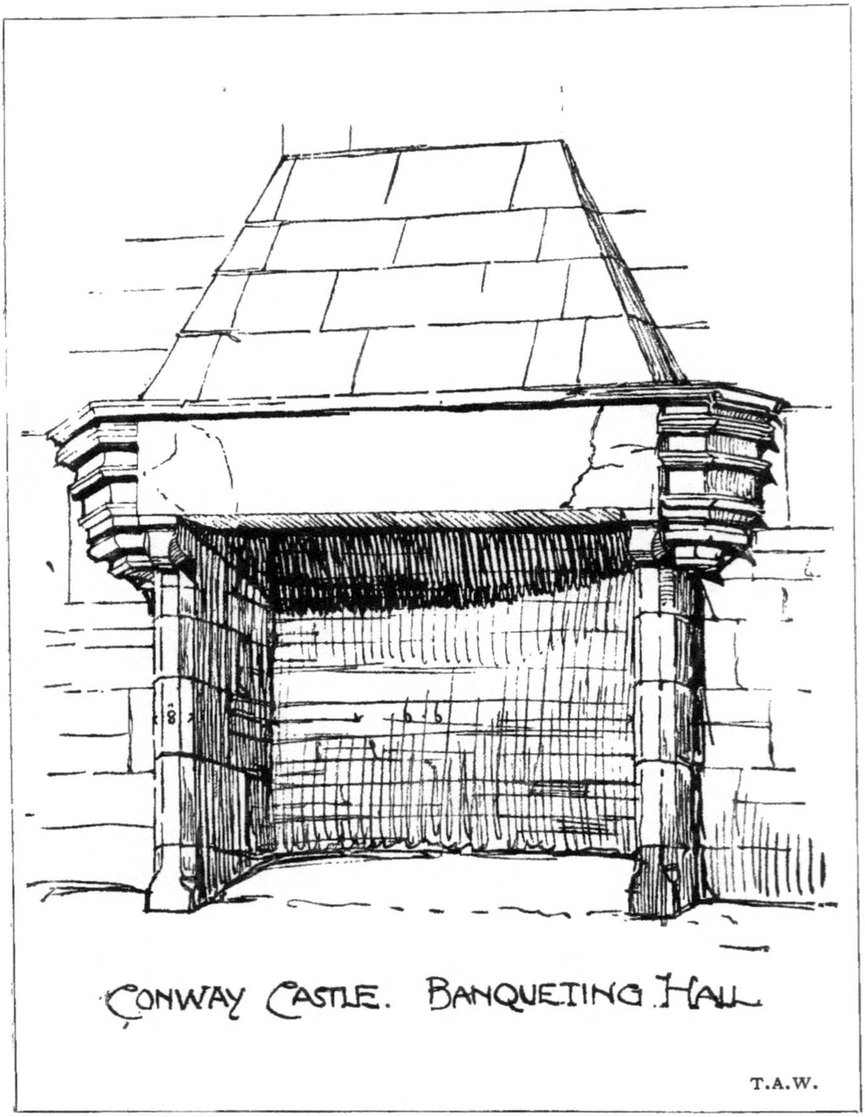
CONWAY CASTLE. BANQUETING HALL
T.A.W.

FIG. 30.

CHIMNEYS OF THE "DECORATED" PERIOD

The chimneys of this middle period of Gothic architecture were very varied in design. The shafts were frequently short, octangular, or square, with battlemented cornice. That at Northborough, Northants shown in Fig. 33, is hexagonal on plan and rises from

FIG. 31. CONWAY CASTLE.

the apex of a gable. It is richly ornamented with gablets and finials, and in the cornice is the characteristic ball flower of the period.

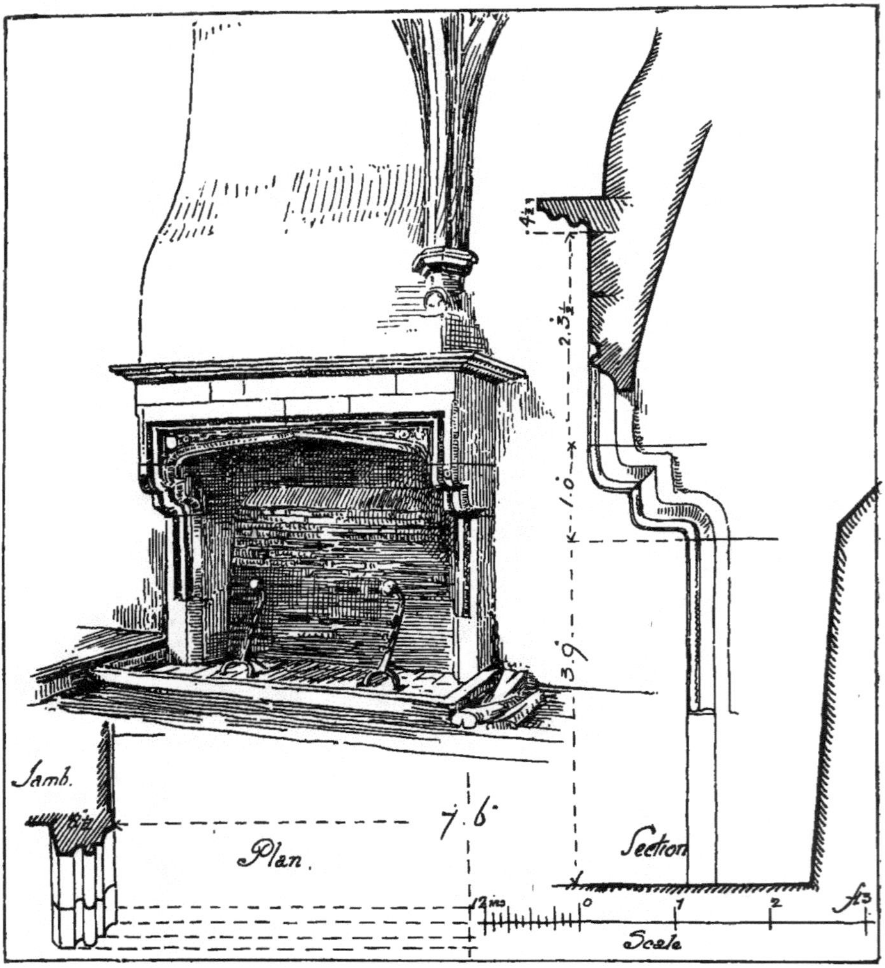

FIG. 32.

There existed, until a few years ago, a good example of a Decorated turret chimney at Burford, the base of which only now remains. Fig. 34 is taken from a sketch made before its demolition. That shown in Fig. 35 is now on a thatched cottage at Harringworth, Northants, and is said to have been removed there from the demolished castle;

TURRET CHIMNEYS

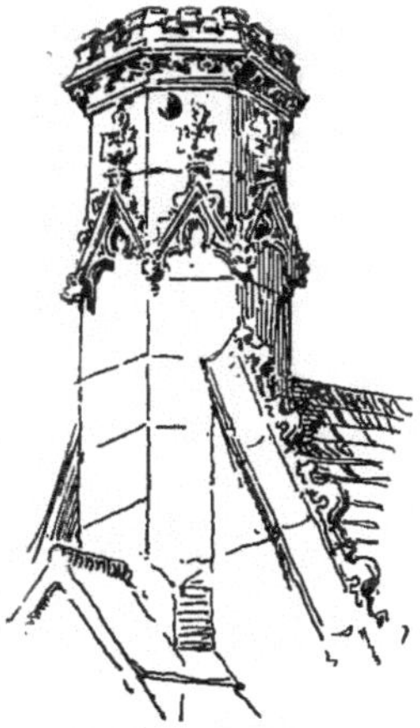

FIG. 33. NORTHBOROUGH, NORTHANTS.

FIG. 34. BURFORD.

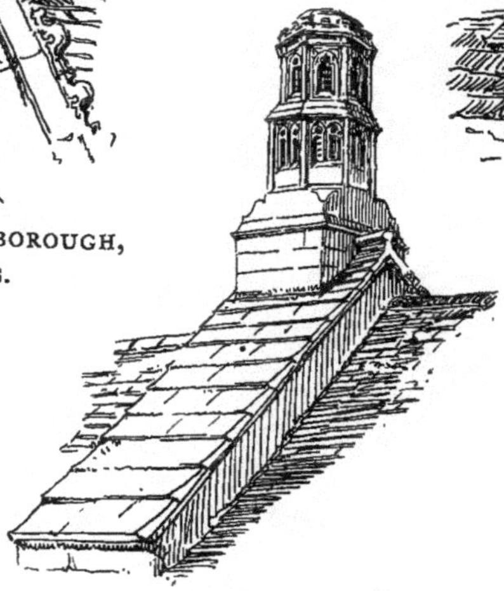

FIG. 36. PRESTON GRANGE, YEOVIL, SOMERSET.

FIG. 35. HARRINGWORTH.

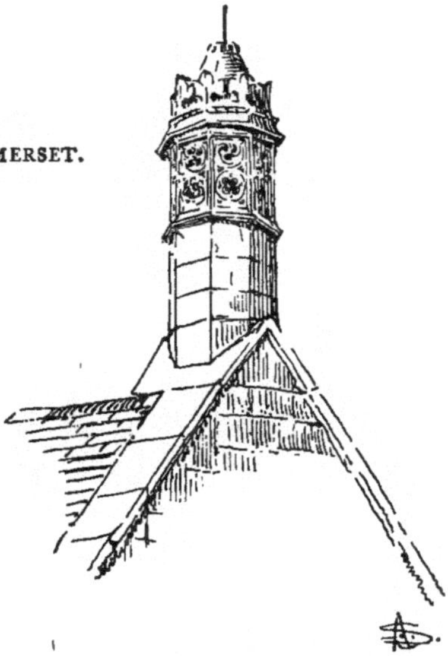

FIG. 37. CHILDS WICKHAM.

others from Preston Grange and Childs Wickham are shown in Figs. 36 and 37. The examples of this type of chimney which still remain are naturally to be found in the stone districts, and it is probable that they were originally more numerous, but the action of sulphurous coal smoke, assisted by rain and frost, has corroded the stone, and, getting unsafe, they have been taken or have fallen down. The form is thought by writers on the subject to have been copied from the smoke louver, but the reverse may have been the case, as the examples of conical stone chimney terminations with lateral apertures which have been referred to at Aydon Castle and Sherborne (Figs. 22 and 23), are of earlier date than any smoke louvers remaining and as

FIG. 38. BODIAM CASTLE.

early as those referred to in the Liberate Rolls of the time of Henry III.

"PERPENDICULAR" FIREPLACES

The plan of placing the hearth against, or only slightly recessed into, the wall, practised by the Anglo-Normans and continued during the early Gothic periods with the hood projected over it, gradually changed, and as the recess was deepened the necessity for a hood became less, until it was finally abandoned. In buildings erected towards the end of the fourteenth century we find the fireplaces entirely recessed and the arch or lintel flush with the face of the wall, as at Bodiam Castle (Fig. 38).

The chambers, on the different floors one above the other, in Guy's Tower, Warwick Castle, all have fireplaces with straight lintels flush with the face of the wall. The great thickness of the walls in these fortified buildings made it possible to get sufficient recess without any projection either in front of or at the back of the wall.

During the fifteenth century recessed wall fireplaces were introduced into dining halls, although the central hearth fire with louver continued to be used. The most usual position was in the side wall near the bay window and below the dais, as at South Wraxhall and Great Chalfield, Wilts. These fireplaces were both wide and deep, and very generally lined with herring-bone brickwork. The hearth space or halpas was often raised a few inches from the floor, bounded in some instances by a low stone curb, and on it stood the andirons for supporting the ends of the logs of wood, to enable air to pass beneath them and quicken their combustion.

In the Lancastrian Hall of Kenilworth Castle there are two wide fireplaces opposite each other between the windows in the side walls (Fig. 39). These are of red sandstone, the same as the

FIG. 39. FIREPLACE IN HALL, KENILWORTH CASTLE.

walls of the building, and the backs of firestone, which still shows the red colour caused by the action of the fire. Their design is singular, in respect of the way in which a very large bead is carried up from the splayed jambs to a square angle, making a pointed arch on each side, the spaces so formed being filled with delicate tracery. The chimneys which terminated the flues carried up in the thickness of the wall do not now remain.

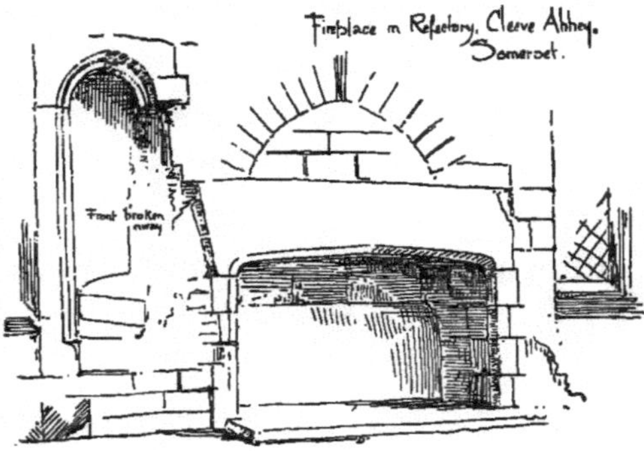

FIG. 40.

In their simplest form these fifteenth-century fireplaces consisted of a four-centred arch, with chamfer on the angle which ran down the jambs on each side (Fig. 40). These were generally of stone, but sometimes of brick, both plastered and unplastered. The jamb mouldings became elaborated and were stopped on a splay well up from the floor, and the head was enriched with tracery enclosed in the square form, as at Minster Lovell, Oxon (Fig. 41), and at the

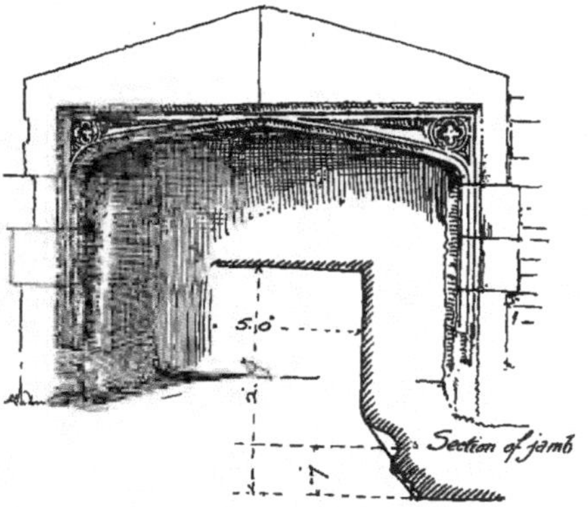

FIG. 41. TUDOR FIRE-PLACE AT MINSTER LOVELL, OXON.

FIG. 42.

Bede House, Lyddington, formerly a palace of the Bishops of Lincoln (Fig. 42). The four-centred arch was the most convenient for a fireplace, and the deep lintels required to span the wide openings presented a suitable field for elaboration.

FIG. 43.

These were enriched with tracery and shields, as in the Upper Chamber of the same building (Fig. 43) and in Fig. 44 from Salisbury. In this latter some projection from the face of the wall has been given to the chimney-piece and a cornice added. A further development consisted of enclosing the composition above described with pillars at the sides, which have base mouldings, and a cap formed by breaking round them the members of the cornice which crowns the whole as in Fig. 45, from the Church House, Salisbury. This arrangement, in a more elaborate form, is seen in Fig. 46, being a drawing of one of the four fireplaces which remain at Tattershall Castle, Lincolnshire, plaster casts of which are in the Victoria and Albert Museum, South Kensington (see Plates I and II). Tattershall Castle is a brick castellated building erected between the years 1433 and 1455 by Lord Treasurer Cromwell, and the purse which frequently occurs in the panels refers to the office held by him. These are, perhaps, the

FIG. 44. AT SALISBURY.

FIG. 45. CHURCH HOUSE, SALISBURY.

finest remaining examples of late Gothic fireplaces which we possess; the carved ornament and heraldic work are of the most interesting description, and may fairly be considered to represent the high-

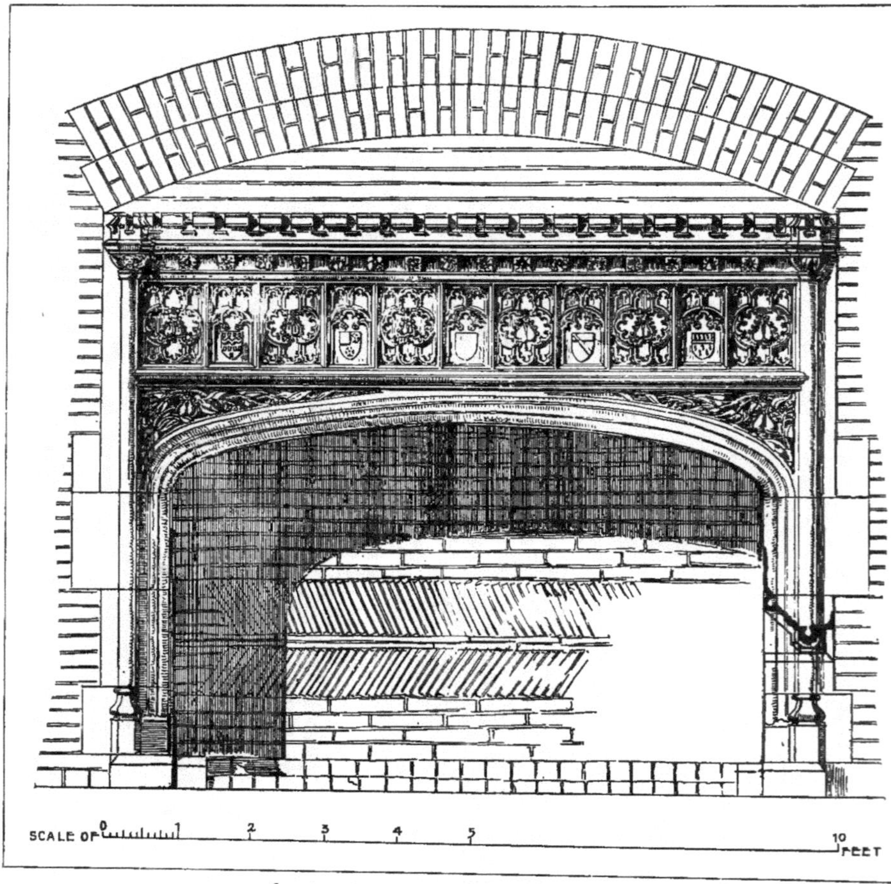

FIG. 46. TATTERSHALL CASTLE, LINCOLNSHIRE.

water mark of Gothic fireplace design and ornamentation. The chimneys have disappeared from the building, which is now roofless.

Fig. 47 shows the stone fireplace in the hall of the Vicar's

ARCHED LINTEL TO FIREPLACE, ON GROUND FLOOR, TATTERSHALL CASTLE, LINCOLNSHIRE.
From a plaster cast in the Victoria and Albert Museum.

ON THE SECOND FLOOR, TATTERSHALL CASTLE, LINCOLNSHIRE.

From a plaster cast in the Victoria and Albert Museum.

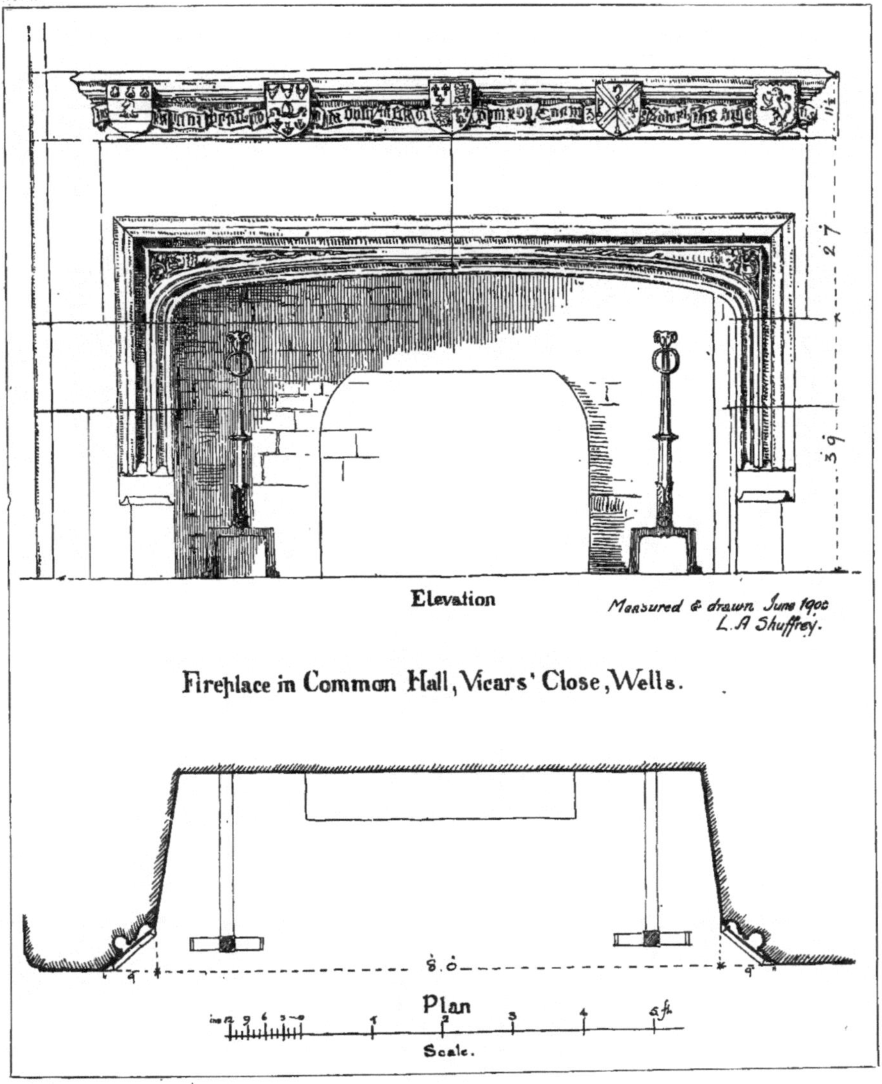
Elevation
Measured & drawn June 1900
L.A Shuffrey.
Fireplace in Common Hall, Vicars' Close, Wells.
8.0
Plan
Scale.

FIG. 47.

Close, Wells, Somerset, which is another fine example of this period and has its original andirons. The arched opening, 8 ft. wide, has well moulded jambs and arch, the latter being formed of two very deep stones with a joint in the centre, surmounted by a moulded cornice on which are carved five shields emblazoned in colour and connected by a riband "bearing an inscription which solicits the prayers of the vicars in favour of Sir Richard Pomroy and expresses solicitude for the safety of his soul." On the right-hand side of this fireplace is a window from which is approached a small chamber used as a pulpit, where grace was said at meal times. At Cleeve Abbey, Somerset (Fig. 40), there is a similar pulpit with steps up to it on the left side of the fireplace, the position chosen showing consideration for the warmth of the brother or monk who had to read whilst the others partook of their meal. The chimney of this fireplace in the Vicar's Close, as shown in Pugin's *Examples*, part i, originally had an octagonal shaft finishing with a battlemented cap, with openings in the vertical faces for the exit of smoke similar to the other chimneys, rows of which form such a striking feature of these dwellings (Fig. 52).

There is built into one of the walls of the ruined Abbey at Reading a handsome fireplace made of clunch. This was brought from a building also in Reading, called the Oracle. Being exposed to the weather, it is fast falling to pieces, but fortunately a scale drawing of it was made in 1878 by Mr. W. T. Walker, of which Fig. 48 is a reproduction. It will be noticed that the design is quite exceptional, the traceried cove formed in the lintel at the back of the three-centred arch being unique, and the sinkings on the inner returns of the jambs met with elsewhere are here elaborated with arches and cusping. In the fireplace at Ludlow Castle (Fig. 49) a remnant of the hood is retained, and an incipient mantel-shelf appears.

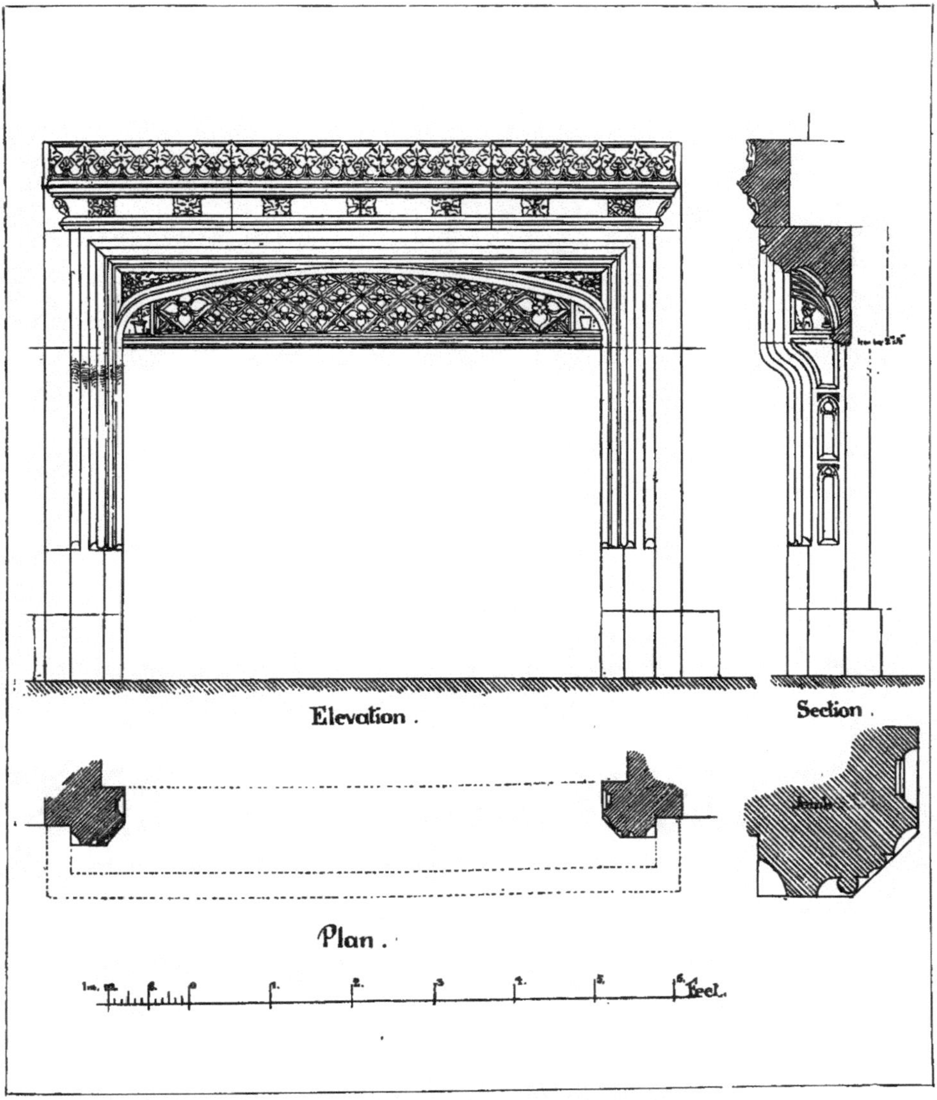

FIG. 48. FIREPLACE AT READING ABBEY.

Fireplaces were sometimes built in churches. At Grantham Church, Lincolnshire, is a singular one in a library over the south aisle, which is placed in the angle of the room and has a stone hood (Fig. 50).

FIG. 49. FIREPLACE AT LUDLOW CASTLE, SHOWING INCIPIENT MANTEL-SHELF.

Plate III shows the stone fireplace in the Board Room of St. Peter's Hospital, Bristol. The present building is a timber-framed Jacobean structure incorporating an earlier one of the first half of the fifteenth century, to which the lower part of the chimney-piece belongs. This is a vigorous piece of work, with bold bosses of foliage at each end of the traceried mantel. The upper part is Jacobean, but the general proportions of the masses being satisfactory, the mixture of the two styles is less incongruous than might be expected, providing an object lesson which is well worth attention.

There was but little change in the general type of fireplace during the latter half of the fifteenth century, or indeed until well into the sixteenth, for in the Great Hall at Thornbury Castle in Gloucestershire we find the same characteristics as at Tattershall and Wells[1]; the same richly moulded four-centred arch, with

[1] Pugin's *Examples*, vol. ii.

THE BOARD-ROOM FIREPLACE, ST. PETER'S HOSPITAL, BRISTOL.

traceried panels and cornice mouldings above. This building was left unfinished by Edward Stafford, Duke of Buckingham, who was beheaded on Tower Hill in 1521, the date on one of the brick chimneys being 1514. Carved bosses in the hollow of the surrounding mouldings and in the traceried panels show the Stafford knot and other badges connected with the family.

The simple shaft on each jamb of the fireplace as seen at Tattershall (Fig. 46) became more elaborate, and in a fireplace of the time of Henry VII at Windsor Castle[1] was made octagonal with hollow faces and detached from the jamb (Fig. 51), becoming a veritable *chimney-piece*. This is ornamented with the united roses of York and Lancaster and the portcullis, the badge of the Beaufort family, from whom Henry VII was descended by his mother.

FIG. 50. GRANTHAM CHURCH.

This chimney-piece is compared by Pugin with those at Tattershall. He contrasts them with those of his time " set up to adorn

[1] Pugin's *Specimens*, vol. i.

our best rooms, that here the greatest skill, both in design and workmanship, was bestowed on common stone. '*Materiam superat opus*' might truly be said of these ancient works, whilst we seek the rarest foreign marbles, and are content to see them in slabs of the most shapeless forms." This paragraph was written by a rigid Goth in the early days of the Gothic revival, about 1821, a time when the marble chimney-piece had sunk to its most degraded condition.

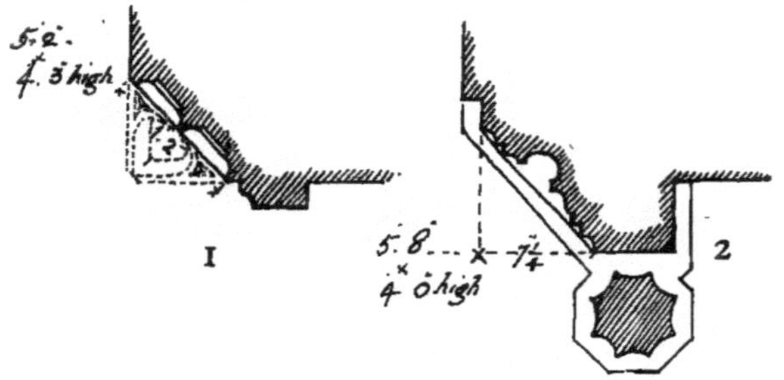

FIG. 51. SECTIONS OF FIREPLACE JAMBS, WINDSOR CASTLE, SHOWING: 1, PANELLED JAMB; 2, DETACHED SHAFTS.

It will be noticed that the fireplaces hitherto mentioned have been in all cases part of the structure, probably built in as the work proceeded, and supplying illustrations of the Gothic principle of "ornamented construction." As so many of the buildings in which they are found are or have been at some time in a ruinous condition, it is due to this that they remain to this day for our edification.

STONE CHIMNEYS OF THE "PERPENDICULAR" PERIOD

The stone chimneys of the Perpendicular period were built taller than those preceding them and varied greatly in design. In colleges and almshouses stacks are numerous, octagon in couples as at All Souls College, Oxford, and single as at St. Cross. Those in the Vicar's Close, Wells, with single octagonal shafts, have been previously referred to (Fig. 52) with their vertical apertures for the escape of the smoke.

As fireplace recesses were deepened and walls were built of

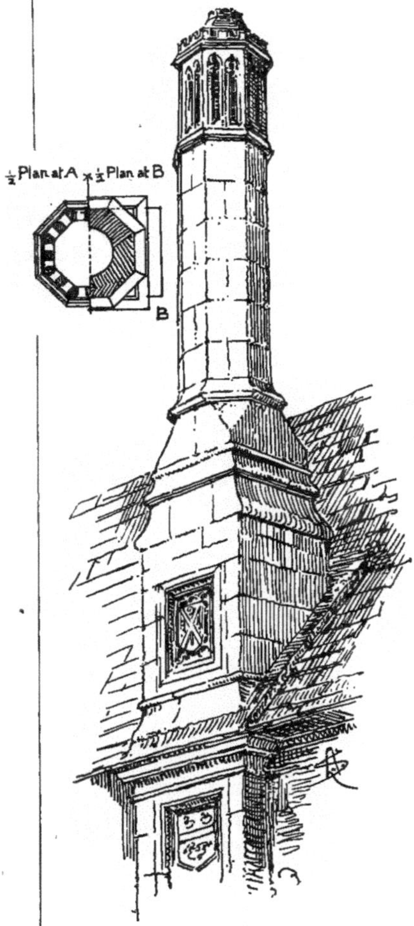

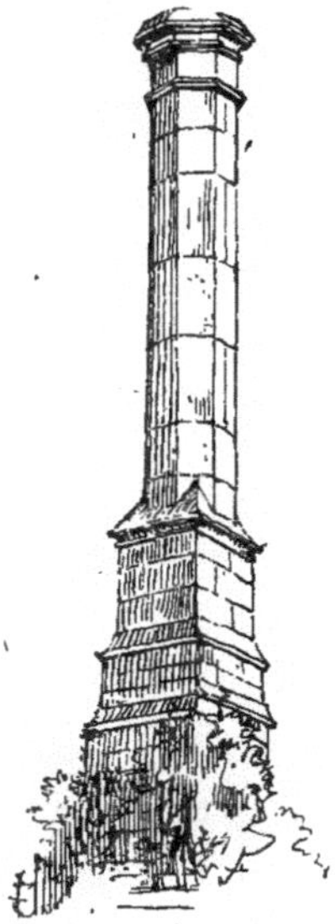

FIG. 53. CHIMNEY AT BISHOP'S PALACE, SOUTHWELL.

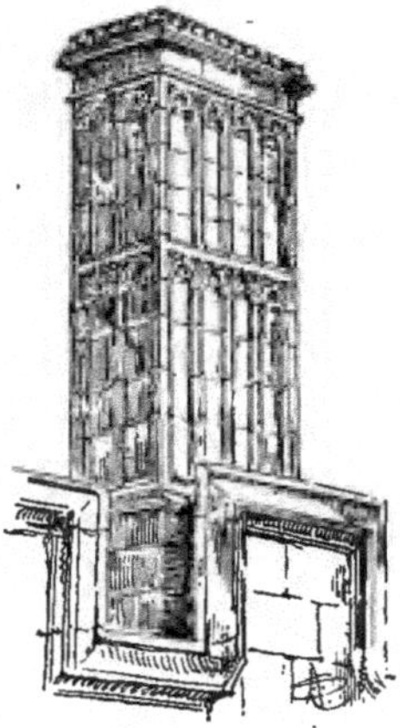

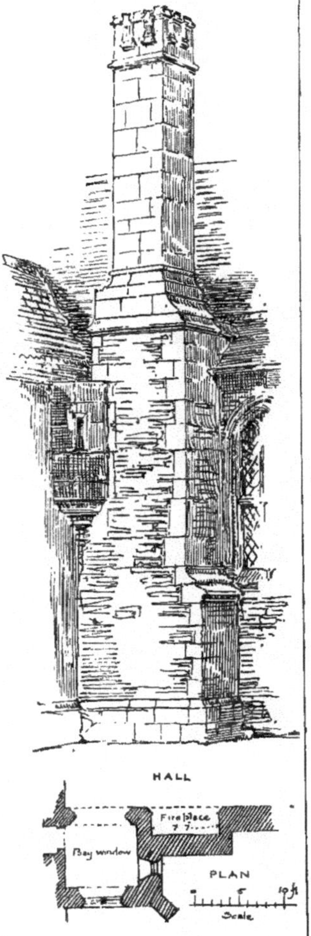

FIG. 52.

FIG. 54.

FIG. 55.

FIFTEENTH-CENTURY STONE CHIMNEYS.

less thickness, it became necessary to project the chimney either on the outside or inside of the wall, and the former plan was the earlier. At Great Chalfield the Hall chimney which comes in the angle adjoining one of the bay windows is projected outside from 2 to 3 ft. to form a recess for the wide open fireplace, and is carried up boldly with set-offs above the eaves, and surmounted by a tall shaft 2 ft. 9 in. square, finished at the top with battlements and a string course (Fig. 55). The battlemented cap was very prevalent, and gave great richness when seen dovetailing into the sky.

At Bodiam Castle (Fig. 38) we find an early example, which consists of tall coupled octagonal shafts with richly moulded caps. Frequently the chimneys were carried up the turret walls, as many are in this building, and show as short excrescences on the parapet walls, doubtless adding to their efficiency, but detracting from their appearance. Many single shafts are met with, generally octagonal in form, with moulded cap and spreading base—as at Bishop's Palace, Southwell (Fig. 53).

The panelling of walls with tracery, so prevalent during the fifteenth century, was extended to the chimneys, as in the example from Wells Cathedral buildings (Fig. 54).

The introduction of the brick chimneys, which present such an important feature in buildings of the sixteenth century in England, belongs to the last phase of Gothic architecture. As the number of fireplaces increased, chimney stacks containing several shafts clustered together were built. In the earlier ones, as at East Barsham, Suffolk, and Thornbury Castle, Gloucestershire (Figs. 57 and 58), the shafts are attached; but in later, detached, and connected at cap and base only—a practical improvement, as the wind passing between them was less likely to eddy and blow down the chimney—

BRICK CHIMNEYS

became more general. Great variety is found in the form of these: shafts are round, octagonal, spiral, zigzag and diapered, with their bases and caps elaborately moulded. The greater number are built of moulded bricks in courses, but at East Barsham the shafts are composed of blocks about 6 in. square with an ornament on each forming a diaper, in contradistinction to others, in which the courses run through independently of the design, the latter being the truer brick method.

Good examples of these are to be seen in the earlier part of Hampton Court, at Eton College, and elsewhere. East Anglia, where there is a scarcity of building stone, was the chief seat of their manufacture. The bricks were generally moulded but sometimes rubbed also as at Hengrave.[1]

Many of these old chimneys having become dilapidated, their top caps have been removed and they have been finished off at a lower level, no regard being paid to the original form.

In considering the origin of the forms adopted for the ornamentation of these shafts, which appear to have come into existence without any previous leading up to, the markings on the pillars of Norman arcades suggest themselves as a prototype, such as are seen in Durham Cathedral and in the crypt of Canterbury Cathedral. The spiral form which, in a pillar, is wanting in appearance of support, is more suitable for a flue, suggesting the upward course of the smoke which it is intended to convey. Decoration of the shaft akin to that found in chimneys is to be seen also in the shaft screens of this period. The spiral form was adopted for stone chimneys as well as brick, as seen in Figs. 58A and 58B.

We have seen that the later Gothic fireplaces finished with a cornice at no great height from the floor, the space of wall

[1] In Gage's *Hengrave* the cost of a brick chimney i sgiven. "Itm paide to Thom. Lyng for making the chymne in the back house for xiijs. iiijd. A bargain was made betwixt Thomas Kytson, Knight, and John Eastawe. Ye said Jhon must macke . . . and of roubed brick all the shank of the chymnies."

FIG. 56.
HAMPTON COURT.

FIG. 57. EAST BARSHAM.

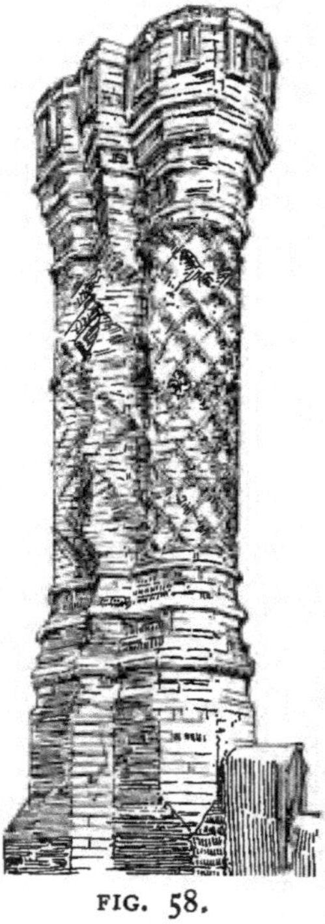

FIG. 58.
THORNBURY CASTLE.

FIG. 58A. BARRINGTON COURT.

FIG. 58B. LAYCOCK ABBEY.

TUDOR BRICK CHIMNEYS.

above was sometimes decorated with tapestry specially designed for this position and called a chimney-piece. Among the furniture belonging to Henry VIII at Wanstead in Essex was "an old chymney piece of tapestrye,"[1] and "a hanging clothe of tapestrye for the chymneys of the storye of Danea" was at Hengrave Hall.[2] These tapestries bore the arms of the owner, as in the great chamber, also at Hengrave. "Item two pieces of like arras which hangs ouer ye chimnees wheof one hath Sir Thos Kitson's and the Cornwallis their armes in the border of it, ye other wrought with great beasts." In the inventory of the belongings of Sir Richard Weston, at Sutton Place, dated 1542, is mentioned: "In my masters chamber vj pec^s of hangyngs w^t a lytle pece on the chemenye of birds and bests of grene and yalowe."[3] The chimney-piece was sometimes a tablet of wood upon which a fabulous scene or armorial insignia were carved or painted, and was not always a fixture, but, like the hangings of the walls, taken down when the owner was absent from the mansion.

CHIMNEY OVER-DECORATIONS

When in the early part of the sixteenth century the wainscoting of walls became general, it superseded tapestry for this position over the fireplace, the whole space around being panelled frequently right up to the ceiling. The favourite form was the linen fold panel, examples of which can be seen at Thame Park, Oxon; Wolsey's Closet, Hampton Court; and in some of the halls of the Colleges at Oxford and Cambridge. The panelling of the space over the fireplace received special attention, and was enriched with armorial bearings and other carving. Henry VIII expended large sums on this feature of the royal apartments, and in an undated roll of that monarch is an entry "to certain ffrenche men working upon the ffronts of chemneys for the privye chambre vjli.

[1] Parker, Fifteenth Century, vol. i, p. 17; *Rot. Reg.*, 1413, 4a.

[2] Gage's *Hengrave*, p. 27.

[3] Harrison's *Annals of an old Manor House.*

FIG. 59. DINING-ROOM, HADDON HALL.

xjs. xjd."[1] At Haddon Hall, Derbyshire, in the wainscoting over the fireplace in the dining-room (Fig. 59), the panels contain the arms of Henry VIII, and in a side panel a shield with plume of feathers and the letters E.P. for Edward, Prince of Wales; also carved on the rail below the motto "Drede God and honor the Kyng."

KITCHEN FIREPLACES

There are many examples of the mediaeval kitchen still remaining with their original fireplaces. In important buildings, the kitchen was frequently a detached building approached by

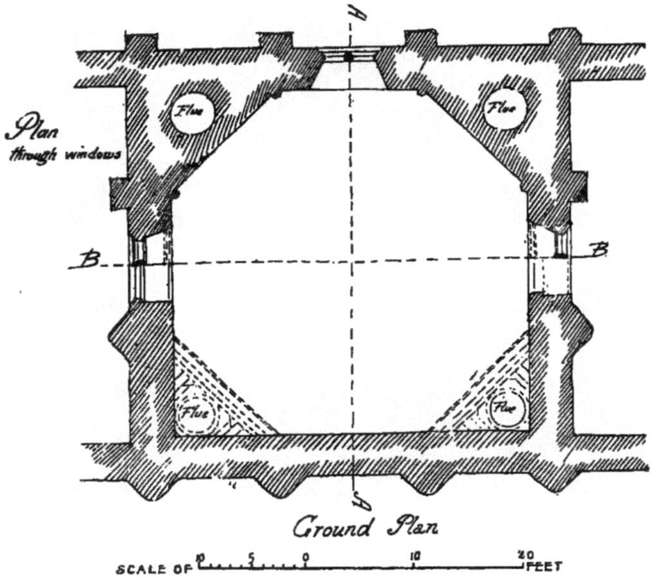

FIG. 60. PLAN OF THE ABBOT'S KITCHEN AT GLASTONBURY.

a passage. The abbot's kitchen at Glastonbury is of this description, and is probably the finest remaining. It is built entirely of stone, square on plan, at the floor level, with a fire-

[1] Parker, Fifteenth Century, vol. i, p. 17; *Rot. Reg.*, 1413, 4a.

place in each corner (Figs. 60, 61, 62). The pointed fireplace arches are built across each corner, forming the chamber into an octagon, and from the eight angles rise arched ribs to a great height carrying the stone lantern above. This is ingeniously constructed to form a cylindrical shaft within the larger octagon, helping to

FIG. 61. ONE OF THE FIREPLACES IN THE ABBOT'S KITCHEN.

carry the top stage, each part being pierced with apertures for the exit of foul air or any smoke which may have escaped into the chambers. The central shaft, probably designed so for constructive reasons, would prove a more efficient ventilator on account of its walls not being exposed to the outer air and rain. The smoke was carried away from each fireplace by a flue in the thickness of the stone angle, but the chimneys above the roof do not now remain. This remarkable building is a fine example of Gothic construction, and an illustration of the thoroughness with which the prin-

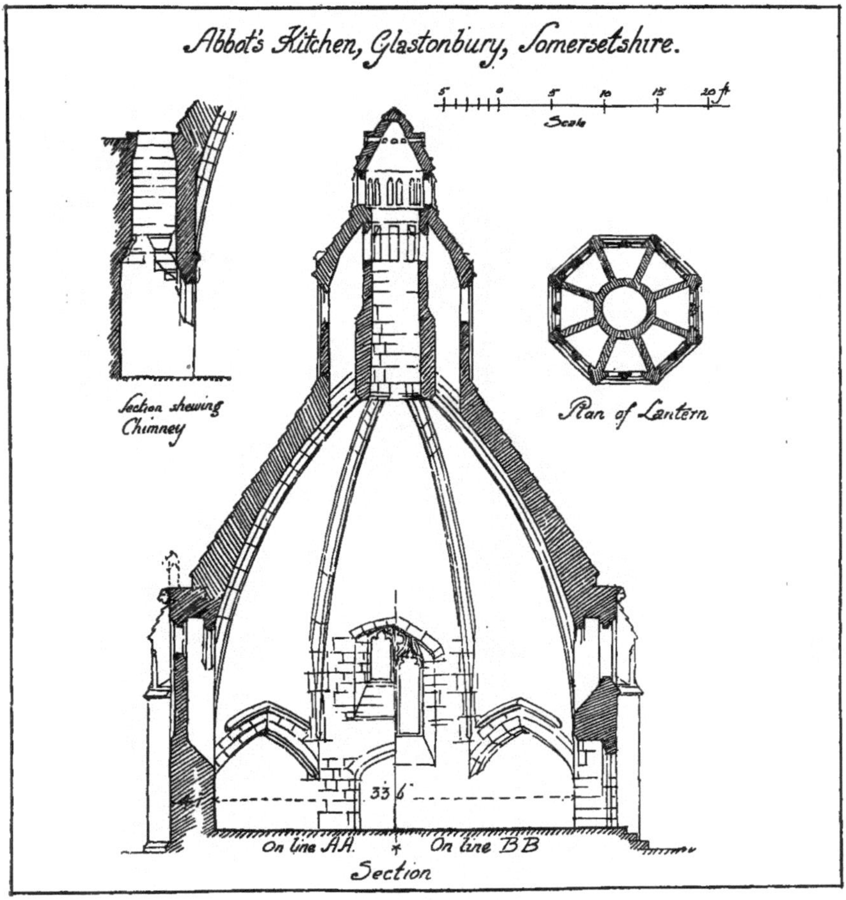

FIG. 62. SECTION.

ciple was carried through the whole of the monastic buildings. Glastonbury was an important abbey, where the finest work would be expected, and with a supply of good building stone near to hand.

The plan and section shown in Figs. 60 and 62 are traced from the very complete measured drawings of this building in Pugin's *Examples*, vol. ii. Fig. 63 is a sketch of the exterior as it now

FIG. 63. ABBOT'S KITCHEN, GLASTONBURY.

remains. The destroyed chimney shafts would have helped to furnish the corners where there is now a void. The date of the building is attributed by Pugin to the time when Abbot Chinnock governed the Abbey from 1374 to 1420.

FIG. 64. KITCHEN, ST. MARY'S HALL, COVENTRY.

Fig. 64 shows the interior of the kitchen at St. Mary's Guildhall, Coventry. It is attached on two sides to the adjoining hall, and in the two external walls are the four fireplaces shown in sketch. These are each 9 ft. wide, large enough to roast a whole beast at a time. The grates, seen on the right-hand side, belong to the eighteenth century, and superseded the earlier form of rest for the spit irons seen in Plate IV in Wolsey's kitchen at Hampton Court. These fireplaces have flues to carry

FIG. 65. SCREEN WALLS AT STANTON HARCOURT.

away the smoke, the lower parts of the massive chimney stacks still remaining. This kitchen is ventilated by means of an original rectangular louver in the middle of the roof, of oak, with gabled ends and openings in the sides.

Another fine example of the kitchen as a distinct building open to the roof remains at Stanton Harcourt, Oxon. It formed part of the Manor House of the time of Edward IV, the greater part of which has been destroyed. The kitchen is a square of about

27 ft., very lofty, with fine open timber roof which rises from an octagon made by arching across the angles as at Glastonbury. Here there are no fireplace recesses, only screen walls as in Fig. 65, about 6 ft. high. The fire was made against the wall, and the smoke ascending found its way out through louvers in the vertical sides of the octagonal roof. Opposite the fireplace are the ovens, the smoke from which when the fire was drawn must also have had to find a similar exit. Fig. 66 shows the plan and interior view traced from *Parker's Domestic Architecture*, Middle Ages; and Fig. 67 is a sketch of the exterior, the oak louvers opening on to the alure behind the parapet approached by a turret stair at the corner. The fine roof is covered by Stonefield slates and surmounted by a heraldic animal.

FIG. 66. INTERIOR OF THE KITCHEN AT STANTON HARCOURT, OXON.

Plate IV shows the interior of Wolsey's kitchen at Hampton Court, and in it many of the old kitchen utensils. The sloping brick piers in the large central fireplace have irons built in, notched for the long iron spits to rest upon. These in early days were probably turned

FIG. 67. EXTERIOR OF THE KITCHEN AT STANTON HARCOURT.

by hand. In an illumination from the MS. of the Romance of Alexander, Bodl. 263, a boy sitting cross-legged is turning a spit on which are threaded two large birds roasting over a fire

WOLSEY'S KITCHEN, HAMPTON COURT.

outside an inn. "Roasted meat when served up in joints was usually taken to table on the spit. This is evident from paintings in contemporary manuscripts, and it was on that account that spits were sometimes made of silver."[1] On the extreme right hand of Plate IV will be seen a spit-jack. This piece of mechanism was for the purpose of turning the spit when the operation of roasting before the fire was in progress, and was fixed on the wall at the side of the fireplace. See also Fig. 70 which is a smaller one. A heavy weight suspended from a cord was wound over a cylinder by means of a handle. The power was conveyed by a series of cogged wheels to another cylinder connected by a cord with a grooved disc on the end of the spit (Fig. 72), which it slowly turned. This weight was sometimes suspended outside the kitchen wall. Many of these spit-jacks are in existence of almost the same design, apparently belonging to the early part of the seventeenth century. The fronts were often of brass and some more elaborated than others. Two charcoal braziers may be seen in Plate IV. In the kitchen, which is all that remains of old Bucklebury House, the weight is dispensed with, the motive power for turning the spit being derived from a fan placed in the mouth of the chimney, which was tapered to a circular shape. The draught from the large open fire passing up the chimney turned this fan, which was connected by means of a rod through the front wall with the jack which turned the spit. Some of these are still in use in our City Halls, the old cooking arrangements at the Hall of the Brewers' Co. being very complete.

Another plan for turning the spit was by means of specially

NOTE.—The following "Item" from the Inventory of the goods of Sir Thos. Middleton gives a good idea of the implements used in a Jacobean kitchen:—"A paire of fire irons, 3 bars of iron, 4 pothangers, a paire of racks, fire shovell, tongs, fire forks, 7 spitts, a jack, and weights and other iron things belonging to the chimney, with five dripping pans."

[1] *Parker's Domestic Architecture*, Middle Ages.

FIG. 68

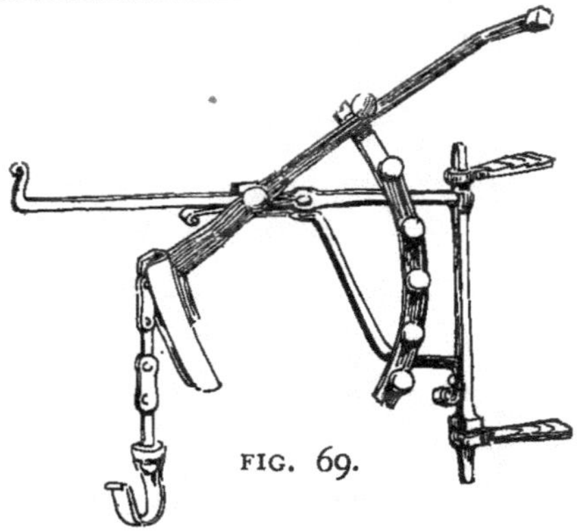

FIG. 69.

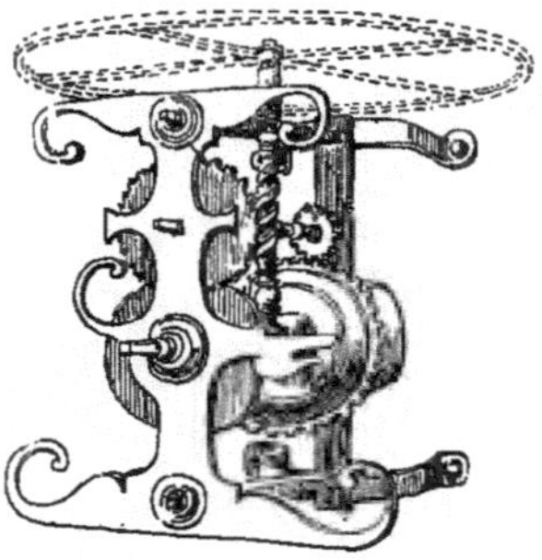

FIG. 70.

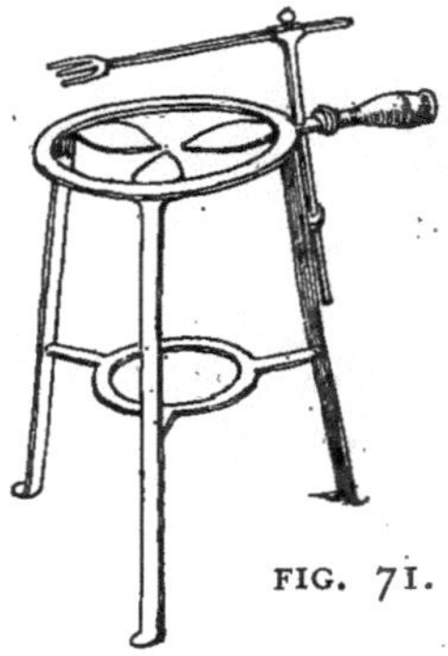

FIG. 71.

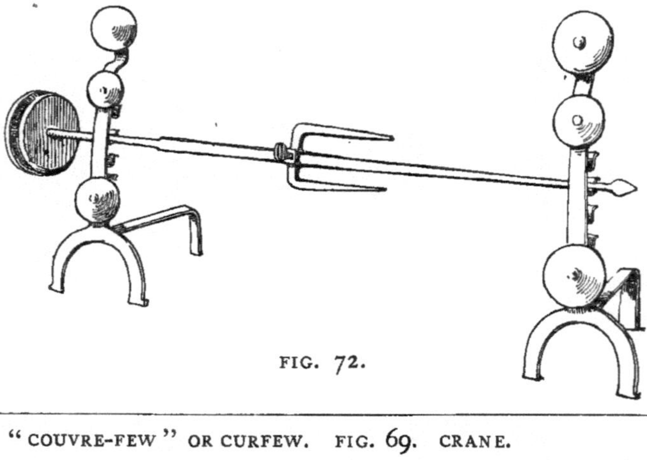

FIG. 72.

FIG. 68. "COUVRE-FEW" OR CURFEW. FIG. 69. CRANE.
FIG. 70. SPIT-JACK. FIG. 71. TRIVET WITH TOASTING-FORK.
FIG. 72. ANDIRONS AND SPIT.

trained dogs known as "turnspits." The dog was placed inside a wheel or drum fixed high up on the wall containing the fireplace, which he had to make revolve with his feet, after the manner of a treadmill. A spindle passing through the dog wheel was connected to the spit by a chain passing over a block by which it was made to turn the joint of meat in front of the fire.[1]

The large size of the fireplaces in the mediaeval kitchens and their number is accounted for when it is taken into consideration how many retainers and menials had to be fed from the kitchen of the lord, and in days when flesh formed a larger proportion of the food eaten than it does at the present day.

THE OVEN

An early accompaniment to the kitchen fireplace was the oven, the operation of baking being shown in old manuscripts, where cakes are being drawn out of an oven on a long-handled fire-pan. The oven has its prototype in the space under the brick or stone hearth. Bernan says: "When Alfred was in the cottage at Athelney, the swaines wife, as a Latin MS. gives it, 'placed as necessity required, a few loaves, which some call *loudas*, on a pan, with a fire underneath, to be baked.'" Matthew of Westminster writes "that the peasant's wife placed her bread under the ashes of the fire to bake" (Turner, *Hist. Ang. Sax.*, vol. i, p. 509). In farmhouses in Norfolk, and other parts where wood is burned, the hearth is swept; and the piece of dough is placed on the hot stone and covered with an iron pan, round and about which the burning embers are carefully raked. The practice still

[1] Dog Wheels, by Edward Laws, Esq., F.S.A. Within the memory of man dog wheels were generally used in the kitchens of Pembrokeshire houses. One survives at Bukor Hill, the property of Mr. George Roch of Maesgwyn, made of wood 2 ft. 4 in. diameter and a width of 9 in. The wheel is smooth inside and 9 ft. from the floor. An iron spindle runs through the wheel, resting on two wooden brackets. The chain went over a wooden block and through a square hole in the mantel-piece. A pure breed of turnspits was in Pembrokeshire, but curs were often used.

is in many cottages and farmhouses to light a faggot in the brick-lined oven, the door of which is in the wall of the fireplace recess, the smoke having to find its way out of the oven door. When

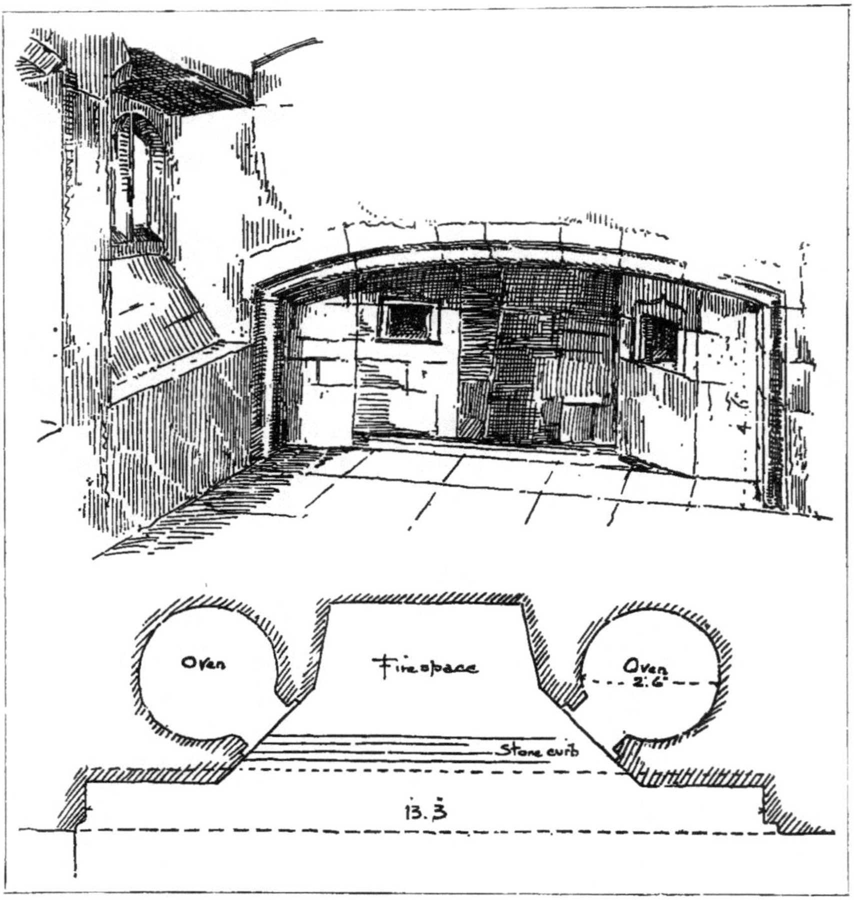

FIG. 73. OVENS AT SKIPTON CASTLE, YORKS.

the wood is burned the ashes are raked out, and the loaves or cakes take their place on the oven floor. Although many ovens are still used, probably none are now built in the old manner.

At Barnstaple, Devon, a complete oven of fire-clay is still made in shape like an arched trunk with a small door at one end. Fig. 73 shows one end of the sixteenth-century kitchen at Skipton Castle, Yorks, where two stone-built ovens are formed in the wide fireplace recess with a fire space and flue in the centre. There is another large fireplace in the kitchen on the opposite side for roasting.

In cottages on the Chiltern Hills, Bucks, an old form of oven is still to be seen, set between the low hobs of the open fire and made of iron in the form of a box with a door in front. The top being level with the hobs, a flue is formed under it, which comes up into the chimney at the back. The fire can be made either beneath or above the oven. In the chair manufacturing district the shavings from the beech wood are used for heating this oven. This oven was afterwards placed at the side of the fire and became a part of the kitchen-range introduced at the end of the eighteenth century.

THE INCREASE OF FIREPLACES

The recessed fireplace with chimney, which, as before stated, was introduced into the hall of the manor house during the fifteenth century, and three centuries earlier into other rooms of castles and important buildings, found its way during the sixteenth into the hall or house place, the general living room, of the yeoman. There are in Kent houses which originally had a central hall or living room of one storey open to the roof, between wings of two stories, into which a floor and at the same time large fireplaces with chimneys have been inserted. It is supposed that these were previously supplied with a central hearth fire only, the smoke from the fire of wood finding its way out through window openings or hole in the roof. Mr. Reginald Blomfield [1] says that "the change can be followed closely in the half timber houses of the Weald of Kent."

William Harrison, writing about 1577, says: "There was an old man yet dwelling in the village where I remain which have

[1] *Short History of the Renaissance.*

noted three things to be marvellously altered in England within his sound remembrance, and other three things too much increased. One is the multitude of chimneys lately erected, whereas in their young days there were not above two or three, if so many, in most uplandish towns of the realm (the religious houses and manor

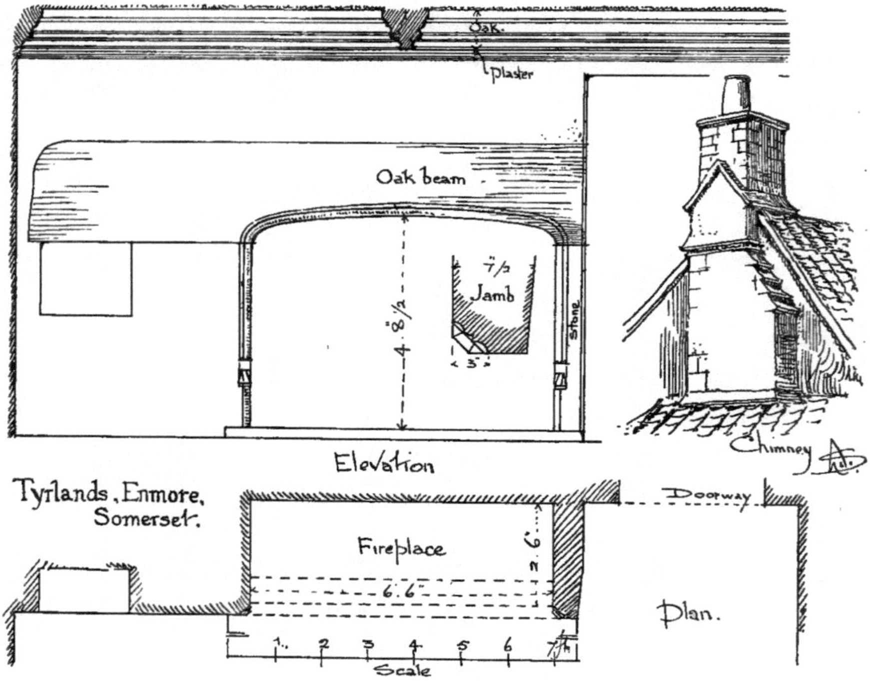

FIG. 74. TYRLANDS FARM.

places of their lords always excepted, and peradventure some great personages), but each one made his fire against a reredos in the hall where he dined and dressed his meat."

We may assume that the memory of this old man extended back fifty or sixty years before Harrison's time, or to the early part of the sixteenth century, and that it was during this interval that fireplaces or chimneys were becoming common in houses of the smaller kind; and we find in Somersetshire farmhouses examples which appear from the style of the buildings to belong to this period. These are in the principal living rooms, which have original ceil-

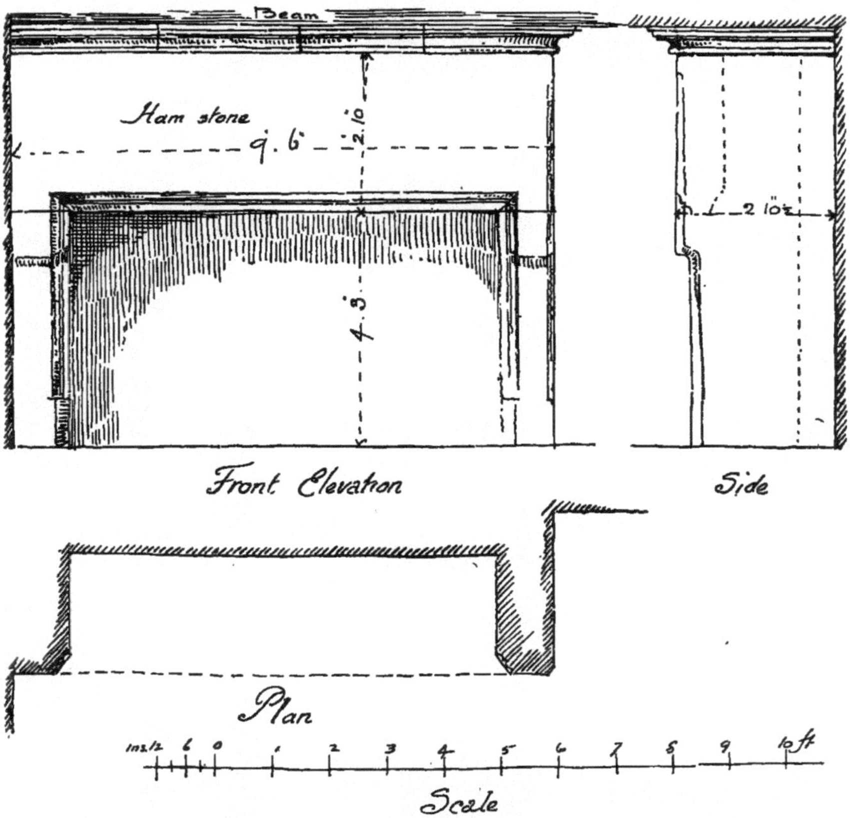

FIG. 75. FIREPLACE IN THE PRIEST'S HOUSE, MUCHELNEY, SOMERSET.

ings constructed of moulded beams and joists to carry the floor above and are not converted as in the yeoman's houses in Kent, previously referred to (see Figs. 76 and 77).

At Tyrlands, Enmore, the fireplace jambs are of stone, but the

FIG. 76. SMALL FARMHOUSE, SAMPFORD BRETT, SOMERSET.

mantel beam is of oak, cut to an arched form and moulded the same as the jambs (Fig. 74).

The plan of placing the fireplace against one side wall of the room was a usual one, and we meet with it again at the priest's house, Muchelney (Fig. 75), the relative positions of door and fireplace being the same as in the preceding. Here both jambs and the huge lintel are of stone from the Ham Hill Quarries in

FIG. 77. SAMPFORD BRETT: INTERIOR OF FARMHOUSE.

the neighbourhood, as also the cornice which finishes under a beam of the ceiling.

At Sampford Brett (Figs 76 and 77) we find another example with stone jambs and wood lintel. An oven is built out at the back of the fireplace and a small opening in the wall admits light to the fire-space. Stone hobs and fire-bars have here taken the place of the fire on the hearth.

The chimney (Fig. 76) lacks any details to associate it in date with the Gothic doorway and window, or the moulded beams in the ceiling, so may be a later addition, a supposition strengthened by the existence of the plaster ornament of frieze which would not be earlier than Queen Elizabeth's time.

These three Somersetshire fireplaces, although of considerable width, have not sufficient height in the openings to be used as chimney corners, which appear to have been a later development.

Harrison deplores the change of the fire, from the central position to the side, with its attendant chimney to take away the smoke, and attributes to it the softening of men's characters from "oke" to willow, and says: "Now have we many chimnies; and yet our tenderlings complain of rheums, catarrhs and poses. Then had we nothing but reredosses; and yet our hedes did never ake. For as the smoke in those days was supposed to be a sufficient hardening for the timber of the house, so was it reputed a far better medicine to keepe the good man and his familie from the quack or pose, wherewith as then verie few were oft acquainted."

When discussing the central hearth we have given the fireplace in the middle of a Shetland cottage as illustration of the reredos referred to by old writers. It is thought that "covers" were sometimes erected over these, the term being used by Leland when describing an arrangement at Bolton Castle, which differed from them, for carrying away the smoke by "Tunnells" made on the sides of the wall between the windows.[1] Parker, when referring to this, states: "The walls of this hall are standing, and there are no chimneys or fireplaces in it, either between the

[1] From *Leland's Itinerary*, 1538. "One thinge I muche noted in the Haulle of Bolton, how chimneys were conveyed by Tunnells made on the syds of the wauls betwixt the lights in the Haull; and by this means, and by no Covers, is the smoke of the Harth in the Hawle wonder strangly conveyed. There is a very fair cloke at Bolton *cum motu solis et lunæ*, and other conclusyons. It was finiched or Kinge Richard the 2 dyed."

windows or anywhere else." So we are unable to learn from the building what these were like; but from the wonder created in the mind of Leland, an experienced observer, we may assume that they were quite exceptional in his time—1538. Fig. 78, from a MS. of the Romance of Alexander in the Bodleian Library, shows a fire burning under a canopy which is continued up as a chimney with a stork's nest on the top: as may still sometimes be seen over disused chimneys on the Continent. There is nothing to show whether this was in the centre of the room or against a wall; if the former, it would be a difficult thing to construct, and the obvious advantage of placing it against a wall except in the case of wooden buildings must soon have occurred to the old builders. Some such arrangement seems to be described by Carew in his Survey of Cornwall in 1602, when he says "the ancient manner of Cornish building was . . . to set hearths in the midst of the roome for *chimneyes* which vented the smoake at a louer in the toppe."

FIG. 78. FIRE-PLACE AND CHIMNEY, FROM AN ANCIENT MS.

Another supposition in that "covers," as mentioned by Leland, may have been another name for hoods. Aubrey says: "Antiently, before the Reformation, ordinary men's houses as copyholders and the like had no chimneys but flues like louver holes; some of them were in being when I was a boy." These flues probably went obliquely through the external wall, with aperatures under the hood or cover as at Abingdon (Fig. 19), or as in the Early Norman fireplaces. Circumstances varied, such as, whether the wall was an external one, whether constructed of stone or brick or of timber and plaster. For examples of simple hooded fireplaces we must go to those districts which are least affected by modern methods, as in the crofter's dwellings of Scotland or in the Irish cabins. Fig. 11 shows a crofter's fireplace with hobs set against the wall enclosed by stone jambs which carry the hood. This is seen in a somewhat different form in an Irish example (Fig. 79), where brick corbellings support the mantel-tree, from which rises a plastered hood. The next stage in the development of the fireplace is seen in the familiar illustration from Shakespeare's Birthplace (Fig. 80), where the mantel, resting on brick piers built up from the ground, carries the front of the chimney enclosure. We thus arrive at the ordinary chimney breast, which is stated by a writer in the Architectural Publication Society's Dictionary to be peculiar to this country. The wooden beam was superseded by the brick arch on an iron chimney bar, such as is still used.

FIG. 79. FIREPLACE IN IRISH CABIN.

Town houses being mainly of wood, and the floors strewed with straw or rushes, fires were frequent, especially in London, and the magistrates, says the *Chronicle of London*, quoted by Strutt, " are empowered to enquyre if there be any house in the ward that is tiled without other thing than tile or lead, and if there be any chemini that hath a reerdos made uncomli, otherwise than it ought to be." The scavengers' oath of office was, that they should examine that all " chemys, reedossys and furnessys be made of stone for defent of fire." That chimneys of plaster were made we have seen, as Henry III ordered one to be made in the Queen's Chamber at Kennington. In Mr. Ralph Nevill's book on *Old Surrey Cottages*, he refers to a " curious form of wattle and clay chimney," and gives extracts from the records of a court leet held at Clare in Suffolk in 1621, where a Mr. Skinner, of Sudbury, is stated to have erected a dangerous chimney and is ordered to amend it and afterwards fined for not doing so, and an order is made by the Court, " That no man shall erect and build up any chimney within the borough but only of brick, and to be builded above the roof of the house fower feete and a halfe, upon the pain for every such offence to be hereafter committed the summe of vl." and on April 7, 1719, other clay chimneys are ordered to be rebuilt of brick.

FIG. 80. FIREPLACE IN SHAKESPEARE'S BIRTHPLACE, STRATFORD-ON-AVON.

The mantel-tree or beam was often richly carved. Fig. 83

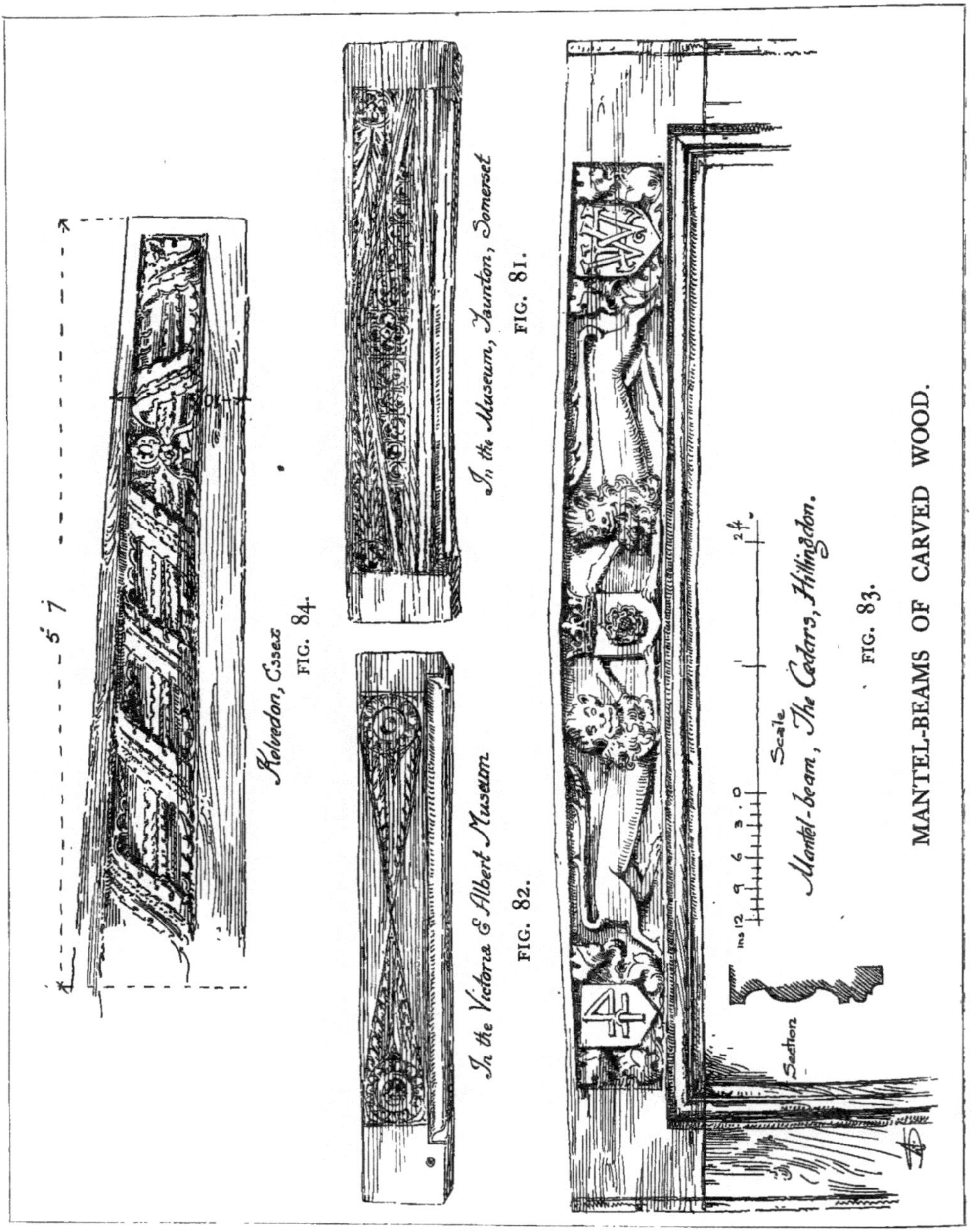

Kelvedon, Essex
FIG. 84.

In the Museum, Taunton, Somerset
FIG. 81.

In the Victoria & Albert Museum
FIG. 82.

Mantel-beam, The Cedars, Hillingdon.
FIG. 83.

MANTEL-BEAMS OF CARVED WOOD.

shows an interesting one from Essex now at the Cedars, Hillingdon, which has a crowned shield bearing the Lancastrian rose and lion supporters, the jambs in this case being of oak as well as the beam. Others are shown in Figs. 81, 82, and 84.

THE MANTEL-TREE

In the example from Faversham a richly moulded oak beam spans the opening 10 ft. wide, the spandrels showing early renais-

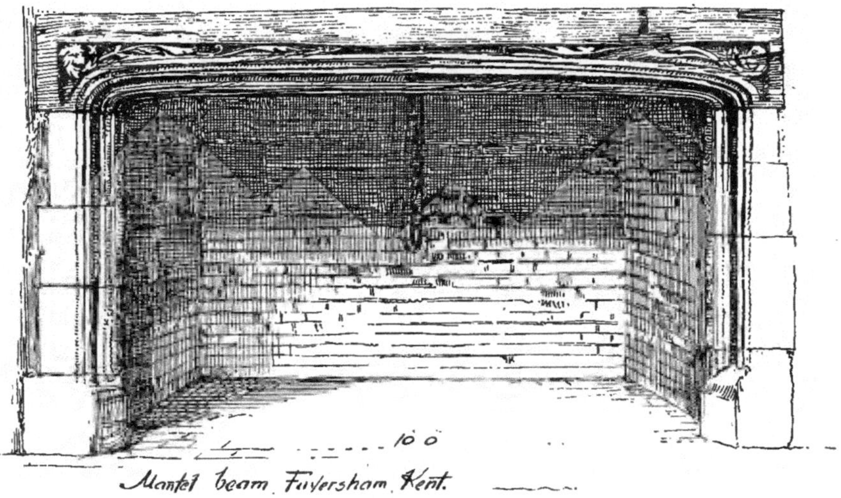

FIG. 85.

sance ornaments (Fig. 85). Mottoes were sometimes carved on mantel-beams. A curious beam was found in an old mansion in Kent, on the ends of which were carved the words "Wass heil" and "Drinc heile," with a wassail bowl in the middle, on which were shown two hawks, intended as a rebus of the builder's name, Henry Hawkes.[1] The provost of Eton says:—

"Always, if we touch any tender matter, let us remember

[1] *Antiq. Repertory*, vol. iii, p. 155.

his motto that wrote upon the mantel of his chimney, where he used to keep a good fire, Optimus Secretariorum." [1]

THE CHIMNEY CORNER

To provide the ample space required for the work which had to be carried on in connexion with the fireplace of the living room or house part in houses of the smaller kind, a large part of one side was given up to the chimney corner. A fire of logs or peat burned on a raised hearth of brick or stone in the middle of the wide recess.

Fire dogs were used for raising the ends of the logs, and in many instances for supporting iron spits which rested on hooks at the back of their standards (Fig. 72). A brick-lined oven often adjoined the chimney corner, with an opening into it, through which the smoke had to pass out, and thence up the chimney, and this was provided with an iron door. Plate v shows a typical example from near Petworth, Sussex. The oven in this case is on the right, and on the opposite side a small window gives light to the fireplace. The pot-hangers were suspended from an iron bar carried lengthwise across the throat of the chimney, which rested on two transverse bars built into the front and back walls.[2] A substitute for this longitudinal bar was the iron crane (Fig. 69). This had a back standard pivoted on iron staples built into the wall at top and bottom, so that it could swing round over the fire. In the simpler forms a fixed arm stiffened by a diagonal brace was the only means of support for the pot-hangers, but the more elaborate were provided with a lever working on a pin; the long arm, being held in position by a quadrant ratchet, controlled the pot-hook which

[1] *Relequiæ Wottonianæ*, p. 363.

[2] Miss Gertrude Jekyll, in whose book, *Old West Surrey*, many interesting illustrations of fire-side utensils may be seen, mentions that a pole of chestnut was used for this purpose in the simpler cottages.

A COTTAGE CHIMNEY-CORNER NEAR PETWORTH, SUSSEX.

was suspended from the short arm, which it raised or lowered. Many of these chimney cranes are good examples of artistic smiths-work. These fireplace openings, 7 ft. wide by 4 ft. 6 in. high as at Dunsfold (Fig. 86), were usually spanned by mantel beams slightly cambered, with bevelled edge; and projected from the face, on simple brackets, was the mantel-shelf. The height of the opening was seldom sufficient for a person to enter without stooping, and this was often reduced by a small curtain suspended from the

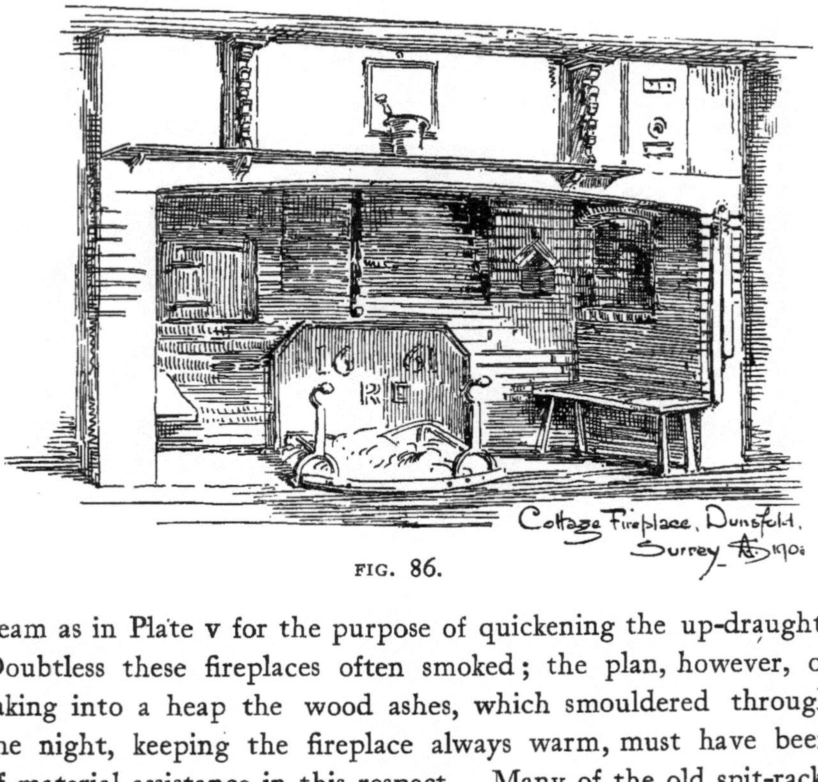

FIG. 86.

beam as in Plate v for the purpose of quickening the up-draught. Doubtless these fireplaces often smoked; the plan, however, of raking into a heap the wood ashes, which smouldered through the night, keeping the fireplace always warm, must have been of material assistance in this respect. Many of the old spit-racks remain as in Fig. 86. These were for resting the bright roasting spits upon when not in use, and often showed interesting design in simple joiners' work. In Fig. 86 the marks remain where the spit-jack was fixed, the mantel-shelf having been cut away for the cord to pass down to the pulley block. A large cast-iron back of simple character was placed behind the fire to protect the back wall. Seats often occupied the space right and left between the fire and the side walls, from which the sky could be seen through the vast sooty funnel. These large chimneys are now often found

FIG. 87.

blocked up as in this instance (Fig. 87), the smoke having to pass through the modern brick hood shown in sketch. The little recesses in the back wall, forming shelves on which to place a cup of ale or pipe, are often found. This capacious mouth to the chimney was sometimes utilized for hanging up flitches of bacon to be smoke cured from the wood fire. Boys were employed to ascend the chimney for the purpose of sweeping, and in some instances iron bars were built in to form steps. With a blazing log fire the draught at the back of any one sitting in front of it must have been considerable, and this inconvenience was obviated by the

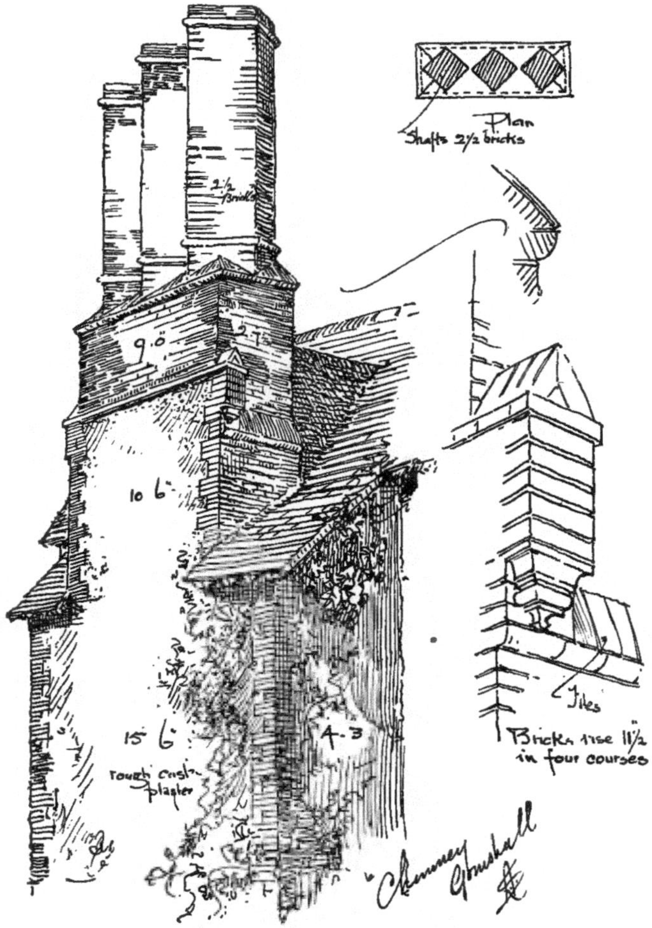

FIG. 88.

use of high-backed settles, some being fixed and others movable. The sketch (Fig. 87) shows one on either side of the fire-hearth. The left mantel jamb has been cut away and an iron support inserted. This sketch, made in 1886, shows the fireplace at the *Bull's Head Inn*, Ewhurst. The writer well remembers the skill with which the landlady produced a hot meal of bacon and eggs for a party of pedestrians at the wood fire shown; the plates being ranged around the raised hearth to warm whilst the cooking was in progress. The fire dogs are of good design with cresset tops, which, whether intended for the purpose or not, are convenient for standing a cup in or for placing a candle on to light the pot.

FIG. 88A.

The converging sides of the mouth of the chimney were sometimes formed of wood and plaster, as in an old house at Worksop, the slope starting from the floor level of the chamber above.[1] A screen or "speer" forming one side of the chimney corner sheltered the occupants from the draught from the door.

When projected from the outside wall of the house these wide and deep chimney stacks have a great artistic value, rising with a mass of plain brickwork from the ground, the earlier ones built of thin bricks, and diminishing with many a weathering and set-off to form a base for the shafts above (Fig. 88). Probably no feature so readily bespeaks an old building, or contrasts so favourably with modern examples. The shafts are never less than two and a half bricks the narrowest way, and many clever devices of plan were resorted to to give scale to stacks on the ridge, as in Fig. 88A, which would otherwise have looked heavy and uninteresting.

[1] *Evolution of the English House*, by Sidney O. Addy.

The Early Foreign Influence

HITHERTO the development of our subject has proceeded on quite traditional lines. Fireplaces of the time of Henry VII at Windsor Castle are quite Gothic in character; as also are those at Thornbury Castle, Gloucestershire, the date of the latter being 1514, as seen on one of the brick chimneys previously referred to. At Samlesbury Hall, near Preston, a large Gothic chimney-piece of granite bears the date 1545 (Fig. 89).

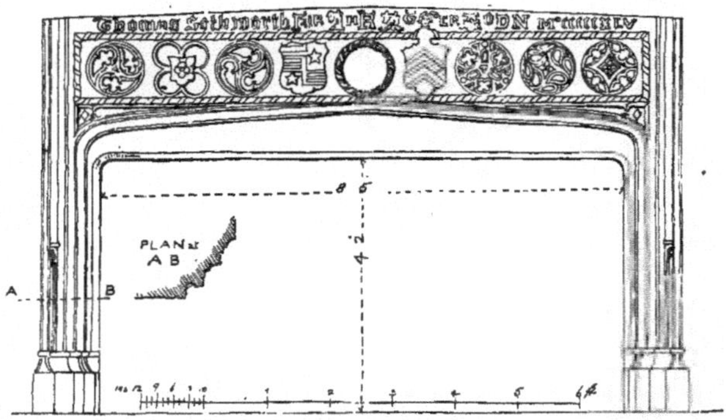

FIG. 89. CHIMNEY-PIECE AT SAMLESBURY HALL, NEAR PRESTON.

With some few exceptions, no great change in the design of fireplaces took place until Elizabeth's reign; the Tudor arched form continued in use until the end of the sixteenth century, in combination with Renaissance woodwork, as seen in Fig. 101. It is occasionally met with still later, as in the stone fireplace from Gloucestershirenow at Ockwells Manor, dated 1673, Plate XXV. The craft of the mason, which hitherto had been almost exclusively employed in the construction of fireplaces, that

FIG. 90. STONE FIREPLACE, BREWER STREET, OXFORD.

of the carpenter being confined to the mantel-beams which we have seen sometimes took the place of the stone arch or lintel, longest retained its traditional style. The example from Brewer Street, Oxford (Fig. 90), ornamented in the spandrels with the rose of England and thistle of Scotland, is probably of James I's time, and has on the stops to the mouldings above the plinths the fleur-de-lys and portcullis. This shortening of the jamb mouldings upon moulded plinths was a pleasing and characteristic feature of Tudor fireplaces; they were often kept high up from the floor, thereby giving the opening an appearance of great breadth. A late form of the Tudor arch is seen in Plate VI, from Ockwells, Berks; and in Plate XXXIX from the Star Hotel, Great Yarmouth.

In the early part of the reign of Henry VIII foreign artists were introduced into England by that monarch and Cardinal Wolsey, who worked in the style of the Italian Renaissance, and were employed principally on tombs, tablets, and busts. We have no evidence to show that the best known of these Italians, Torigiano, Majano and Benedetto da Rovezzano, worked on chimney-pieces here; but an important one by the last named in the National Museum at Florence, composed of a single order, with columns at the sides ornamented with Arabesque carving, represents a type which became general here before the end of the century.

Hans Holbein, who was sent to England by Erasmus in 1526,

Plate VI.

THE DINING-ROOM, OCKWELLS, BERKSHIRE.

combined with his great talent as a painter and decorative artist some skill as an architect; and a drawing of a chimney-piece by him is preserved in the British Museum, of which the frontispiece of this book is a reduced copy. This design is thought to have been made for a palace at Bridewell for Henry VIII, whose cypher it bears, but it is not known to have ever been carried into execution. A description of it from the Museum catalogue is given below.[1] The design shows a masterly treatment of the subject both in general design and particularly in the ornamental details; the same skill, however, is not shown in the architectural parts, the profiling of the entablatures being clumsy and the columns unduly large for their purpose. In the original these are drawn with ink of a different colour from the ornament, and may have been by a different hand.

It is singular that this, probably the first design made in this

[1] DESIGN FOR CHIMNEY-PIECE, PROBABLY FOR HENRY VIII PALACE AT BRIDEWELL.

Two stages flanked by coupled pillars with entablatures. Doric on pedestals below, with Ionic above. The upper part is divided into six panels, richly decorated; the upper three contain the Royal Arms of England, with the motto Dieu et mon Droit in the centre; H and a fleur-de-lys, l.; H.R. and a portcullis (one of Henry's badges), r. The lower panels have a relief of a cavalry combat in the centre; medallions of Charity l., and Justice r. In the centre of the entablature between the two stages of the chimney-piece is the letter H, and the space under this above the fire-place where logs are burning is decorated as a lunette with spandrels; the lunette contains a relief of a battle with a wreathed medallion in the centre, representing Esther and Ahasuerus; the spandrels have l. the head of a warrior, r. the head of a lady, on medallions. The bases of the lower pillars on each side have blank tablets with scroll work. It is of pen and ink with Indian ink wash and colour in parts, about 21¼ × 16¾ ins. The presence of the royal arms, monograms, and badges proves that this superb chimney-piece was designed for some building occupied or planned by Henry VIII. Peachem in his notes on Holbein, in the *Compleat Gentleman*, mentions having seen "of his own draught with a penne a most curious chimney-piece K. Henry had bespoke for his new built pallace at Bridewell"; and there can be little doubt that, as Walpole conjectured, this is the drawing in question. Purchased July, 1854. Formerly in the Richardson and Horace Walpole collections.

FIG. 91. STONE CHIMNEY-PIECE AT WHISTON PARK, SUSSEX.

country for an important Renaissance chimney-piece, should have attained such a high level of excellence. The fire of logs burning on andirons, shown with much artistic verisimilitude, represents the custom at this time.

Holbein worked for the King at St. James' Palace, the ceiling of the Chapel Royal being attributed to him; and in the spandrels of an arched fireplace, a position where Renaissance detail first crept into fireplaces, we find the letters H. & A., standing for Henry and Anne, tied together in a true lover's knot quite in the style of Holbein.

The Italian artists worked largely in terra cotta, and at Sutton Place, Surrey, in addition to much external detail, the fireplaces in the great and panelled halls are of this material. The spandrels of the four-centred arches contain Saracen's heads, the crest of Sir Rd. Weston the owner, and bunches of pomegranates, the badge of Catharine of Arragon, implying a date not later than 1527, when Henry VIII was actively promoting her divorce.[1]

Few important buildings were erected during the latter part of the reign of Henry VIII. The times were too unsettled; the uncertain temper of that monarch and his treatment of Wolsey with regard to his acquisition of Hampton Court probably acted as deterrents to those of his subjects who were disposed to spend their new-gotten riches in building.

One of the few was the palace of Nonsuch near Ewell in Surrey, begun after 1537 by Henry, and left unfinished at his death, when it passed into the hands of Lord Arundel, who completed it. The name associated with its design is Toto del Nunziata, an Italian. The building afterwards came into the possession of Charles II, and was given by him to Lady Castlemaine, who ordered it to be pulled down and sold as old materials. The chimney-piece shown in Plate VII, now at the Priory, Reigate, is said to have

[1] *Annals of an Old Manor House*, Harrison.

come from Nonsuch.[1] This shows a strange medley of features, making up an ambitious whole such as existing descriptions of the palace would lead us to expect. The Tudor arched fireplace of stone is retained, but otherwise the forms are all of Renaissance character and of oak. A well designed order, with detached Corinthian columns standing on consoled pedestals, extends the whole height from floor to ceiling, and between the columns on each side seats are placed, which, surmounted by pediments set diagonally, terminate with a pyramid of models of Italian architecture done to a small scale. John Evelyn, who visited Reigate in 1655, refers to it: "The chimney-piece in the Greate Chamber, carv'd in wood was of Hen. 8 and was taken from a house of his in Bletchinglee." This does not agree with the tradition mentioned by Brayley that it came from Nonsuch, but Bletchingly is in the same district, and it may have been taken there on the demolition of Nonsuch before being removed to Reigate.

There were probably many chimney-pieces at Nonsuch, and it is not likely that all others than the one referred to were destroyed. At Whiston Park, Sussex, an elaborate composition of architectural parts carved in stone is built up against an external wall. This work has the appearance of having formed parts of two, or perhaps three, chimney-pieces (Fig. 91); it is in the style of the Italian Renaissance, and shows great richness and refinement in its details.

It might be expected that there would be many examples showing the fusion of the native and imported styles, but with the exception of the retaining of the Tudor arch previously referred to, this is so to a very limited extent. A chimney-piece now in the Gate House at Kenilworth, removed there from the Castle, shows this mixture (Fig. 92). The letters stand for Robert Leicester, with his badge the "ragged staff," and motto

[1] Brayley's *Surrey*.

Plate VII.

THE PRIORY, REIGATE.

THE BANQUETING HALL, PLAS MAWR, CONWAY.

"Droit et loyal" on the frieze of the chimney-piece, which is now surmounted by an elaborate wooden overpiece in the style of the Italian Renaissance.

One of the few chimney-pieces belonging to the period immediately preceding the reign of Elizabeth is at Laycock Abbey, Wiltshire. It consists of flat panelled pilasters on pedestals which break up through the entablature, framing a rectangular opening, which is perhaps the earliest of its kind. Caps, architrave and cornice have enriched members, but the whole is restrained in design and quite free from Flemish exuberance. The hearth is ornamented in a singular way, a pattern is formed by letting lead into the stone. Mr. Gotch gives a drawing of this chimney-piece in his smaller work on the English Renaissance, and dates it previously to 1553.

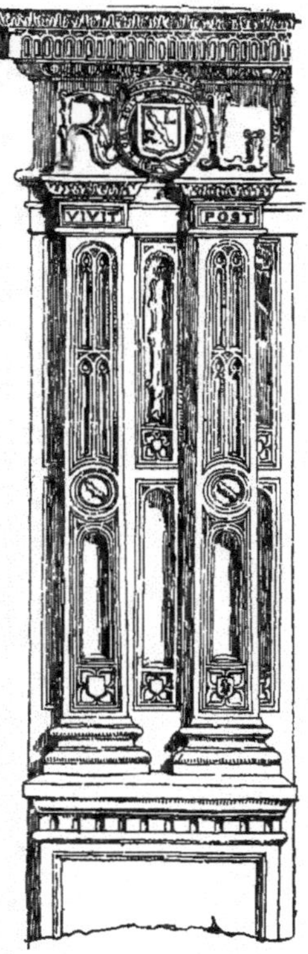

FIG. 92. PART OF THE CHIMNEY-PIECE AT THE GATE HOUSE AT KENILWORTH CASTLE.

At Plas Mawr, Conway, there are several interesting chimney-pieces which, although showing foreign influence in the sections of the mouldings, are quite Gothic in principle, being structural hooded fireplaces (see Plate VIII). The applied ornamentation of the overmantel (dated 1580) is made up of plasterers' models, and may be some years later than the chimney-piece. The chimney-piece Fig. 93 is in the Withdrawing Room of the same building, and retains the structural hood, but treated in quite a Flemish manner with its supporting columns and corbels.

Belonging to the first half of the sixteenth century is the fire-

FIG. 93. CHIMNEY-PIECE IN THE WITHDRAWING ROOM, PLAS MAWR, CONWAY. Date on ceiling, 1580.

place, shown in Fig. 94, at Woodsome Hall, Yorkshire. The fine oak mantel-tree spans the wide chimney corner, and on it are carved the names of the owner and his wife, Arthur Kay and Biatryx Kay, in letters of French character. So similar are these

FIG. 94. HALL FIREPLACE, WOODSOME HALL, YORKSHIRE.

letters to those over a doorway of a church at Oyron of the time of Francis I as to suggest a common origin. The beam rests on stone corbels, forming a canopy from which the chimney recedes; and the fireplace shows a feature commonly met with in Normandy, the back wall being arched, so that the filling-in can be renewed from time to time as is found necessary for repairs.

Fig. 95 shows a stone chimney-piece which was saved from the fire at the old Manor House, Bucklebury, Berks. It appears to belong to the early Renaissance period, showing French influence, but the building from which it was removed having been destroyed it is difficult, in the absence of documentary evidence, to assign it to its historical position. It stands quite alone as to design so far as we have been able to discover.

As might be expected, the chimney-pieces which belong to this period of transition show but little connection one with another, but are rather odd examples whose existence is due to accidental circumstances.

FIG. 95. FORMERLY AT THE OLD MANOR HOUSE, BUCKLEBURY, BERKS.

The Elizabethan Renaissance

THE era of building which commenced in the early part of Queen Elizabeth's reign produced a great revolution in fireplace treatment, in the consideration of which the reigns of Elizabeth and James I may be grouped together, as, although great diversity of design is found, no chronological distinction can be made. The renaissance of classical architecture which had spread from Italy through Europe during the previous century, a foretaste of which had reached England in the reign of Henry VIII by the introduction of Italian and French artists, came in greater force with the advent of Germans and Netherlanders during Elizabeth's reign. Many of these to escape religious persecution in their own country came over and found occupation for their talents here. The spoils of the monasteries which had passed into the hands of court favourites on their dissolution by Henry VIII provided the funds for the erection of numerous stately mansions throughout the country by men who tried to outrival one another in the magnificence of their abodes. The chimney-piece provided a suitable object for display second only to the sepulchral monuments of the period. The only limiting conditions being a fireplace recess some 6 ft. wide by 4 ft. high, great liberty of design was possible. That this liberty resulted in license many ambitious examples show, the executed works being monsters in more senses than one. Many examples of large Elizabethan chimney-pieces, in both stone and wood remain, varying very much in their approximation to regular classical forms of architecture, but almost all showing a complete severance from the Gothic in principle, in not forming an integral part of the structure. So great is their variety that it would be difficult to classify them. Our plates have been selected to illustrate the various types, which will be referred to taking those of stone or marble first. Many are quite out of harmony with their surroundings, being probably the work of men who were responsible for the chimney-piece only. The local materials continued to be used, and were supplemented by marble from abroad, black, white, and coloured. Alabaster, so largely used for monuments, was used for chimney-pieces also. The more important designs consist of two stages, which often occupy the entire height of the room, each being an architectural order. In the lower stage, coupled columns standing on pedestals on each side of the fireplace support an entablature, the cornice of which forms the mantel-shelf; in the upper, a lighter order is used, the place of the columns being frequently taken by caryatides representing in varying degrees the human form, the lower extremities being merged in a pillar. On the heads of these figures rest in many instances baskets of fruit or flowers which form capitals for the upper entablature to rest upon as at Loseley (Plate IX). The space over the mantel-shelf between the upper columns was frequently filled with the arms of the reigning sovereign as at Enfield (Plate XVII) or of the noble owner as at Cobham Hall (Plate XIV).

Shield with garter, helmet, crest and mantlings, with supporters at the sides resting on strapwork or cartouche, and bearing the family motto, supplied an effective composition for this important position, its appearance being sometimes enhanced by the addition of gold and colour. The absence of an heraldic subject for this place of honour was attended by loss of artistic effect, as will be seen in succeeding illustrations. In the drawing-room at Bramshill House a geometric arrangement of marble rather tamely fills this space (Fig. 96), and in both ball-room (Plate XVI) and cartoon gallery at Knole, although elaborately framed, flat pieces of marble fill this position. At Hatfield House, in the chamber which takes its name from this circumstance, a bronze figure of James I occupies a niche over the mantel-piece.

FIG. 96. BRAMSHILL HOUSE, HANTS.

The Netherlanders delighted in representations of some moral truth or maxim of worldly wisdom, and these, as well as biblical subjects, frequently took the place of heraldry for the embellishment of their chimney-pieces. At Stockton House, Wilts, in the Shadrach room the subject carved in the overmantel is taken from Daniel iii. 25, with the words, "Loe I see foure men walking in the midst of the fire."

At Burton Agnes, Yorkshire, this fondness of the Renaissance designer for sculptured allegorical subjects is very fully exemplified in the great hall chimney-piece. This is of three stages, reaching almost to the cornice of the two-storied hall; the middle stage is occupied by a representation of the parable of the wise and foolish virgins; the five wise with their lamps burning are following their usual avocations, the five foolish with their lamps out are playing and dancing. The upper part of the panel, divided from the lower by a bank of clouds, portrays the ordering off of these virgins by angels to their respective abodes of bliss and woe. Figures to a larger scale, one with a book and the other a dove, stand on each side, carrying up the line of the coupled columns below. The top stage is divided into three panels containing armorial bearings divided by armless caryatides. There are many other carved subjects at Burton Agnes: representations of Faith, Hope and Charity occupy the panels of the oak dining-room overmantel, and in a detached piece, a solid block of oak about 10 ft. long by 5 ft. high, the subject is the Dance of Death.

At Speke Hall, Lancashire, Sir Wm. Norris memorialized the fact of his having been blessed with nineteen children by having them carved in the panels of his drawing-room overmantel.

Representations of historical events sometimes took the place of allegorical subjects. In the *Gentleman's Magazine* for 1812 is a description of an important chimney-piece which was at Gosfield Hall, Essex. The central compartment above the fireplace, 5 ft. 10 in. long by 2 ft. high, contained a representation of the battle of Bosworth Field carved in wood in high relief with a statue on the left of Henry VII and on the right of Elizabeth his Queen. Nothing now remains of this fine chimney-piece at Gosfield, but the large subject panels with the figures of the King and Queen are at Stowe House, in Buckinghamshire, having been removed there by the first Duke of Buckingham and Chandos, then owner of Gosfield, in the early part of last century and erected over his library entrance. This carving is the subject of an interesting article by the Rev. T. G. Gibbons in the *Essex Review*, where an illustration of the carving is given.[1] Horace Walpole, writing to his friend, George Montagu,

[1] "An Essex Relic," *Essex Review*, No. 45, vol. xii.

refers to the carving enthusiastically, "It is all white except the helmets and trappings, which are gilt, and the shields, which are properly blazoned with the arms of all the chiefs engaged. You would adore it." From the description in the *Gentleman's Magazine* we gather that this was a Renaissance chimney-piece, having "on each side detached Ionic columns fluted, with bases and capitals, and behind them compartments of warlike trophies." The lunette over the fireplaçe in the Holbein design similarly contains a battle-piece.

When the cornice of the upper stage of the chimney-piece finished below the ceiling of the room it was often surmounted by a pierced cresting of strapwork, as in Plate III, from S. Peter's Hospital, Bristol, and in Fig. 96, from the drawing-room, Bramshill, Hants.

RENAISSANCE CHIMNEY-PIECES OF STONE.

An early example of an Elizabethan Renaissance chimney-piece of stone is in the great chamber, Loseley, Surrey, built by Sir Wm. More, 1562–68 (Plate IX). It is noticeable that this is very similar to the Holbein design in its main divisions; this similarity extending to the cutting up of the space over the shelf into six compartments, which at Loseley are filled with the heraldic bearings of the More family. The caryatid with the fruit basket capital which occupies a subordinate place in the Holbein design takes an important position at Loseley. No feature is more characteristic of the period; it was seized on its introduction with the greatest avidity by designers of chimney-pieces and soon found its way into all parts of the country for execution in both wood and stone. In another chimney-piece at Loseley, shown in Plate X, caryatides take the place of columns in the lower storey, the fruit basket capitals are omitted and trusses rest uncomfortably on the heads of the figures, without any intervening horizontal moulding. The central compartment is here occupied by shields, and between them is a representation of a mulberry tree with Latin epigram referring thereto, forming a rebus on the owner's name More; implying, says Brayley,[1] that the family would, like the tree, be of long endurance, but that its individual descendants would, as is the common lot of humanity, be subject to steady decay.

These Loseley fireplaces retain their original fire dogs, but the larger one has been filled in at some later date with an arched iron front, probably to prevent a smoky chimney by reducing the size of the opening, thereby increasing the draught.

There is in the great hall at Longleat a large two-storied white marble chimney-piece which shows a kinship with that in the great chamber at Loseley, both being early Elizabethan examples which show in their columns and entablatures a direct adoption of the Italian Renaissance style, rather than the Dutch or German rendering of it, which will be seen in many succeeding examples. The Loseley design (Plate IX) suffers from the crowding of rather incongruous features and the disturbing appearance of the caryatid figures paired in different attitudes, but is in its main divisions fine and well proportioned. The overpiece at Longleat has in the centre a caryatid in the form of a mermaid dividing it into two arched compartments, one containing a clock and the other a wind gauge. Coupled Ionic columns in the lower stage and paired caryatides above support heavily enriched unbroken entablatures.

In the example from Little Moreton Hall, Cheshire (Plate XI), a well designed heraldic composition fills the centre compartment, with figures for side supports which represent Justice and Learning. The design is much marred by the clumsiness of the side pilasters.

Plate XII shows a later example at the Red Lodge, Bristol,

[1] Brayley's *Surrey*.

FIG. 97. DODINGTON HALL, SOMERSET.

where the usual breaking forward of the side divisions is absent, with loss of effectiveness to the design, and the decorative arrangement of the upper stage with its heraldic centrepiece and caryatides is poorly conceived and executed.

Fig. 97 shows a stone chimney-piece at Dodington Hall, Somerset, on the northern slope of the Quantocks. The work suggests the hand of a tyro who has succeeded very well with his mouldings, but whose figure work is crude in the extreme. The date 1581 is carved beneath the coat of arms. The andirons of brass are fine ones of this period.

At South Wraxall Manor House, Wilts, several important chimney-pieces remain in the additions made to an earlier Gothic house about the end of Elizabeth's reign, that in the hall bearing the date 1598. The most important of these is in the great chamber or withdrawing-room, shown in Plate XIII. This shows the Dutch influence in its most pronounced form. Coupled caryatides of singularly ungraceful proportions support a heavy entablature with coarse foliated frieze, and a central feature, starting from a head with volutes with mouldings breaking round it, forms a pedestal for a figure of Pan. The side projections are carried up, and the entablature breaking forward rests on enriched columns, which by their diminutive scale emphasize the coarseness of the details of the lower stage. Figures representing "Prudentia, Arithmetica, Geometria and Justicia" as named by lettering cut in the stone fill semicircular-headed niches with Latin mottoes beneath. Cartouches or strapwork cover all the remaining surface of this enormous structure, leaving no resting place for the eye. The fireplace recess is stone panelled, as was frequently done in districts where stone was more plentiful than brick. Another of the series of large Jacobean stone chimney-pieces in this house is in the guest chamber (Fig. 98), which is more restrained design than the preceding, but is lacking in interest in its treatment of the space over the fireplace. It is

FIG. 98. GUEST CHAMBER, SOUTH WRAXALL MANOR, WILTS.

an early example of the type in which one order enclosed the whole composition, both mantel and overmantel.

There was, until recently, when it was removed for erection elsewhere, a very fine stone chimney-piece in John Langston's House,

Welsh Back, Bristol.[1] This presents points of resemblance to the large one at South Wraxhall, but is superior to it in unity of scale and proportion. The single corbel in the latter is doubled, and from these a projecting centrepiece is carried up containing the royal arms boldly carved. It is of somewhat later date than those at South Wraxall, probably about 1625 when John Langston was Mayor of Bristol, and shows a considerable advance in design. The main cornice reaches the ceiling of the room and a plaster rib follows round it. To the same place and period belongs the overpiece at S. Peter's Hospital, Bristol (Plate 111).

The question, who were the persons responsible for the designs of the buildings of the Elizabethan period? is one not less fertile in discussion than that of the merits or demerits of the executed work. Although the native or traditional style succumbed but slowly, in the mass, to the foreign influence, it is remarkable how quickly and almost universally its details became impregnated with it; and this was particularly so with chimney-pieces.

A comparison of these stone chimney-pieces of Wilts and Somerset indicates that they were the work of a group of native masons whose work, crude at first as at Dodington, progressed in both design and execution.

The upheaval of social and religious institutions by Henry VIII had caused a partial cessation of building on the part of his subjects long enough for a generation of Gothic masons to have passed away; since, for example, the building of Henry VII's Chapel. Old traditions were weakened and new formed. The desire for the revived antique became the new fashion, which attracted wealthy patrons who had travelled and become acquainted with the Renaissance abroad. Recourse was had to pattern books and works on architecture published on the Continent. The

[1] *In English Homes*, vol. ii.

Architecture of J. V. Frisius of Antwerp was published in 1563; a book, says Mr. Reginald Blomfield, "which was used with such disastrous readiness by the English builders of this period. And it was unfortunate that the treatises most in use in England at that time were German rather than Italian." Mr. Gotch gives extracts from the state papers of Queen Elizabeth, in a letter from Lord Cobham to Williams, his clerk of works, which show that one Giles de Whitt was employed on a tomb at Cobham, and that when, being in want of work, it was decided to start him on a chimney-piece his price was cut down from £65 to £50, which he accepted rather than lose the job. Plate XIV shows one of the large marble chimney-pieces in the long gallery at Cobham Hall which may have been the work of the Dutchman referred to, being in the typical Dutch manner. The date 1599 is on the central cartouche of the main cornice. Finishing as this cornice does against a coved ceiling, its heavy section appears singularly unsuitable, and the pedestals of the caryatides, out of which the figures appear to rise, are unduly heavy; the lower stage, however, shows some familiarity with the orders, and the nakedness about the fireplace opening may be due to the price having been cut down. Another of these Dutch chimney-pieces is at Charlton House, Kent (Plate XV). Male and female figures stand in front of, rather than support, the entablature, into which a segmental pediment is introduced. A dark marble background effectively contrasts with the alabaster of which the chimney-piece is made.

At Knole House, Sevenoaks, the ball-room chimney-piece is a striking one (Plate XVI), its lower stage having coupled Ionic columns of dark marble with architrave, frieze and inverted cornice mouldings forming a pseudo mantel-shelf; the overpiece, which extends to the ceiling, is richly carved with strapwork, festoons and trophies of white marble set in a contrasting ground of dark marble. The lintel over the fireplace is decorated with surface ornament with shield in centre, produced by the ground being slightly sunk in dark marble. As is frequently the case with chimney-pieces of this period the whole composition cuts ruthlessly through all the architectural lines of the side panelling, showing a want of connection between the different trades, and suggesting for authorship the monumental mason and that the blank central panel still awaits its inscription. The andirons at Knole are fine ones of this period, those in the ball-room being of silver.

An important stone chimney-piece, which differs very much in proportion and details from any of those previously referred to, remains in a house at Enfield, said to have been attached to a manor granted to Princess Elizabeth and afterwards by her, when Queen, to Sir Robert Cecil, first Earl of Salisbury (Plate XVII). The arms of Elizabeth occupy the centre panel, and the Tudor badges, the rose and portcullis crowned, appear in the left and right hand panels respectively, and in the panels beneath the letters E and R. In this work the decorative carving is far superior to the architectural details, the mouldings, and the caps particularly, showing considerable ignorance of the style adopted. The treatment of the crowned badges reminds us of the work at King's College, Cambridge, and may have been executed by a native craftsman who, accustomed to the Tudor badges, had picked up his limited knowledge of Italian work from the screen in the chapel. Native and Italian carvers must often have worked side by side and each learned from the other. The chimney-piece appears to be contemporary with the oak wainscoting of the room, although harmonizing but indifferently with it.

In the style under consideration a somewhat barbaric richness of effect was often produced when the various parts of which it was composed will not bear critical analysis. The example from Wakehurst Place, Sussex, is an instance of this, where the general appearance is much helped by fine proportions. The arms of the Culpeper family make an effective decoration in the upper frieze, the broad fireplace opening with enriched architrave and curtain, and the old wrought andirons, complete a very picturesque composition (Plate XVIII).

Hardwick Hall, Derbyshire, erected for that great builder Elizabeth known as "Bess of Hardwick," contains a series of important chimney-pieces, that shown in Plate XIX being in the great hall. The stone mantel, of great size, as seen by comparing it with the chairs standing on either side, is well proportioned and restrained in design, and the Doric order adopted is treated with some freedom to bring it into harmony with the then prevailing taste; strapwork being the order of the day. In the mantel this strapwork is kept subservient to the general design, but in the stucco overpiece the craftsman has let himself go, in a presentment of the family arms which overpowers even the large chimney-piece. Other chimney-pieces which have this fret ornamentation are to be seen at Quenby Hall, Leicestershire, Hardwick House, Oxfordshire, and elsewhere.

The long gallery which so frequently formed part of the large Elizabethan mansion gave great scope for chimney-piece design, being often furnished with two fireplaces, which were necessary or desirable on account of its great length. The gallery at Hardwick has two of similar design which are 15 ft. wide and 19 ft. high. These are of two stages, each founded on the Doric order, having coupled fluted pilasters on either side of the fireplace, and in the central compartment over a strapwork composition with figure in an oval niche standing on a key block. A decorative effect is produced by the contrast of light and dark marble in blocks and panels.

In the long gallery at Cobham Hall the chimney-pieces, both on the same side of the room, are quite different, producing an unsatisfactory effect; similarity of design for the position when on the same wall is required, but not necessarily an exact likeness of parts. Plate XIV shows one of them.

One of the two fireplaces in the long gallery at Aston Hall, Warwickshire, is shown in Plate XX, belonging to the latter part of James I's reign and illustrating the last phase of Jacobean work. This design, executed in alabaster and made up of strapwork, spirals, roundels, blocks, grotesque faces and pigeon-breasted figures with capitals on their heads, represents the acme of taste in the style which succumbed to the purer Italian of Inigo Jones and Wren.

Plates XXI, XXII, XXIII, XXIV and XXV show the very varied forms which the chimney-piece took during the fusion of the foreign with our native style. Many such simple and reasonable designs as at Iccomb (Plate XXI) are to be found in the stone districts about the Cotswolds. That in the drawing-room of Burford Priory, built by Speaker Lenthall, is of a more ambitious character; the well-shaped Corinthian columns doubtless followed closely an Italian example, but the designer was sadly lacking in imagination who could not do better than place a pair of them in the middle to be cut off by the shelf.

In the gatehouse of Guildford Castle the craftsman has again been successful with his Corinthian order, pilasters being used in this instance, and the retention of the Tudor arch points to his having been an Englishman. This chimney-piece, which is of clunch, was giving way, when the curtain piece bearing the date 1898 was added to support the lintel.

There is much merit in the example from Salisbury Museum

(Plate XXIII) with its dignified figures, although appearing incomplete at the top and weak in the mouldings which span the fireplace opening.

The chimney-piece at Ockwells, removed there from Gloucestershire, is dated 1673, and is a late instance of the retention of the Tudor arch in a design of good scale and proportion.

There is an interesting series of chimney-pieces at Bolsover Castle, Derbyshire, which stands very much alone as to design. These are of stone and alabaster, and have projecting hoods which slope back to the main wall face, which is of dressed stone; a rectangular space is enclosed by a stone moulding which frames the chimney-piece and stops the wall panelling on each side. This bounding line is continued at the base of the chimney-piece in the form of a raised hearth (Plate XXVII). The design of Bolsover, attributed to Huntingdon Smithson, shows some originality which extends to the chimney-pieces. These are varied in plan, some being square, others part octagon, and where they occur in the angles of the rooms quadrant shaped with conical hoods. The hoods originally built to perform their true function as receptacles for the smoke in its passage up the chimney have now been filled in with substantial stonework which appears to have been necessary for support as well as to reduce the aperture for use with coal fires.

The impression given by these Bolsover chimney-pieces is that the designer was inspired by Italian work, but had a very limited knowledge of classical enrichments which we find applied in an unusual manner, as on the sloping member of the main cornice in Plate XXVII. The Gothic influence is seen in the section of this cornice, as also in the arched lintel and, still more pronounced, in the trefoiled opening of one of the angle fireplaces. The difficulty appears to have been found in designing a satisfactory form of fireplace opening, since in no case has a graceful result been achieved, that shown in Plate XXVII being the most satisfactory. The chimney-piece in the star chamber is like a sepulchral monument placed against the wall.

There is in the old Charterhouse a fireplace which forms a striking feature in the great dining hall (Plate XXVIII). The chimney-piece, with its black sarcophagus-like lintel spanning an opening 8 ft. wide, shows a type differing from any of the foregoing. The hall, built in the time of Henry VIII, originally with a central hearth fire, the smoke louver still remaining, was altered during the ownership of the Duke of Norfolk, who in 1571 erected the handsome oak screen, and purchased by Sir Thos. Sutton who founded the hospital in 1610 and died the same year. As the chimney-piece bears the arms and crest of the latter we may assume that it was erected after his acquisition of the property, and that the cannon and casks of gunpowder, seen on the overmantel, refer to his appointment as Master-General of ordnance in the north. A monument was erected to Sutton's memory in 1615, the work of Nicholas Stone and others, from the designs of Bernard Jansen, a Dutch architect. The chimney-piece, in some of its details, shows a similarity to Jansen's work and may have been designed by him. The standards of the firegrate of cast iron terminated with Sutton's crest, a talbot's head, closely resemble the finials to the posts of the gallery above. If original, this is an early example of the grate for burning coal, and a fitting object in a fireplace of Sutton's who made his great wealth by bringing coals to London. The illustration shows the good effect produced by raising the back hearth a step above the front.

The sculptors of this period, who produced the many fine monuments which still exist, worked upon chimney-pieces also, as in the case of Giles de Whitt, the Dutchman at Cobham, previously alluded to. In Nicholas Stone's pocket-book, preserved in the

THE DRAWING-ROOM, LOSELEY, SURREY.

THE DINING-ROOM, LOSELEY, SURREY.

THE RETIRING-ROOM, LITTLE MORETON HALL, CHESHIRE.

THE DRAWING-ROOM, THE RED LODGE, BRISTOL.

THE GREAT CHAMBER, SOUTH WRAXALL, WILTSHIRE.

THE LONG GALLERY, COBHAM HALL, KENT.

THE SALOON, CHARLTON HOUSE, OLD CHARLTON, KENT.

THE BALL-ROOM CHIMNEY PIECE, KNOLE PARK, KENT.

THE OLD PALACE, NOW THE CONSERVATIVE CLUB, ENFIELD, MIDDLESEX.

THE LIBRARY, WAKEHURST PLACE, SUSSEX.

THE GREAT HALL, HARDWICK HALL, DERBYSHIRE.

THE LONG GALLERY, ASTON HALL, WARWICKSHIRE.

THE DINING-ROOM, ICOMB PLACE, GLOUCESTERSHIRE.

THE DRAWING-ROOM, BURFORD PRIORY, OXFORDSHIRE

IN THE GATEHOUSE, GUILDFORD CASTLE, SURREY.

Plate XXIV.

STONE CHIMNEY-PIECE IN THE MUSEUM, SALISBURY.

THE BILLIARD-ROOM, OCKWELLS, BERKSHIRE.

IN THE MANOR-HOUSE, UPPER SWELL, GLOUCESTERSHIRE.

THE SOUTH ROOM, BOLSOVER CASTLE, DERBYSHIRE.

THE HALL OF THE CHARTERHOUSE, LONDON.

Soane Museum, mention is made of many chimney-pieces made by him, for which he received considerable sums of money. In 1634 one was made for Sir John Holland and set up at "Godnon (Quidnam), in Norfolk, for which he had £100, and another for Mr. Paston at Osnett, in Norfolk, for which he had £80," and the following shows that he carried one out for Inigo Jones, "Agreed with Mr. Jones, servier of his M^ty^ workes, for one chemnee pees of whit marbell according to direction for him given to be set up at Somerset Hous in ye Quenes Ma^ty^. bed chamber for ye which I am to have ye som of £40, and Received of M^a^. workes this 14th of October, 1631, ye white marbell provided by me." Stone also made a chimney-piece for Windsor Castle during the time that he was clerk of works there in 1633. Mr. Bullock in his work on Nicholas Stone says: "It is very difficult now to attribute with certainty any existing examples to Stone." At the same time it is very unlikely that all the important chimney-pieces made by him have been destroyed.[1]

RENAISSANCE CHIMNEY-PIECES OF WOOD

In many districts, where stone was not easily procurable and brick was the building material used, chimney-pieces were made of oak, as at Blickling Hall and Holland House. To protect the woodwork from the heat of the fire an inner lining of stone was used, and this became an important feature, both jambs and lintel being often richly ornamented, as in the chimney-piece from Bromley Palace, now in the Victoria and Albert Museum (Plate LIII); others were plainly moulded, as at Levens Hall (Plate XXIX), and in the China Room at Holland House the Tudor arch is retained with carving in the spandrels (Plate XXXV). The practice of panelling

[1] The work of Stone belongs rather to the succeeding period to this. A chimney-piece in Old Somerset House, given in I. Vardy's *Designs of Inigo Jones and Kent*, has the folded leather ornament seen in Stone's monuments and the grotesque mask so much affected by Inigo Jones.

FIG. 99. THE QUEEN'S CHAMBER, SIZERGH CASTLE, WESTMORLAND.

walls with oak, which came into use in the beginning of the sixteenth century, continued and increased, fresh varieties were introduced, and the chimney-piece formed an enriched part of this panelling.

At Sizergh Castle, Westmorland, some rooms in the old peel-tower were panelled with oak during the first part of Queen Elizabeth's reign by Walter Strickland; the late Gothic stone fireplaces were retained and over them elaborately carved chimney-pieces were erected of Renaissance character, following Italian rather than Flemish models. In the Queen's Room, dated 1569, single detached columns of the bedpost type stand on each side of the fireplace, and on them, without any intervening shelf, lighter columns, over which the main cornice of the wall

FIG. 100. GREAT CHAMBER, GILLING CASTLE, YORKSHIRE.

panelling breaks. The Royal arms, richly carved, occupy the central panel and highly relieved carving amply fills the surrounding ones. In Fig. 99, which shows this chimney-piece, tapestry covers the wall panelling which exists beneath it.

Of the early Elizabethan wood chimney-pieces, that in the great chamber of Gilling Castle, in Rydale, Yorkshire, is probably the largest, if not the most important, its central pediment rising into the plaster cornice, which is 15 ft. from the floor of the room. As seen in Fig. 100, it is a well conceived design, of good proportions, and well carried out in most of its details. The heraldic decorations for which this room is celebrated extend to the chimney-piece, the arms of Queen Elizabeth occupy the top panel, and below are the Fairfax shield and crest with goat supporters.

Another important chimney-piece, which, from the likeness of some of its parts, notably the treatment of its lowest stage, can hardly fail to have been connected with the preceding, is at Levens Hall, Westmorland (Plate XXIX). It is dated 1595; rather later than that at Gilling Castle, if the latter is of the same date as the stained glass in one of its windows, 1585. At Levens both chimney-piece and panelling are carried up to the ceiling of the room, producing a quite different proportion to that at Gilling Castle, where the side wings are ramped down. Fireplaces hitherto have been generally recessed into the wall, which, if not sufficiently thick to allow enough depth, has had a projection on the outside; but at Levens the projection is into the room—the beginning of a practice which afterwards became general. The overpiece is divided vertically into three equal compartments, the lower ones containing the arms of the Bellingham family. The wide enriched bands or friezes cut the overpiece into low horizontal divisions, making the height of the columns, reduced by their being placed on pedestals, unduly small; a sturdy not to say stumpy proportion is produced which found favour at this period. The Doric, Ionic and Corinthian orders are made use of.

The same low horizontal divisions and sturdy columns may be seen again in the example from Old Place, Sandwich (Plate XXX), far away, geographically, from Levens. Here crude figures, surmounted by fruit basket capitals, form the vertical divisions for curiously arched panels of equal size. The mantel mouldings and main cornice show a well-ordered richness and the supports at the sides of the fireplace a typical form of pilaster. This and succeeding illustrations show this downward tapering pilaster in various forms, ornamented by strap carving, reeds, flutes, bosses and nailheads; sometimes of exaggerated form, as in Plate XXXIII from Audley End, in others, when more nearly approaching the proportions of the human figure, more graceful, as in Plate XXXII.

The overmantel from Dogpole, Shrewsbury (Plate XXXI), bears the date 1553, and, if this can be relied on as correct, shows an early example of Renaissance woodwork of pleasing proportion, with an absence of the surface ornament which is so frequently found in later examples. The tall pilasters at the sides have probably been added at a later date. A picture, with painted ornament on its frame, occupies the central compartment.

There was a great development of the joiner's craft during the period under review; wood chimney-pieces, which, belonging to the early part of Elizabeth's reign, are seldom met with, became common towards the end of it, and still more so during that of James I. The name "Jacobean" given to this work is therefore a suitable one. In some instances there is but little difference between the designs of wood and stone. At Blickling Hall the drawing-room chimney-piece has large coupled Ionic columns of oak below and Corinthian above quite in the manner of stone, and another is in the dining-room which is dated 1627. Two important chimney-pieces in the long gallery at Hatfield differ but slightly in detail from others of marble in the same house.

In the drawing-room at Audley End, which has the singular "Fish" ceiling, a lighter style is adopted for the chimney-piece (Plate XXXII). The great height of the room provided the opportunity for having a tall central panel, which is filled with the arms of Thomas, Earl of Suffolk, impaling Knyvett. The side compartments have small enriched columns with entablatures, forming niches with shell tops, supported on twin grotesque figures and surmounted by a pierced cresting. This otherwise fine design is disfigured by side scrolls of coarse meandering foliage quite out of scale with the rest of the work. The fireplace arrangement is of later date than the chimney-piece. Plate XXXIII shows the great hall fireplace in the same building. This has the usual divisions, consisting of a wide central compartment with lesser ones at the sides, but, unlike those previously referred to, has the inner supports carried down to the floor instead of being stopped on trusses beneath the shelf; thus necessitating either giving greater width to the chimney-piece, or unduly curtailing the fireplace opening.

The two examples from Holland House, Kensington, shown in Plates XXXIV and XXXV are typical examples of the best work of this period, the former being of painted wood and the latter of oak. The banded columns with their lower parts ornamented with strapwork or rustications, the bellied mantel mould with blocks at intervals, the side niches with shell tops and the small architectural composition in the centre of Plate XXXIV, are all typical features. The way the plinths of overmantel in the same are connected together is unusual, and the removal of the block to the centre of shelf moulding is hardly satisfactory. The cornice of side panelling returns at the sides of the chimney breast in a singular manner. Plates XXXVI and XXXVII show chimney-pieces in the Victoria and Albert Museum which with others were removed from some merchants' houses in Lime Street, E.C., previously to their demolition in 1875.[1] These formed part of completely panelled rooms on the first floor, their cornices ranging with that of the panelling. They are singular as to their jambs and lintels, which are of stone, the overmantels being of oak. To

[1] A visit of the Architectural Association was made to these houses before they were demolished, in which the writer took part, and measured drawings of the woodwork and plaster ceilings may be seen in the *A. A. Sketch Book*, vol. viii, by Mr. R. Phené Spiers and the late G. H. Birch.

follow the process of evolution from an order of architecture in

FIG. 101. A SUSSEX FIREPLACE.

this stonework would be difficult. Probably the work of a German or Dutchman, the designs are harmonious as a whole and show the handling of one who had assimilated his style and could use it freely.

Although all the wood chimney-pieces of the Jacobean period show Renaissance influence in some of their mouldings and details, an English style was evolved which shows a very suitable treatment of the oak of which they were made. Many are to be found in the small manor and farm-houses of the time, as in the Sussex example, Fig. 101. The projections are all very slight, pilasters being sometimes ⅝ in. only in thickness, and although there may be some monotony in this design through excessive repetition of the flutings, this is remedied by the interest gained in the figure of the oak, and in some instances by the addition of box or ebony inlay to the panels.

This treatment so frequently found in old chests is seen again in the overmantel from Burford, Oxon (Plate xl). In this and the preceding example it is seen in connexion with the Tudor arch.

At Eastgate House, Rochester, where that excellent plan has been adopted of turning into a museum an old mansion, which, from altered circumstances, is no longer wanted for its original purpose, several old oak chimney-pieces remain which have had paint stripped off them and are now taken care of. One of these, shown in Plate xxxviii, is in the flat style last referred to, but with the favourite caryatides dividing the panels. Great ingenuity was bestowed upon the elaboration of this feature, and Fig. 102 shows one of its many varieties. The side panels of the overmantel in Plate xxxviii and following plates show a form much in vogue during this period, a square within a cross. This form and a semicircular arch on pilasters, as in Plate xi, were most used for filling in compartments. The andirons and fireback in Plate xxxviii are examples of old Sussex cast iron, the latter bearing the crest and arms of the Dacres of Hurstmonceux; the stone arch is singularly coarse in its details and out of scale with the oak chimney-piece.

Fig 103 is a drawing to scale of a fine oak chimney-piece which forms part of a richly panelled room at Uxbridge, known as the "Treaty Room" from its having been used in an unsuccessful attempt to arrange a treaty between the Commissioners of Charles I and Parliament in 1645. This appears to have been made for a higher room than that in which it is now fixed, as the pedestals have been reduced, and the opening of the mantel is too large for the fireplace. Jacobean carving, which is often very crude in both design and execution, as in Plate XLIII, its principal quality being a certain vigour and directness of expression, is in this example well subordinated to the architectural members, going rather to the other extreme. The ornaments of the central panels, which are now missing, may have supplied the note of interest which the work now lacks. The surface ornament on the columns, copied from Italian work, was a favourite form of enrichment of this period, and a comparison of Plates XLIV and XLV shows the wide difference in examples whether in cultured or uncultured hands.

FIG. 102.

A quite different type of work, and one frequently met with, is seen in the mantel from Cross Street, Barnstaple (Plate XLI), dated 1617. Carving covers the entire surface; the ornament, although rude and uninteresting in detail, is so harmonious in scale and relief that a rich and restful effect is produced. A

Chimney Piece of oak in the "Treaty House", Uxbridge.

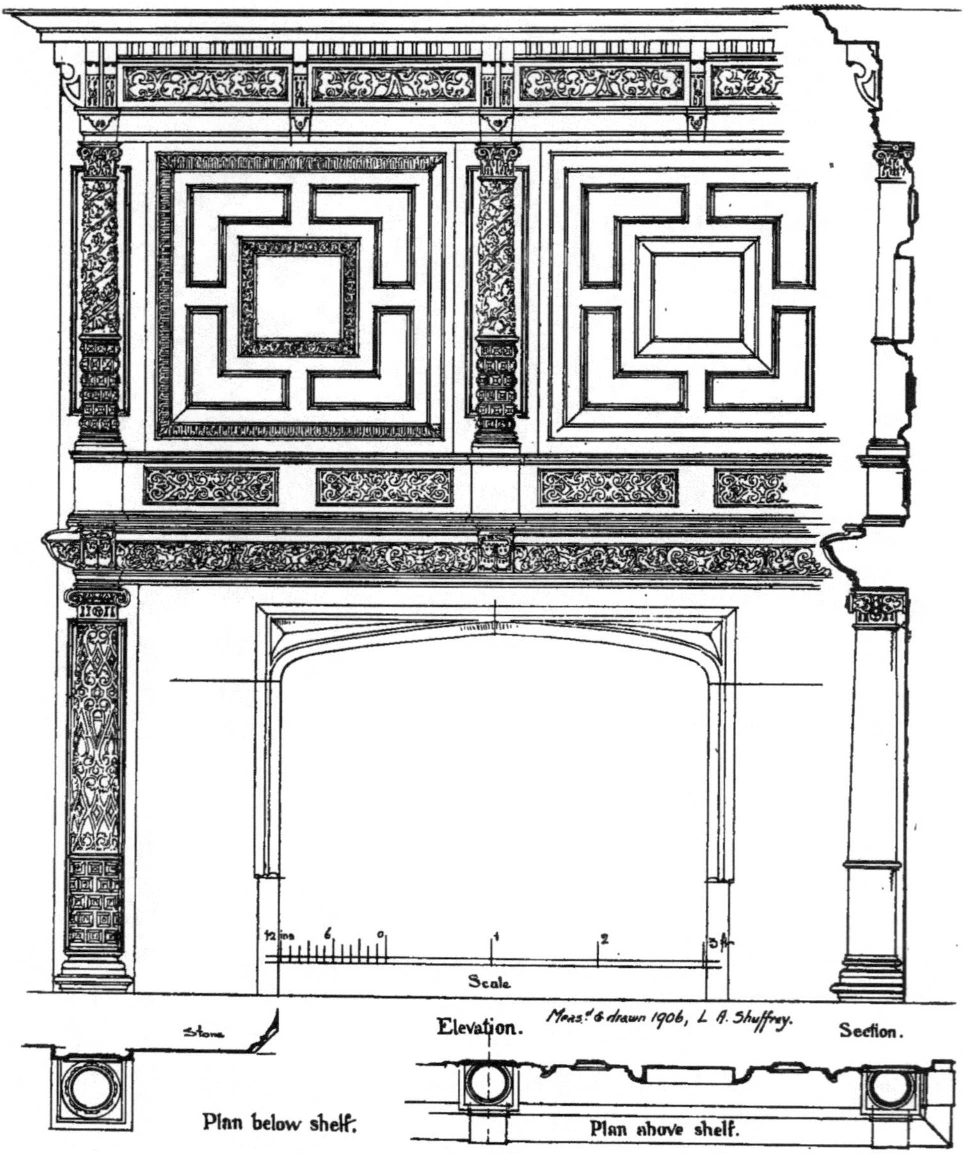

FIG. 103.

satyr was often placed at the sides of overmantels to produce a picturesque outline, as seen in both this and Plate XLIII.

At Stokesay Castle, where Jacobean panelling has been somewhat clumsily added to one of the rooms of the Early English tower, similarly enriched work may be seen in Plate XLII.

Jacobean chimney-pieces were sometimes decorated with colour. Horace Walpole says: "The rooms at Holland House were decorated by eminent artists, including Francis Cleyn." Of this painter's work he remarks: "The compartments in the chimney at Holland House are in the style and not unworthy of the hand of Parmegiano." The large chimney-piece in the Governor's Room of the old Charterhouse, originally the Duke of Norfolk's drawing-room, was richly decorated with colour, now almost obscured by the effects of the London atmosphere. Plate XLVII is from a drawing of Richardson's, who says that it was the work of Rowland Buckett, a limner, who received £50 from the governors of the Charterhouse for his performance. Brayley [1] mentions that the arms of Sutton and James I, seen in the illustration, are posterior additions to the other parts, which belonged to the Duke of Norfolk's work in the building. The fine grate and andirons shown in Richardson's drawing are not now existing in this fireplace.

Another example of colour applied to chimney-pieces is seen in Plate XLVIII, which shows a fireplace in the library attached to the church at Langley, near Slough. In the central panel, emblazoned on a gold ground, are the heraldic insignia of the Kederminster family, to whose private pew the room is connected by a screened passage, and in the spandrels representations of Prudence, Temperance, Justice and Fortitude. The ornament on the chimney-piece shows considerable executive talent, is very

[1] *Londiniana*, by E. W. Brayley, F.S.A., M.R.S.L.

pleasing in colour, and still in very good condition. The brick-lined fireplace, with its stone jambs, lintel and hearth, appears to be in its original condition and has its original brass andirons.

Illustrations of Scriptural subjects and symbolical representations, which we have seen formed part of the ornamentation of stone chimney-pieces, are found in wood also. At the Manor House, Woodstone, near Peterborough (Plate XLIX), Africa, Asia, Europe and America are represented by carved figures standing under semicircular arched canopies over which the cornice breaks. A coat of arms occupies the central panel, and in the right and left respectively are the " Sacrifice of Isaac " and the " Daughter of Herodias dancing before Herod."

For the position of honour in the centre of the overmantel the Royal arms continued in favour as in Plate L, from a room over the Butterwalk, Dartmouth, built in 1643 as inscribed on one of the granite pillars. The ground of the panel is ornamented with the rose, shamrock and thistle. Like so much of the Jacobean woodwork this picturesque piece of light and shade does not improve on close inspection, the parts appearing to have been " made up " into their present form.

Plate LII shows an oak chimney-piece in the Globe Room of the *Reindeer Inn*, Banbury, which appears from similarity of details to be by the same hand as two fine ones at St. John's College, Oxford, in the wing built by Archbishop Laud.[1] It represents the last phase of Jacobean woodwork which preceded the change in design brought about by Inigo Jones and Wren. The proportions and mouldings show an able handling of the free classic style of woodwork which had developed in this country mainly during the reign of James I. By comparing Plates LI and LII with

[1] Tanner's *English Interior Woodwork.*

THE DRAWING-ROOM, LEVENS HALL, WESTMORLAND.

THE DINING-ROOM, THE OLD PLACE, SANDWICH, KENT.

Plate XXXI.

FROM A HOUSE IN DOGPOLE, SHREWSBURY.

THE DRAWING-ROOM, AUDLEY END, SAFFRON WALDEN, ESSEX.

THE GREAT HALL, AUDLEY END, SAFFRON WALDEN, ESSEX.

THE WHITE PARLOUR, HOLLAND HOUSE, KENSINGTON.

THE CHINA ROOM, HOLLAND HOUSE, KENSINGTON.

CHIMNEY-PIECE FROM A DEMOLISHED HOUSE, LIME STREET, LONDON.
Now in the Victoria and Albert Museum.

CHIMNEY-PIECE FROM A DEMOLISHED HOUSE, LIME STREET, LONDON.
Now in the Victoria and Albert Museum.

THE SOUTH-EAST ROOM, FIRST FLOOR, EASTGATE HOUSE, ROCHESTER.

THE NELSON ROOM, THE STAR HOTEL, GREAT YARMOUTH.

AN OVERMANTEL AT BURFORD, OXFORDSHIRE.

IN CROSS STREET, BARNSTAPLE.

THE DRAWING-ROOM, STOKESAY CASTLE, SHROPSHIRE.

AN ELIZABETHAN OVERMANTEL IN SUSSEX.

THE NORTH-EAST ROOM, FIRST FLOOR, EASTGATE HOUSE, ROCHESTER

AT PETERSFIELD, HAMPSHIRE.

AT PETERSFIELD, HAMPSHIRE.

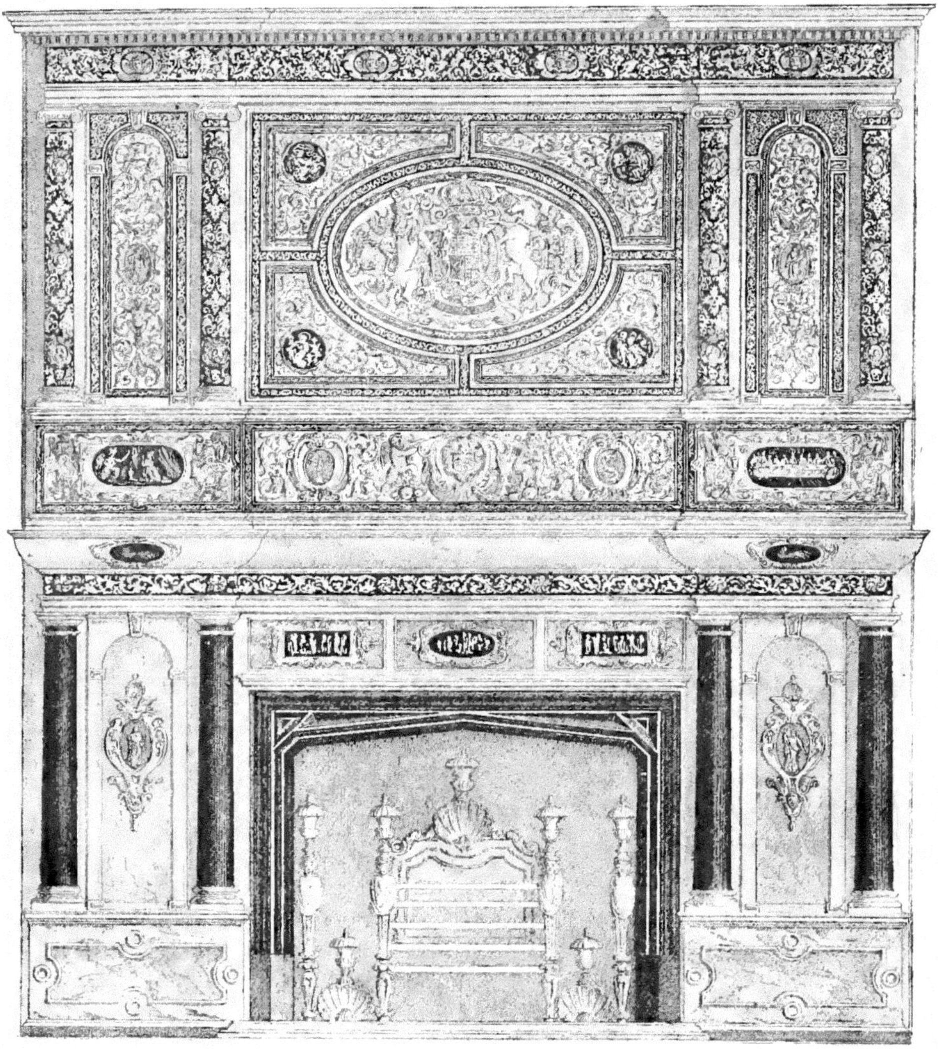

CHIMNEY PIECE IN THE "GOVERNOR'S ROOM," AT THE CHARTERHOUSE, LONDON
Showing its decoration when drawn by C. J. Richardson about 1840.

THE KEDERMINSTER LIBRARY, LANGLEY CHURCH, BUCKS.

Plate XLIX.

IN THE MANOR-HOUSE, WOODSTONE, PETERBOROUGH.

OVERMANTEL IN THE BUTTER WALK, DARTMOUTH, DEVON.

IN THE GUILDHALL, GUILDFORD.

THE GLOBE ROOM, THE REINDEER INN, BANBURY.

the two preceding them the loss in appearance of a dual instead of a triple division of the overmantel may be observed.

ENRICHED STONE LININGS

Interesting examples of the stone linings to oak chimney-pieces, which superseded and to some extent ran concurrently with the Tudor arch, remain. The deep lintel required for the wide openings provided a suitable space for ornament. Fig. 104 shows one of these from the old palace of Westminster. When the old exchequer buildings adjoining

FIG. 104. STONE CHIMNEY-PIECE IN QUEEN'S CLOSET, KENSINGTON PALACE.

Westminster Hall were pulled down this was preserved by the Office of Works; it was afterwards set up in one of the rooms at Kensington Palace, and has now recently been removed to S. James' Palace. It bears the arms of Queen Elizabeth and her cipher crowned. That in the Victoria and Albert Museum from the palace of Bromley-by-Bow (Plate LIII) has been previously referred to. The favourite subjects for ornament were birds, beasts and reptiles combined with foliage.

At Elham (Plate LIV) the lintel takes the form of a flat arch, in the haunch of which is a portrayal of Jonah escaping from the mouth of a big fish, with dogs and cherub in the centre. These lintels were sometimes finished with mouldings forming a mantel-shelf, as in Plates LV and LVI from Norwich. In the latter gorgons' heads supported by wyverns on each side and a vase of flowers and fruit in the centre, are carved on a band of strapwork, producing a rich effect; the composition, modelling and details of mouldings reaching a high standard far removed from much of the ornament of this Jacobean period. In the example from Saffron Walden (Plate LVII) more is made of the cornice, and trusses are introduced at each end of the frieze, filled with naively composed symbolical figures. This type of chimney-piece appears to have been most general in East Anglia, good examples existing at Marks Hall, Coggeshall and Albyns, Essex.

The stone chimney-piece with incised ornament at Charlton (Plate LVIII) is uncommon, especially as to the form of its stops to the jamb mouldings.

OVERMANTELS OF STUCCO

The ornamentation of walls and ceilings with stucco, introduced by the Italians who were employed by Henry VIII at his palace of Nonsuch, developed greatly during the reigns of Elizabeth and the Stuarts, and the space of wall over the fireplace presented a fair field for the operations of the plasterer. Important examples may be seen at Hardwick Hall, Derbyshire (Plate XIX), where a fine heraldic achievement occupies the post of honour over the chimney-piece of the great hall, richly emblazoned. Haddon Hall, in the same county, has an overmantel of stucco in the State Bedroom, surmounting a stone chimney-piece of plain Renaissance character (Plate LIX). The subject, Orpheus with his lute charming the surrounding beasts, is somewhat crudely rendered, and at the sides are the inevitable caryatides. This work was probably

FIREPLACE LINTEL FROM THE OLD PALACE, BROMLEY-BY-BOW.

Now in the Victoria and Albert Museum.

CARVED STONE FIREPLACE LINTEL WITH OAK OVERPIECE, ELHAM, KENT.

CARVED STONE CHIMNEY-PIECE FROM AN OLD HOUSE IN NORWICH.

Now in the Victoria and Albert Museum

CARVED STONE CHIMNEY-PIECE IN THE VICTORIA AND ALBERT MUSEUM.

STONE CHIMNEY-PIECE IN THE MUSEUM, SAFFRON WALDEN, ESSEX.

modelled in position. Fig. 105 shows a plaster overmantel from Gretton, Northants, of pleasing design and proportion. Set between oak panelling, this formed the completion of the stone fireplace.

Devonshire, rich in examples of old plasterwork, retains many

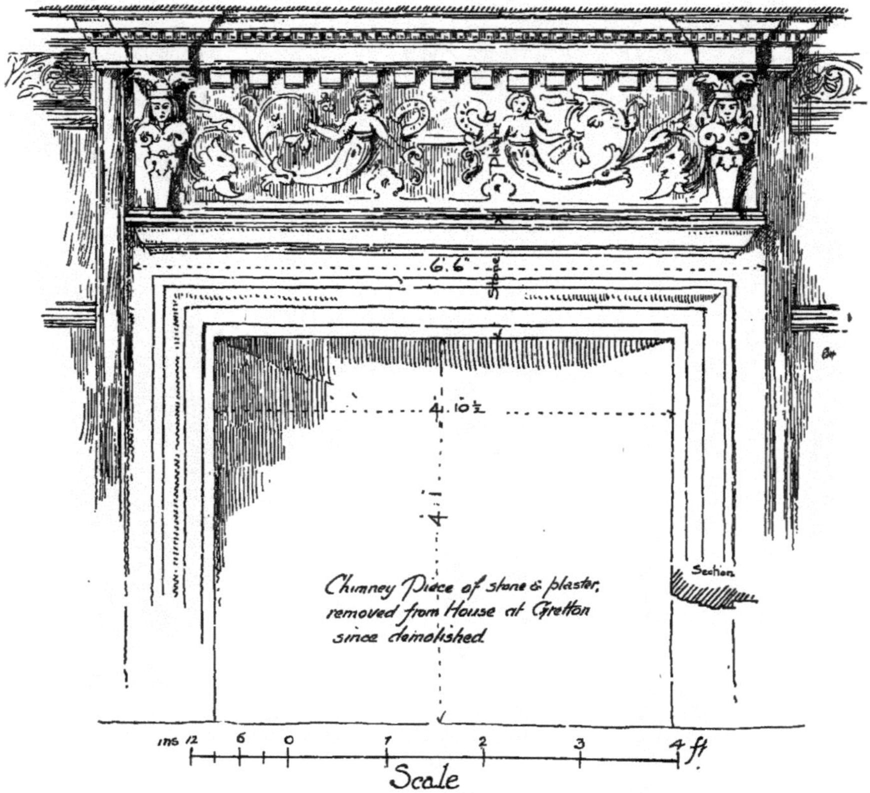

FIG. 105.

examples of overmantels, principally of the time of James I. That at Cross Street, Barnstaple (Plate LX), shows a bold composition of strapwork and foliage, the subject of the centre panel being apparently Caleb and Joshua returning from the "Promised Land." The mantel *shelf* is in this case of plaster, a very unsuitable material for the purpose, as is apparent from its cracked and chipped condition.

In the same style is the example from Chittlehampton (Plate LXI); the frieze of winged horses used here does duty elsewhere, as the main frieze of the room, showing that for repeating ornaments casts were made and set up. These overmantels were often constructed with laths on battens.

In the drawing-room at Langleys, Essex, the plastic treatment is more pronounced. In the overmantel the extraction of Jonah through the side of the whale is portrayed with awful realism, accompanied by music from surrounding female figures, and in the presence of an eagle, stag, dog and monkey.

In the dining hall at Melplash, near Beaminster, Dorset, the royal arms of William III, boldly modelled on the wall surface, form an over-piece to the large open fireplace.

When painted it is often difficult to differentiate the materials of Jacobean chimney-pieces, whether of stone or plaster, as in Plates LXII, LXIII and LXIV, which are of the former. In the chimney-piece of the drawing-room at Boston House, Brentford, the *naïveté* of modelling has disappeared; Abraham with flowing robe and hand uplifted is in the act of striking, when arrested by the angel. This, as the framed centre piece, is surrounded by a swirling mass of hobgoblins, dogs, insects, scrolls and ribands, and beneath it in a panel is the motto of the Clitherows, "Loyal yet free." The fine effect of making the chimney-piece one composition extending from the floor to the ceiling is here seen. The date in one of the panels of this ceiling is 1623, the chimney-piece being apparently contemporary, although about a foot out of centre with it.

The brick chimney stacks which formed such an important feature in the buildings of the Early Tudor period, as at Thorn-

STONE CHIMNEY-PIECE WITH OVERPIECE OF PLASTER IN THE STATE BEDROOM, HADDON HALL.

PLASTER OVERMANTEL, STOWFORD, CHITTLEHAMPTON, NORTH DEVON.

THE DRAWING-ROOM, BOSTON HOUSE, BRENTFORD

Plate LXII

THE DRAWING-ROOM, CHARLTON HOUSE, OLD CHARLTON, KENT.

bury Castle and Hampton Court, continued to be built with some little alteration during the reigns of Elizabeth and James I, as at Moyns Park (Fig. 106), Cobham Hall, Blickling Hall and Bramshill, Hants, where grouped octagonal shafts on bases of the same bulbous form, as in the earlier examples, may be seen. The elaborate diaperings of the shafts, the occasional battlementing of the caps and the panelling of the plinths ceased with the reign of Henry VIII. Designs in brick became more uniform and less fanciful.

RENAISSANCE CHIMNEYS.

FIG. 106.

In chimneys of stone greater change and variety is observable. Burleigh House by Stamford is one of the earliest important Renaissance buildings erected in England by foreigners, and the designer thereof conceived or adopted the unhappy idea of making the chimney shafts in the form of Doric columns with cap and base and entablature complete (Fig. 107); so pleased was he with this idea that a whole army of these columns may be seen on the north front of Burleigh outlined against the sky. This example was followed in other buildings as at Wollaton Hall, Charlton House, Wilts, and at Montacute House, Somerset. In the last mentioned the proportion of the columns is less satis-

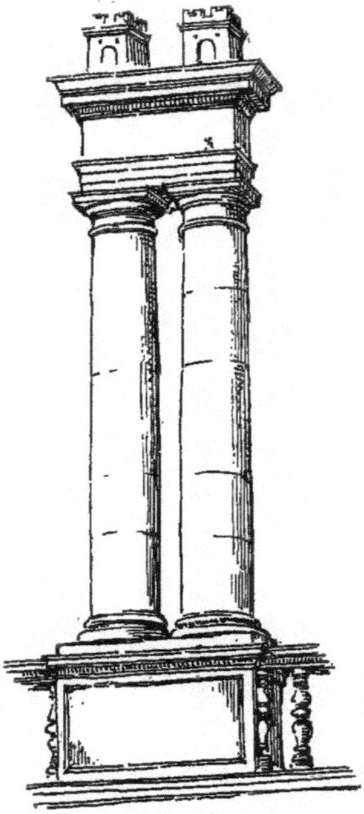

FIG. 107. BURLEIGH.

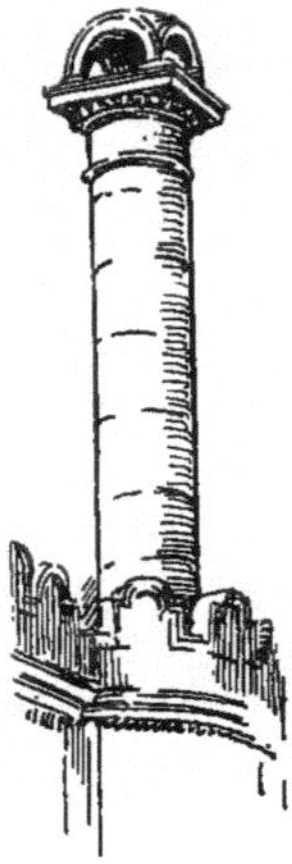

FIG. 108. MONTACUTE.

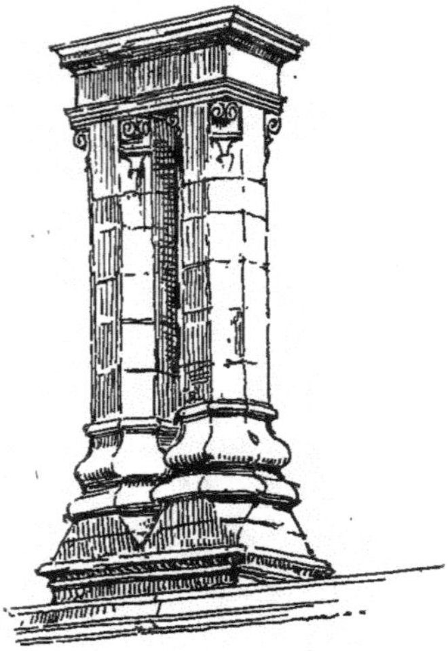

FIG. 109. KIRBY HALL.

FIG. 110. GLINTON.

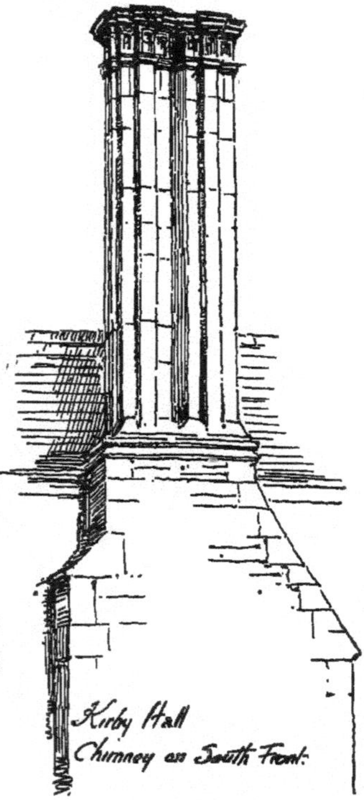

FIG. 111.

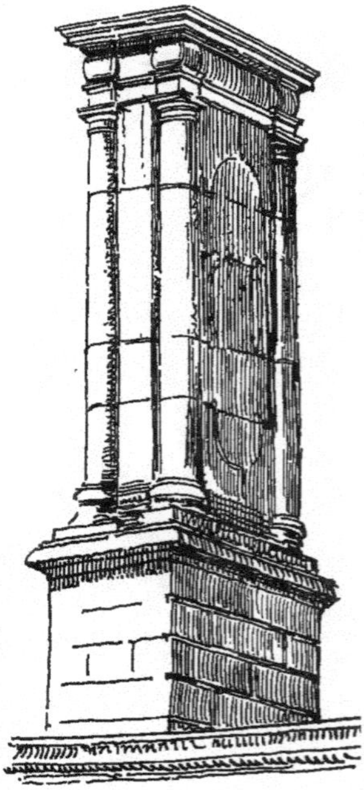

FIG. 112. KIRBY HALL.

RENAISSANCE CHIMNEYS OF STONE.

factory than at Burleigh, the entasis to which the eye is accustomed is lacking (Fig. 108), the shafts which are mostly single and not coupled together by an entablature as at Burleigh, are weak both structurally and in appearance, and have had to be stayed to the roof by iron ties. The absurdity lies not in omitting the entasis but in making the chimneys look like columns.

FIG. 113. MICKLETON, GLOUCESTERSHIRE.

At Kirby Hall, Northamptonshire, the transition from Gothic to Renaissance chimneys may be clearly seen. Fig. 109 shows one belonging to the original building, whereof John Thorpe has recorded that he laid the foundation stone in 1570. This commences with a Gothic base to its octagonal shafts and finishes with a classical entablature rectangular on plan, the corners which overhang the shafts being supported by a volute. In the tall chimney (Fig. 111) on the south side of the hall the Gothic base is absent, and tall pilasters around which the cornice breaks are

FIG. 114. AT SNOWSHILL, GLOUCESTERSHIRE.

formed on each face of the stack. The buildings on the north side of the courtyard which were designed by Inigo Jones have chimneys in which the flues are all massed together without any vertical divisions (Fig. 112), showing an important change of treatment and one favoured by that architect and his immediate successors. At Glinton, Northants (Fig. 110), an unbroken entablature rests upon rusticated shafts but the vertical divisions are retained.

FIG. 115. NEAR GODALMING, SURREY.

In the oolite stone district, of which the Cotswolds form an important section, the chimneys are prominent and pleasing features of buildings, which owe much of their character to them. These are almost universally constructed with rectangular shafts for each flue, formed of thin slabs of ashlar, capped in the simplest example, as at Mickleton (Fig. 113), with a rather fat cyma mould, and with base in which the Gothic section is frequently retained. Very many chimneys are carried boldly up above the apex of a gable, being cleverly bonded in with its coping, as at Snowshill (Fig. 114). Other stacks, projected from the wall, are carried right up from the ground, as also seen in Fig. 114, the shafts being set diagonally on their base. The rather abrupt set off from the square to the octagon is frequently met with. The example

(Fig. 116) from Cote House, Oxon, shows a group of five flues set diagonally on a massive base in the form of a cross.

In the stone districts of the North of England the chimney shafts were generally rectangular and were set both square and diagonally on their bases with mouldings and set-offs of a coarser type than those of the Cotswolds.

The cottage or farmhouse chimneys of brick belonging to this Renaissance period have been previously referred to in connexion with chimney corners. Many small houses were built which bear dates belonging to the seventeenth century, and the original chimneys which remain, becoming fewer every year, well repay careful study, especially those of the Home Counties. The example (Fig. 115) from Unstead Farm near Godalming shows a plan of giving importance and an appearance of stability to the base of a chimney stack by means of stepped gablets or crow steps following roughly the slope of the roof behind.

FIG. 116.

Fireplace Accessories

ANDIRONS.

SO long as logs of wood were used for fuel the andiron or firedog was the necessary accompaniment to the fire-hearth, whether in the lord's withdrawing room or in the yeoman's kitchen or houseplace. Its purpose was to raise the ends of the brands from the hearth to assist combustion, as shown so realistically in the Holbein drawing (Frontispiece). The name, variously spelt,[1] frequently occurs in old inventories, the term used being a "pair of andirons." The Celtic pair of coupled standards at Voelas, previously referred to (Fig. 9), prove the use of these "ancient twin servitors of the hearth" to be of great antiquity. The curious forks, resembling horns, which rise from a rudely-shaped head, were probably for the purpose of resting crossbars upon, others having been found with this peculiar feature, and the loops up the standards were for the same purpose.

FIG. 117. COMMON LITURG 99.

In an assessment made at Colchester, in the 29th Edward I, among the goods of Roger the Dyer, one andiron is valued at 8*d*., and in the wardrobe accounts of the same king an entry occurs of money paid to Thomas de Couvers for repairing the andiron of the King's Chamber.[2]

[1] See inventories of the Priory of Finchall, published by the Surtees Society, andvine, aundhyryns and hawndyrnes.

[2] Parker, vol. ii, p. 39.

The form met with in old manuscripts has a crooked top like a crozier with straddle legs and hooks in front to rest the spit irons upon (Fig. 117).[1]

The fifteenth century andirons with ram's heads in the hall of the Vicar's Close, Wells (Fig. 118), show smith's work of no mean order; but very few mediaeval examples remain. It is difficult to account for this scarcity when we find that

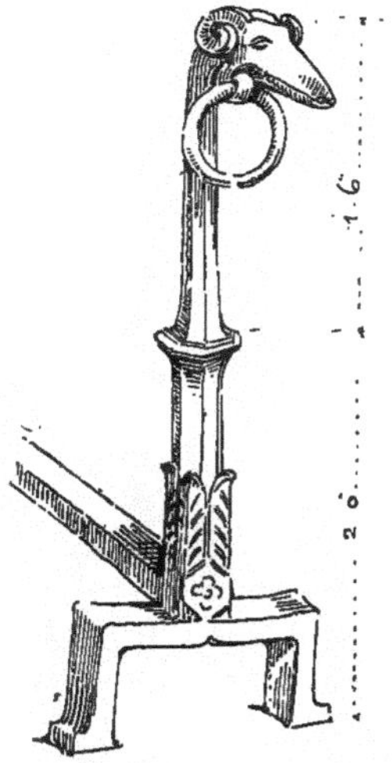

FIG. 118. VICAR'S CLOSE, WELLS.

FIG. 119. KNOLE HOUSE, KENT.

in an inventory of Cardinal Wolsey's furniture at Hampton Court, forty-seven pairs of andirons are mentioned, and these were, as Mr. Law says, "articles on which much decoration was lavished."[2] A sale of the furniture at the palace took

[1] Parker, vol. iii, p. 155.

[2] Cardinal Wolsey had eight pair made of brass, some displaying roses and his own arms, others with mermaids, with lions, with angels, and with fools on the tops. Of seventeen pair more of iron, six were enriched "with my Lordes armes and Cardinall hattes on the toppes," four with his arms and gilt balls, three with lions, five with dragons, two with balls, one with roses, and one with the arms of England. Twenty-

place after the execution of Charles I when these andirons were probably dispersed. The pair which now stand in the hall fireplace at Knole House, Kent, belonging to Wolsey's time, are of wrought steel and brass, and of quite exceptional merit, about 4 ft. high (Fig. 119). They are stated to have belonged to the Boleyn family, who owned Hever Castle in the same county, being ornamented at the top with cabled rings enclosing, in one, the arms of Henry VIII, with the letters H and A, and in the other a falcon crowned, from which issue white and red roses, a cognizance of Queen Anne Boleyn.

FIG. 120. WROUGHT ANDIRON IN BALL ROOM FIREPLACE, PENSHURST PLACE.

The crooked head was superseded by a cup-shaped top with saucer rim, as in Fig. 120, from the Ball Room at Penshurst Place, where they stand in the restored four-

two pair more displayed his own arms, gilt, with balls of metal; and a few had scutcheons and crosses of St. George, and double roses "on either side of their shanks."—*Hampton Court Palace in Tudor Times*, by Ernest Law, B.A., p. 79.

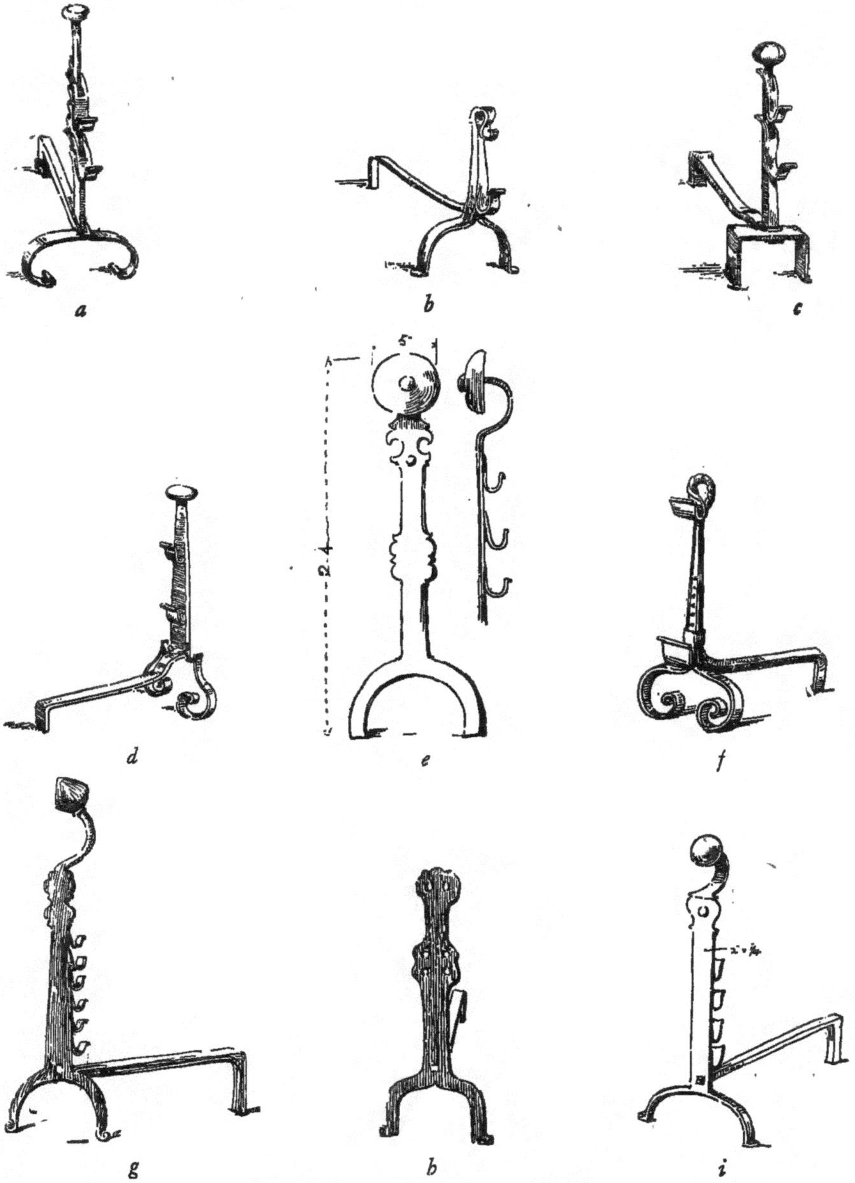

FIG. 121. WROUGHT ANDIRONS.

a, *b*, *c*, *d*, *f*, *h*, *i* in the possession of the Author. *e* at Hoghton Towers. *g* at Lake House, Amesbury.

teenth century fireplace, but are of later date. Another pair at Penshurst, also with cup terminations, may be seen in Plate LXIX. Fig. 121 shows a variety of forms of simple wrought andirons, such as continued to be made by the village smith almost to our own time in districts where wood was burned. These all have character, so simple and satisfactory when arrived at but so difficult to achieve by design on paper, depending solely upon some artistic feeling in the craftsman who made them.

The Early Renaissance period in England appears to have been a somewhat barren one so far as the art of smithing is concerned. The use of gunpowder, which gave the deathblow to the armourer's craft, developed that of the founder in the manufacture of cannon. Iron foundries were started in the Weald of Sussex, where ironstone was found in conjunction with a plentiful supply of timber for converting into charcoal for smelting purposes.

CAST-IRON FIREDOGS

Here cast-iron firedogs or brand-irons, as they are termed in that county, were first produced. "The earliest known dated examples from Cowdray are of the year 1515, and they weigh 200 lb."[1]

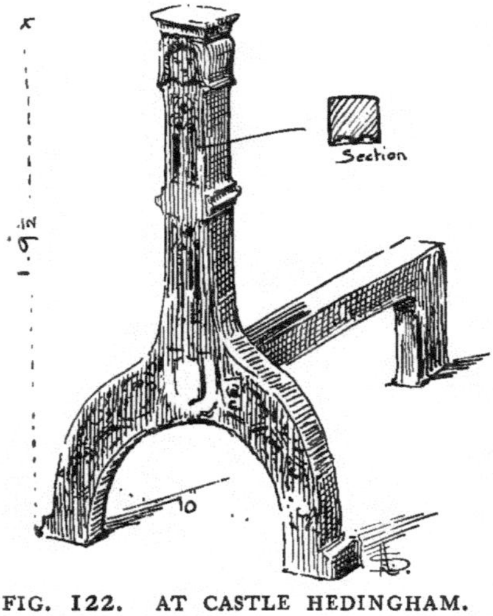

FIG. 122. AT CASTLE HEDINGHAM.

Some few examples are met with that are quite Gothic, as in Fig. 122, a much corroded specimen at Castle Hedingham; but more often some details show the

[1] Article by Chas. Dawson, F.S.A., F.G.S., in *Sussex Arch. Transactions*, vol. xlvi.

FIG. 123.

F.G. 124.

FIG. 125.

FIG. 126.

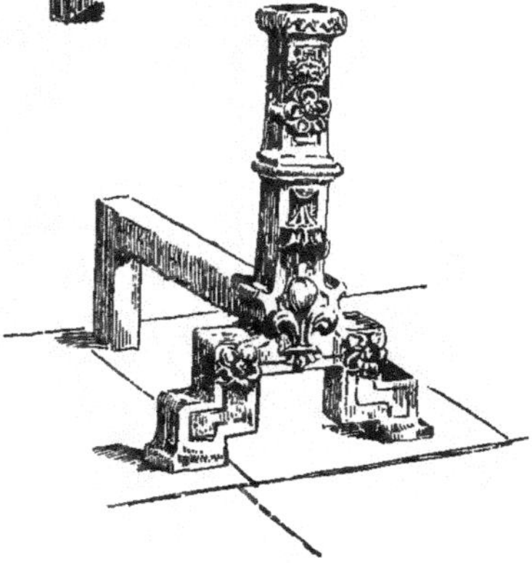

FIG. 127.

FIG 123. IN THE POSSESSION OF THE AUTHOR.
,, 124. FROM COBHAM HALL, KENT.
,, 125. ,, GILSTON PARK, HERTFORDSHIRE.
,, 126. ,, GODINTON, KENT.
,, 127. ,, LEEDS CASTLE, KENT.

From drawings by W. Twopeny.

foreign influence, as may be seen in the first four of the five shown on page 133.

The arched base supporting a column, caryatid or figure, with shield masking the intersection of the standard with the billet bar is the most characteristic form. As models for moulding these firedogs in the sand had to be made the designs were frequently repeated. Fig. 126, which has the sacred monogram on its shield, is often found; the same design may be seen in Plate XXIII from Guildford, but surmounted by recumbent lions. A heavy pair in the hall at Ockwells Manor House have late Gothic mouldings in their caps and the cross of St. George on their shields. At Loseley, shown in Plate IX, we find the downward tapering pillar with voluted heads so common to this period in wood. At Nettlecombe Court, Somersetshire, a pair of warriors with shields, placed lower than when in use, guard the hearth of the hall.

Some cast dogs were very short, as in Plate LXXVIII from Charlton House, Kent, but this sturdy character is lacking in those at Eastgate House, Rochester (Plate XXXVIII), where the straddle legs appear to be standing on their toes. Larger and more elaborate dogs may be seen in Plates XIX and XX from Hardwick Hall, Derbyshire, and Aston Hall, Warwickshire, where we again meet with the caryatid pillar, but to a larger scale and with arched supports, formed of winged heads in the former and cherubs in the latter. The coupled standards with billet bar previously referred to, page 9 (Fig. 8), which stand in the centre of the hall at Penshurst, are of cast iron and probably of the time of Edward VI.

In the Board Room fireplace of St. Peter's Hospital, Bristol (Plate III), stand a large pair of andirons, the supports of which are in the form of a large bird realistically modelled. These are of cast iron and quite different from any of the Sussex examples or from any others we have seen, and may have come from the Forest of Dean foundries.

CAST-IRON FIREBACKS.

The disintegration of the back wall of the fireplace caused by the heat from the hearth fires made renewals necessary; at Woodsome Hall (Fig. 94) we find an arch built to facilitate the taking out of the brickwork, a practice more frequently met with in Normandy. On the development of iron founding in the Weald of Sussex cast-iron plates were made to protect this back wall. The earliest firebacks were rectangular in form, of greater width than height, and are thought to have been suggested by the cast-iron grave slabs of which there are many examples remaining in Sussex. The process of development, of both design and execution, is described in a paper read before the Society of Antiquaries by Mr. J. Starkie Gardner in 1898,[1] who states that, from the unmistakable evidence which these firebacks afford, "the art of iron casting developed step by step there, and was not transplanted as a perfected art from abroad." The earliest backs appear to have been moulded by pressing a board made to the required size and thickness into a bed of sand which, on being removed, would leave a shallow depression, and into this the molten iron was poured, producing a casting with a level back. For decorating the front the nearest ornament at hand was used; roses, fleurs-de-lys, compasses, crossed staples, lengths of cord and sometimes the hand of the moulder, were pressed into the sand and appeared in relief in the casting (Fig. 129). The back shown in Fig. 128 is an important example of one ornamented in this way. It is 4 ft. 8 in. long by 3 ft. wide. The royal arms and supporters are thought to be Plantagenet but to have been used for the decoration of an early Tudor

[1] *Archæologia*, vol. lvi.

back, the lower shield bearing the letters E and H which, so it is suggested, stand for Henry VII and Elizabeth of York. The form of the lion supporters when compared with those in the Plantagenet oak mantel beam at Hillingdon shows close resemblance (Fig. 83). In the Penshurst back (Fig. 130) the surrounding mouldings may have been attached to the wood pattern, but the royal arms, crown and crossed staples have obviously been impressed separately in the mould. This plan of using movable stamps, although generally denoting an early back, continued long after others from complete patterns had been produced, as seen in the back at Charlton (Plate LXXVIII) dated 1602, and still later in Fig. 134, dated 1710, where the out of squareness of the beaded ornament may be attributed to it.

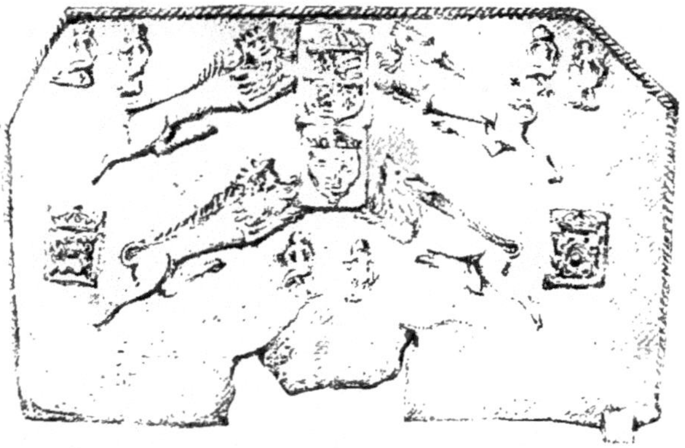

FIG. 128. EARLY FIREBACK ORNAMENTED BY MOVABLE STAMPS AND CABLE BORDER.

Of firebacks made from a complete model the finest are those with representations of the arms of the reigning sovereigns from Henry VII to James II. These are generally rectangular with an arched projection in the centre, which formed a convenient place for the crown. An early example may be seen in Plate VI from Ockwells, which is dated 1548. The arched head to this back is greater in proportion to its width than was usual and in others of this proportion wings with improvised ornamentation

CAST IRON FIREBACK, GROOMBRIDGE PLACE, KENT.

CAST IRON FIREBACK, BREDE PLACE, SUSSEX.

were added to get the requisite width.

Plate LXV shows a fine, but much corroded, example with the arms of James I at Groombridge Place, Kent, and another variety of the same subject is seen in Plate LXVI from Brede Place, Sussex.[1]

FIG. 129. FIREBACK SHOWING IMPRESSION OF HAND IN LEWES MUSEUM.

In the fireplace of the Queen's Gallery at Hampton Court the fireback is of the time of James II, bearing the initials I R and the date 1687 (Plate LXXXII). Mr. Law points out that William III did not hesitate to make use of his dethroned father-in-law's firebacks in his new additions to the palace.

FIG. 130. FIREBACK AT PENSHURST, KENT, WITH ROYAL ARMS.

[1] There was a furnace and foundry at Brede. A fireback dated 1636 shows Richard Lennard of Brede standing with a hammer in his hand and surrounded by the implements of his craft (*Sussex Arch. Collections*, xlvi).

FIG. 131. AT PENSHURST PLACE.

Firebacks with the royal arms were succeeded by others containing those of the noble families on whose estates in Kent and Sussex foundries existed, as in Plate XXXVIII, that of the Dacres of Hurstmonceux Castle, at Eastgate House, Rochester, where a more florid outline may be seen. Fig. 131 has the badge of the Sydneys, with the Earl of Leicester's initials and coronet from Penshurst Place.

Also at Penshurst is the wide and massive back (Plate LXVIII) with the initials only of the owner T. S., a peculiarly English type of which few examples only are to be found. That at Highgate, Kent, shown in Plate LXVII, with arms on a plain field, is another variety.

Events were commemorated, as the Defeat of the Spanish Armada in Fig. 132, with the date 1588, and in the centre an anchor, fleurs-de-lys and roses.

FIG. 132. ARMADA FIREBACK.

The escape

CAST IRON FIREBACK AND HEARTH-PLATE WITH WROUGHT ANDIRONS AND BILLET BAR
HIGHGATE, KENT.

Plate LXVIII.

CAST IRON FIRE-DOGS AND FIREBACK WITH WROUGHT-IRON BASKET-GRATE, PENSHURST PLACE, KENT.

of King Charles forms the subject of a fireback in the Victoria and Albert Museum (Fig. 133). On it are portrayed an oak tree into which three crowns are introduced amongst the foliage, with the letters C.R., and beneath this on a riband "The Royal Oak."

FIG. 133. BOSCOBEL OAK FIREBACK.

Another commemorates his Restoration.[1] The letters C coupled and reversed occupy the centre under a laurel wreath, crossed by palm branches and surmounted by a crown, with the date 1661.

FIG. 134. FIREBACK IN THE POSSESSION OF THE AUTHOR.

Dutch firebacks were imported and largely copied in England. These are of different proportion to the native article, being generally thin, and tall in proportion to their width, with arched top and dolphins reclining on

[1] *Archæologia*, vol. lvi., p. 153.

FIG. 135. FIREBACK FOUND IN PAVING OF COTTAGE FLOOR IN OXFORDSHIRE.

either side. Fig. 136, which has a representation of Charity, shows a large one of this type 2 ft. 6 in. wide and 3 ft. 5 in. high. Plate LXIX shows another at Penshurst ornamented with Dutch tulips and other flowers in a vase and surrounded by a well-designed border and a rather unusual treatment of dolphins around the arch. This fireback appears to have been cast with plain face to form the back of a basket grate.

FIG. 136. FIREBACK IN THE POSSESSION OF THE AUTHOR.

That some of this type were made in Sussex is substantiated by the fact that the wood patterns still exist. The model of that shown in Fig. 137

is in the possession of the Earl of Ashburnham, the subject being Hercules slaying the hydra-headed monster. The Dutch origin of others is proved by one often met which has a figure and the lion of Holland in a wattled enclosure and the words *pro patria Hollandia*, H. H. anno 1665.

Representations of scriptural subjects were frequently placed on the backs which belong to the Dutch variety, as the Nativity and the meeting of Christ and the woman of Samaria at the well; also subjects from the heathen mythology. A favourite example of the latter is Cursius on his charger riding into the jaws of a monster, with the motto *Nil desperandum*. A small fireback was made with a representation of a man masked with a cloak handing a bone to a dog on guard, with the words in the border of the semicircle, *Fides dona superat.*

FIG. 137. HERCULES SLAYING THE HYDRA. A SUSSEX CASTING FROM A DUTCH PATTERN.

A fireback having the arms of France, but otherwise closely resembling English work, is in the Lewes Museum, the habitation of the Sussex Archæological Society's collection.

As coal gradually came into use, firedogs were displaced by firegrates, and the manufacture of both cast dogs and cast backs died out. The charcoal-iron industry of the Weald of Sussex diminished through scarcity of fuel and in competition with coal-iron manufactured in the midlands, where iron ore and coal were found close together.

With the disappearance of the cast-iron back the fireplace lost one of its most picturesque features; the material was very suitable for its purpose and capable of artistic treatment, and its comparative indestructibility in use accounts for the considerable number which are still in existence after from two to three hundred years' wear. The large heraldic examples with the arms of the reigning sovereigns are the finest, such as is seen in Plate LXV from Groombridge Place, bearing the arms of James I. These show great skill in both design and modelling, and when seen either in the firelight or in the gloom of a sooty recess have great artistic value.

FIG. 138. AT HADDON HALL.

EARLY RENAISSANCE ANDIRONS

Of andirons of the Early Renaissance period, other than those of cast iron, we find considerable variety, although the remaining examples are not numerous; and whereas those of cast iron have a strong family likeness the others show great diversity of design, this diversity being perhaps due to some of them being importations from abroad. The greater number belong to the Stuart period, when the andiron was an object on which great skill and costly metals were lavished, remaining examples at Knole House being of silver and others at Hampton Court of silver gilt.

The essential or working parts continued to be made of iron, brass and sometimes silver being employed for their decoration in standards and finials, and the spit hooks disappeared.

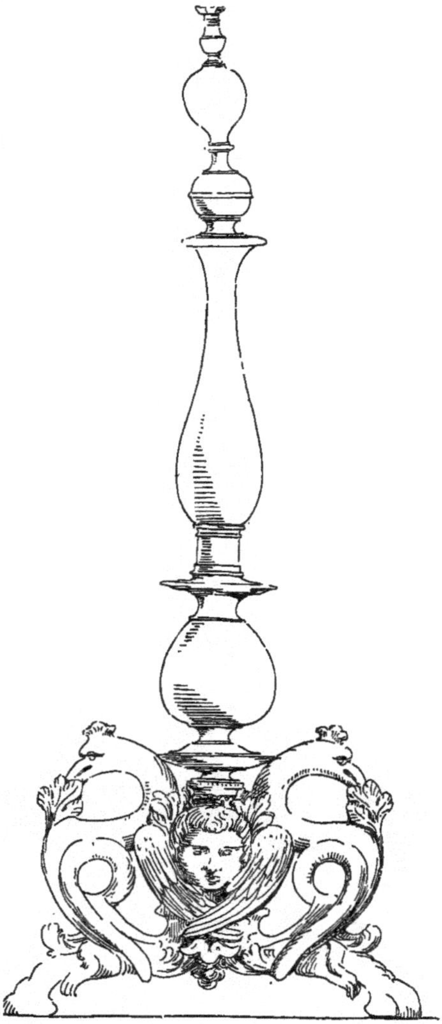

FIG. 139. AT MOYNS PARK, ESSEX.

Haddon Hall, Derbyshire, fortunately retains many of its fireplaces in their original condition; that in the state bedroom, shown in Plate LIX, has andirons, the lower parts of which are of wrought iron, almost identical in design with the Henry VIII pair at Knole (Fig. 119), surmounted by cast brass standards of baluster form. Brass balusters may be seen again in the Long Gallery, but of a heavier and less graceful form, the supports being of cast brass formed of the arched legs and heads of an animal, with head at the intersection with the billet bar (Fig. 138). In both cases these stand on a slightly raised stone hearth, and in the latter there is a front hearth of marble arranged in octagons and squares. This same treatment is met with again in the handsome pair of bronze andirons at Moyns Park, Essex, popularly supposed to have been cast from guns taken from the Spanish Armada (Fig. 139). These are 4 ft. 6 in. high and 2 ft. wide at the base and the workmanship is both vigorous and refined.

FIG. 140. AT HADDON HALL.

Further varieties of this type may be seen in Fig. 96 from Bramshill House, Hants, and in Fig. 98 from Dodington Hall, Somerset, the scrolled feet of the latter terminating gracefully with small figures.

Of quite different character are the andirons which stand in the drawing-room fireplace at Haddon Hall, which have wrought-

FIG. 141. OLD COCK HOTEL, HALIFAX.

iron standards and bases fronted with cast brass openwork and two foliated discs placed one above the other (Fig. 140). This pierced ornament, which is suggestive of a Dutch origin, is very effective as seen contrasted against the plain background of the fireplace recess.

Polished brass and steel discs were much used for the ornamentation of andirons; in an inventory made in 1659 of the goods at Hampton Court Palace, mostly claimed as belonging to Cromwell, the item, "one pair of andirons with double brasses," occurs in many of the rooms, also "one paire of creepers, fire shovell, tongs and bellows."[1] The double brasses referred to may have been of the same kind as at Haddon or plain discs as in Fig. 131.

The term "creepers" was applied to the smaller andirons which stood within the larger ones and did duty for them when the latter became too finely dressed for their work.

The "andirons with double brasses" are not now to be seen at Hampton Court, most of the fireplaces being furnished with simple ones of wrought iron brightened, as in Plates LXXIX, LXXX, LXXXI, and LXXXII. These, although well designed and suitable for their purpose without the assistance of "creepers," are rather insignificant and less than might be expected in a building for which the fine designs in wrought ironwork by Jean Tijou were being executed.

An exceptional pair at Loseley, seen in Plate X, are of forged

[1] *History of Hampton Court Palace*, by E. Law.

FIG. 142. AT KNOLE PARK, KENT.

and embossed iron of obelisk form, terminated with hollow foliated balls and standing on curious arched bases with ball feet. The mulberry, which has been previously referred to as the badge of the Mores figuring in the overmantel, appears again, embossed in low relief and gilt, in the sides of the obelisk.

Fig. 141 is an illustration of a type not often seen, with standards of tablet form. The finest of this kind, at Long Melford Hall, Suffolk, are of cast brass and have small scriptural figure subjects in square compartments one above the other on the face of the standards, with similar arched feet to those in Fig. 141.

Shakespeare, in his description of Imogen's Chamber, gives us a picture of the fireplace of his time :—

> The chimney
> Is south the chamber; and the chimney-piece,
> Chaste Dian, bathing: never saw I figures
> So likely to report themselves: the cutter
> Was as another nature, dumb; outwent her,
> Motion and breath left out.
> The roof o' the chamber
> With golden cherubins is fretted: her andirons
> (I had forgot them) were two winking Cupids
> Of silver, each on one foot standing, nicely
> Depending on their brands.

The silver andirons at Knole, in the Cartoon Gallery (Fig. 142), have cupids holding fireirons in their hands. The ornament of silver repoussé is built up on a structure of iron. Fig. 143 shows a variation of the same type, also at Knole. These are of silver gilt, of exquisite workmanship, and stand about 2 ft. high.

As a further illustration of the luxury of the Restoration period extended to the fireplace, the fire pans for burning charcoal at Ham House, Surrey, are encased with embossed silver (Fig. 144). One of these bears the cypher of the Duchess of Lauderdale beneath a coronet, and in the pan stand andirons with small figure terminations of silver.[1] The addition of andirons as seen in simple form in Fig. 144, enabled logs to be used; the wrought fireirons have silver knops and the bellows are cased with embossed silver.

FIG. 143. AT KNOLE PARK, KENT.

Belonging to King William's Rooms at Hampton Court we have a pair of singularly beautiful andirons, one of which is shown in Fig. 145. These are of silver gilt, standing 16½ in. high, the work is attributed to Andrew Moore and the date of it to 1696–7.

At the dispersal of the furniture of Horham Hall, Essex, a few years ago, a very interesting pair of andirons was sold which

[1] Macquoid's *History of Furniture*, Walnut Period.

have now appeared at the Victoria and Albert Museum (Fig. 146). These are of cast brass, about 2 ft. high, the depressions in the ornament being encrusted with enamel in colours mainly green, blue and white, with red in the arms and crown of the Stuart kings. Described as English, second half of the seventeenth century; they have a rich appearance, but the design is strange and but slightly suggestive of their purpose.[1] Another example of enamel applied to andirons is seen in Fig. 150 from Weald Hall, Essex.

FIG. 144. SILVER-MOUNTED FIRE-PAN, FIRE-IRONS AND BELLOWS AT HAM HOUSE.

Elaborate Italian andirons were imported into England, examples of which are at Wilton (Plates LXXIII and LXXIV) and in the Tapestry Room at Ham House (Plate LXXXIX). The opportunity which the standards gave for play of imagination and line appealed to the Renaissance sculptor, and beside the florid Italian and French examples our native efforts appear but modest.

[1] An interesting article on this type of enamel firedogs, by Viscount Dillon, appeared in the *Burlington Magazine*, January, 1910.

INTRODUCTION OF COAL

In 1239 Henry III is said to have granted a charter to the townsmen of Newcastle-upon-Tyne for liberty to dig coals in the vicinity of that place.[1] In 1281 one hundred pounds per annum was paid to the Crown as a fee farm. In 1306 the use of sea-coal in London was prohibited by proclamation. The nobles and commons in parliament complained against the use thereof as a public nuisance, which was thought to corrupt the air with its stink and smoke. A few years afterwards sea-coal appears to have been used in a royal palace in London, 1321–22, ordered by the clerk of the palace of Richard del Hurst, but had been neglected to be paid for. In 1327 the measure became an object of consideration, and in 1351 Edward III granted a licence to the burgesses of Newcastle to dig coals and stones in a place called the Castle Field without the walls of that town and confirmed it in 1358. In 1365 an order was issued concerning the measure to be used by the vendors of coals. In the household book

FIG. 145. KING WILLIAM'S ANDIRONS AT HAMPTON COURT.

[1] Brand's *History of Newcastle.*

of the fifth Earl of Northumberland, of the date 1512, mention occurs of this fuel, which, it seems they had not then learnt to use by itself, "bicause colys will not byrne withowte wood." In 1536 the price of coals in Newcastle was 2*s*. 6*d*. per chaldron and in London about 4*s*.

FIG. 146. FORMERLY AT HORHAM HALL, ESSEX.

Harrison in 1577 mentions that the "trade in coals beginneth to growe from the forge to the kitchen and halle, in cities and towns that lie near the coast where they have little other fuel except turf and hassocke," and he marvels that there is no trade in them in Sussex and Southamptonshire for there the smiths work their iron with charcoal.

In 1582 Queen Elizabeth obtained the manors of Gateshead and Wickham, with the coal mines, etc. These were afterwards procured by the Earl of Leicester and by him assigned to the famous Thomas Sutton of the Charterhouse, and the price of coals was raised to 6*s*. per chaldron, afterwards in 1590 to 9*s*.

Wood, where procurable, was the ordinary fuel, but in Elizabeth's reign there was a complaint that it was getting scarce for purposes of carpentry through its being so largely felled for fuel. To remedy this, Elizabeth, in the first year of her reign, issued a proclamation that no oak, beech, or ash tree that was one foot square at the stubb, and growing within fourteen miles of the sea or any navigable river should be converted to coal or fuel, "as being a debasing of that which, if nature did not at first intend, necessity must employ for better service."[1]

This waste of timber was noticed by Harrison, who feared that, if the woods decayed as fast in the time coming as in time past, "turf, gal, brome, heth, brake, whinnies, dies, ling, hassocks, flags, strawe, sedge, reede, rushe, and seacole, would soon be good merchandise even in the city of London; whereunto some of them have gotten and taken up their innes in the great merchaunds parlers." The last named of these, seacole, which had been long used by brewers, smiths, dyers and others, was now becoming an article of use for domestic purposes, and the trade in it may be said to have commenced in 1561.[2]

The prejudice against it, however, still continued, the fair sex being most hostile to its use as it was thought to give the "coal tinge" to the complexion, and it was considered a mark of respect when entertaining company to warm the room with charcoal.

Dame Quickly was above this prejudice as she said to Falstaff, "Thou didst swear to me upon a parcel gilt goblet sitting in my dolphin chamber, at the round table by a sea-coal fire on Wednesday in Whitsun week, when the Prince broke thy head for likening his father to a singing man at Windsor."

[1] Fuller, *Worthies*, vol. i, p. 133.
[2] Gray, *Chorographia*, p. 33.

FIG. 147. ASTON HALL, BIRMINGHAM. HOB FIREPLACE IN AN UPPER ROOM.

In an inventory of the furniture of Sir Thos. Kytson of Hengrave Hall, Suffolk, made at his death in 1603, occur the items "In the great chamber one cradell of iron for the chimney to burne seacole w^th^, one fier sholve made like a grate to seft the seacole w^th^, and one other fier sholve, and one payer of tongues."[1]

Hengrave was begun about the year 1525 and completed in 1538. We see that between the latter date and 1603 coal had been introduced and some sort of basket grate in which to burn it. The andirons for burning logs still existed as "two payer of andyornes, with heads and foreparts of copper; one payer being less than the other and two payer of creepers."[2]

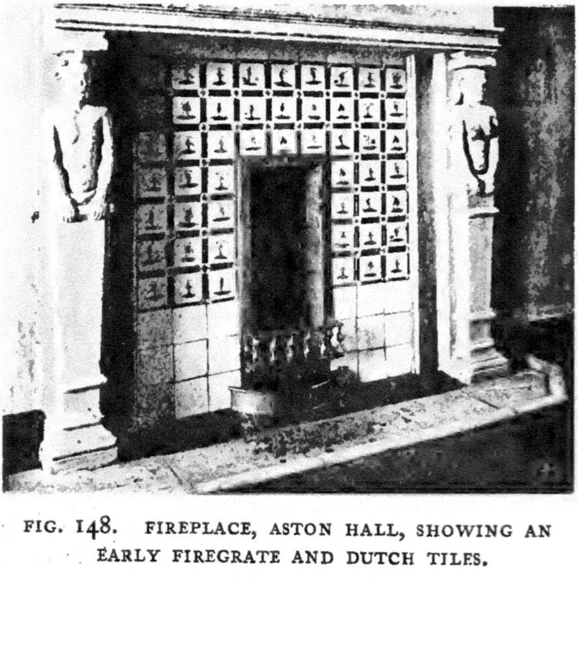

FIG. 148. FIREPLACE, ASTON HALL, SHOWING AN EARLY FIREGRATE AND DUTCH TILES.

[1] Gage's *Hengrave.*

[2] Another interesting item is mentioned showing a custom prevalent at the time: "One p-fuming panne of brass" in the winter parlor. Floors

WROUGHT IRON BASKET-GRATE WITH CAST IRON BACK AND WROUGHT ANDIRONS, PENSHURST PLACE, KENT.

We do not know what the "cradell of iron" at Hengrave was like but the term might not inaptly be applied to the fire baskets at Penshurst, with their side supports, as seen in Plates LXVIII and LXIX. The great chamber at Hengrave had two fireplaces and not a central hearth. This form of fire basket may be seen also at Ockwells (Plate XXV). Grates, perhaps of still earlier form, for burning coal are at Haddon Hall in the state bedroom and long gallery, Plate LIX and Fig. 138 respectively, and in the dining-room of the same building (Fig. 59, page 52) we see probably the earliest form of hob arrangement and the upright bars which find favour at the present time. Fig. 147 shows a quaint hob fireplace in an upper room of Aston Hall, Birmingham, the grate appearing to have lost its side supports, and in

FIG. 149. A GRATE FROM WESTMORLAND.
Dan Gibson del.

were strewed with straw and rushes, which became unpleasant for want of frequent changing, and this was sought to be overcome by burning charcoal in a brazen chafing dish or perfuming pan with a bit of rosin or fir cone placed on the embers. Shakespeare alludes to this when he makes one of his characters say, that he was "entertained for a perfumer when he was smoking a musty room."

the same building we find the earliest form of enclosed grate (Fig. 148) surrounded by Dutch tiles. We are not able to say whether these grates at Aston Hall were the originals, but if not they are judged to be very early additions.

Plate LXX shows to a large scale the fireplace in the hall of the Charterhouse previously referred to with cast-iron standards which follow closely the form of the oak newel terminations of the staircase, surmounted with the Sutton crest.

Fig. 149 shows a form of basket grate, of wrought iron with pierced brass apron and standards, which belongs to the Jacobean period and followed the introduction of coal for use in domestic fireplaces.

FIG. 150. GRATE AT WEALD HALL, ESSEX.

FIREGRATE IN THE HALL OF THE CHARTERHOUSE, LONDON

Later Renaissance Chimney-Pieces

THE SEVENTEENTH CENTURY.

A DISTINCTION has been made by recent writers on English Renaissance Architecture between the work executed previously to Inigo Jones's second visit to Italy in 1613, designated "Early Renaissance," and that executed subsequently, called "Later Renaissance." During the former period, details more or less Italian were being grafted on to our native style of building, through the instrumentality of owners who had travelled on the Continent, artists introduced from Italy, France, Germany and the Lowlands, English craftsmen sent abroad by patrons to study classical architecture, and others who had acquired some knowledge of it from published books, and through working by the side of the foreigner here. It is thought that the Earlier Renaissance buildings were conceived and planned by the owner or his surveyor, and that the details were left to the various trades to carry out, thus accounting for the lack of harmony often found in the executed work; but on the introduction of a more scholarly classical style by Inigo Jones, it became necessary to supply full-size details of the various parts, and so began the practice of the professional architect, which has continued to the present day.

An analogous change took place in the designs of chimney-pieces, regular classical forms taking the place of such ofttimes bizarre productions as have been under consideration.

FIREPLACES BY INIGO JONES.

We have examples of Inigo Jones's designs for chimney-pieces in his executed works, some of his original drawings, and in the published works of his followers. The type of marble mantel devised or introduced by him supplied to a great extent the mode for imitation during the eighteenth century.

At Raynham Hall, Norfolk, built for Sir Roger Townshend about 1630 from designs of Inigo Jones, several chimney-pieces remain which illustrate this change of style, although there is some uncertainty about their remaining as originally designed. The lower parts, which, it may be noticed, follow closely the forms surrounding Italian door and window openings, are of marble and the upper are of wood painted and gilt like other parts of the room

In the dining-room (Plate LXXI) a heavy architecture frames the fireplace opening, with shoulders which stop the side consoles, from the eyes of which hang festoons of fruit. The cornice mouldings which form the mantel-shelf break forward in the centre with a pediment over a heavy central tablet, a questionable feature for this position, but one much favoured by Inigo Jones. As overpiece, a richly-moulded frame containing a portrait is crowned by a strong cornice with opened pediment, and the intervening space is filled with a cartouche and festoons of oak leaves. This chimney-piece is clearly designed to suit the projecting breast, which it does admirably; the main cornice of the room, base and surbase mouldings break round and tie the whole into one composition.

In the red drawing-room, Plate LXXII, there being no projecting breast, greater width is given to the mantel by adding side pilasters, finishing with trusses, over which the shelf mould breaks; emphasis having been given to the wings, the central tablet is kept flat and stops beneath the shelf. The full width of mantel is carried up, side panels in the overmantel flanking the central frame, which is surmounted by a scrolled pediment with head and festoons of oak leaves in the centre. The dining-room mantel suffers from the large size of the centre tablet, with its clumsy ornamentation, and the contour line of the side scrolls stops too abruptly at the top; great skill is, however, shown in adjusting the overmantels to their position in the general design of the room, and it is this that differentiates them from the more ambitious of the Early Renaissance designs.

The south front of Wilton House, Salisbury, was designed for the Earl of Pembroke by Inigo Jones towards the end of his architectural career, and carried out under the superintendence of his nephew and pupil, John Webb. It contains a suite of magnificent rooms, with chimney-pieces which equal them in importance. The largest apartment, known as the "Double Cube Room," designed to receive on its walls the family portraits by Vandyke, contains a handsome white marble chimney-piece, with overpiece of wood, painted and partly gilt, to accord with the rest of the room (Plate LXXIII). Here we see the front and side consoles, with festoons of fruit hanging from their voluted sides, centre tablet with pediment over as at Raynham, but parted in this instance for the insertion of a cartouche containing the Pembroke cypher with coronet. A portrait group of the children of Charles I occupies the central space, in a richly-carved frame surrounded by drapery, and having over the centre the Prince of Wales's feathers. Figures representing "Peace and Plenty" stand one on each side, and behind them fluted Corinthian columns support a rich entablature. The crowning pediment is opened for coronated shield, and on its curved sides recline figures after the manner of those on the tomb of Lorenzo de Medici by Michael Angelo in Florence. A specially-designed grate with coved cheeks and marble hearth of geometrical pattern complete this sumptuous composition.

Plate LXXV shows the chimney-piece of the "Corner Room,"

which is in some respects a finer design than the preceding ; it encases a projecting chimney-breast, of which full advantage has been taken. The way in which the pediment works in with the room cornice and the poise of the central cartouche are superb ; there is no more striking illustration of the work of Jones's master hand.

A third important chimney-piece is in the "Colonnade Room" (Plate LXXVI), a variation from the preceding, of which the gilt dragons on the slopes of the pediment form an important feature. The fire-grate is of this period. The marble mantel, so well shown in Mr. Davies' photograph (Plate LXXVII), forms a worthy pedestal for the works of art it supports. The grate, fender and fire-irons, although suiting their position well, are of later date.

We are told in Colin Campbell's *Vitruvius Britannicus* that these marble chimney-pieces were carved in Italy and brought over by the first Earl of Pembroke, and this is confirmed by the style of the carving, but there is no doubt that the design of the decorations of these rooms was influenced by the work of contemporary French architects. In a French book on Architecture, by J. Barbet, dedicated to Cardinal Richelieu in 1633, there are several designs for chimney-pieces engraved by Abraham Bosse which can hardly have been unknown to the designer of those at Wilton. One shows important points of similarity to that in the "Double Cube Room," such as the reclining figures on the curved pediment with cartouche between, Corinthian columns with figures standing on pedestals in front of them and other smaller details. The consoles with heads, forming the side supports of chimney-piece in Plate LXXVII, figure in Barbet's book, as also the running ornament of the frieze, and the dragons above the pediment in the "Colonnade Room."

Plate LXXVIII shows one of the chimney-pieces at Charlton House, Kent. Barbet gives this design, but with an elaborate overpiece and with the caryatid support repeated in profile at the sides. The designing of Charlton has been attributed to Inigo

FIG. 150A. CHIMNEY-PIECE DESIGNED BY INIGO JONES FOR KING CHARLES I. AT GREENWICH.

FIG. 150B. CHIMNEY-PIECE DESIGNED BY INIGO JONES FOR SIR GEORGE PRICE.

Jones, but it is not authenticated; there are, however, strong points of similarity between this chimney-piece and designs of his given by Vardy. The cut leather scrolls forming grotesque masks appear in a design for chimney-piece in old Somerset House and again in another at Greenwich.

The designs shown in Figs. 150A and 150B are taken from Vardy's book, where they are described as by Inigo Jones, although a drawing of that for Sir George Price with figured dimensions by John Webb is in the R.I.B.A. collection, where it is inscribed, "Sr George Pratt his Guest Chamber," and dated 1660.

These designs show a fine sense of proportion and a freedom of handling of classical forms of architecture, the most questionable feature being perhaps the cartouche in the Greenwich design with its exaggerated horns. Inigo Jones had a facile pencil, but before allowing it free play was careful to first get his mass and proportions right, and we feel that but little would be lost if the ornaments were removed from his designs. We find the influence of his early training as a designer of masks and prosceniums in the questionable trick of passing drapery in and out of the architrave mouldings, afterwards much copied by his successors; and in another design for King Charles I.'s Drawing Room at Greenwich festoons of foliage are suspended from the claws of an eagle and wind around the side columns in a quite theatrical manner.

Mouldings much broken and mitred appear frequently in his designs. Fig. 151 shows a bold chimney-piece in the Victoria and Albert Museum, taken from a house in Great St. Helen's, which, from similarity of details to other works of his, may be thought to have come under the influence of Inigo Jones, who designed the entrance doorway to the church of that name. The cut scrolls are almost identical with others in the chimney-pieces of his at West Woodhay. The mantel is of deal, and is an early example of the use of that wood for the purpose in place of oak, of which wood mantels had hitherto been made.

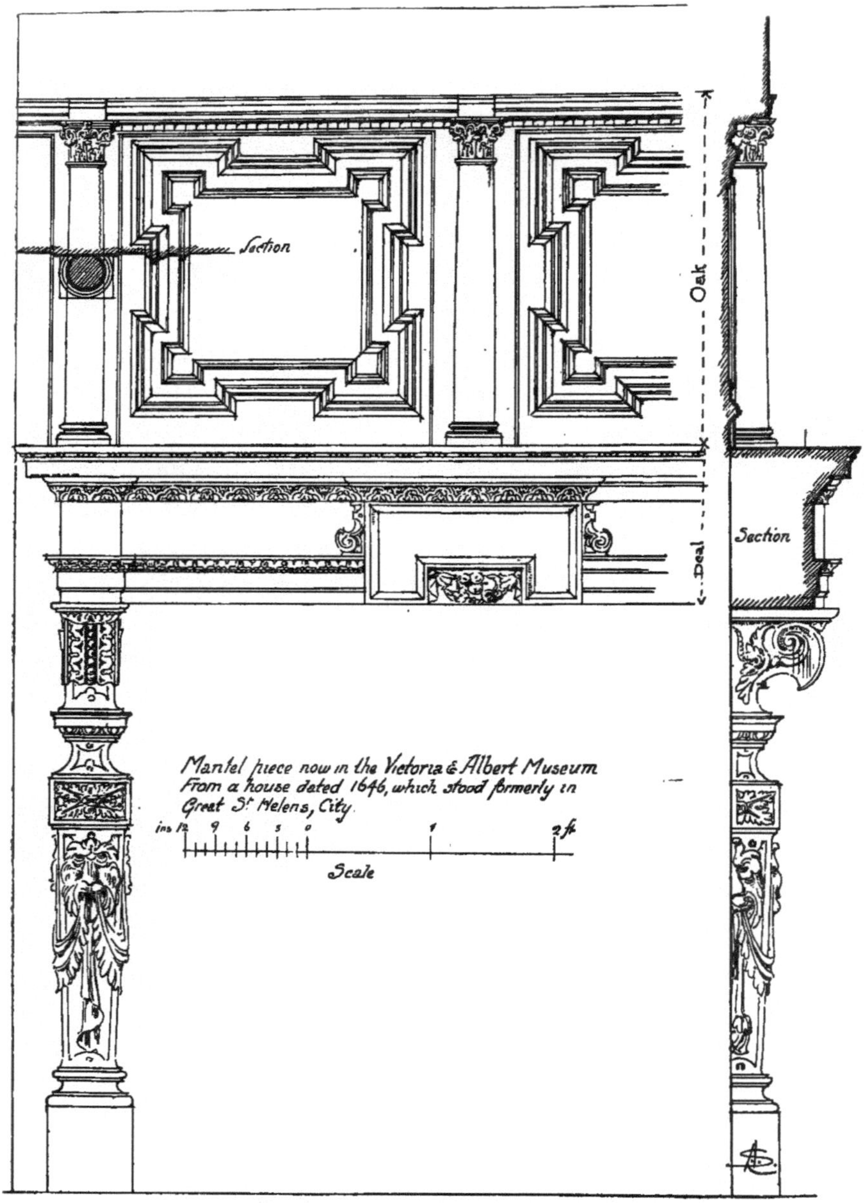

FIG. 151. FORMERLY AT GREAT ST. HELEN'S.

THE DINING-ROOM, RAYNHAM HALL, NORFOLK.

THE RED DRAWING-ROOM, RAYNHAM HALL, NORFOLK.

THE DOUBLE CUBE ROOM, WILTON HOUSE, SALISBURY

DETAIL OF CHIMNEY-PIECE IN THE DOUBLE CUBE ROOM, WILTON HOUSE, SALISBURY.

THE CORNER ROOM, WILTON HOUSE, SALISBURY.

THE COLONNADE ROOM, WILTON HOUSE, SALISBURY.

THE ANTE-ROOM, WILTON HOUSE, SALISBURY.

THE DINING-ROOM, CHARLTON HOUSE, OLD CHARLTON, KENT.

The overpiece bears signs of not having been made for its present position.

An interesting fragment of a plaster overmantel probably by Inigo Jones remains at Kirby Hall (Fig. 152), which has a niche in the centre as at West Woodhay.[1] The cornice has fallen away, showing the wooden construction beneath. This is a somewhat rare example, showing the continuance of the custom of constructing overmantels of plaster, which was more usual in the early part of the seventeenth century.

FIG. 152.

FIREPLACES BY SIR CHRISTOPHER WREN

In the hands of Wren chimney-pieces took a form differing from any which preceded them; he followed the practice of his talented predecessor, Inigo Jones, in embracing the whole height of the room as his unit of design, but does not otherwise appear to have been influenced by his designs for chimney-pieces. The broad manner of wainscoting took the place of the small panel style of the Elizabethan Renaissance; the low dado, with base and

[1] *Inigo Jones*, by Triggs and Tanner, p. 21.

surbase, and long panels above extending to the cornice, became almost universal. The rebuilding of London after the Great Fire provided the requisite opportunity; and it was a most fortuitous circumstance that the services of Wren, who had just then commenced his architectural career, were available for its rebuilding.

Wren's fireplace openings were generally enclosed by a heavy bolection moulding of stone or marble, as seen in the King's Drawing-Room at Hampton Court (Plate LXXIX); he seldom provided a mantel-shelf at the ordinary height, and his overpieces were limited to an enriching only of the panelling of the room. The state rooms at Hampton Court Palace, which he designed for King William and Queen Mary, provide illustrations as seen in Plates LXXIX, LXXX, LXXXI. In the King's Drawing-Room, where great height had to be dealt with, a panel portrait of the Archduchess Isabella of Austria occupies the place of honour, surrounded at the top and sides by festoons of carving in limewood by Grinling Gibbon, laid on to the oak wainscoting. Simple wrought andirons stand in front of a cast fireback on a marble hearth, and stone side linings of a moulded section complete the fireplace opening.

In the King's private dressing-room the mantel is projected forward, its cornice providing a shelf for china, and a mirror is placed below it at a convenient height from the floor. It was about this time that mirrors for this position were coming into vogue, and they were used by Wren both at Hampton Court and Kensington Palaces. Jno. Evelyn mentions that in 1676 he visited the Duke of Buckingham's glassworks at Lambeth, where they made "looking glasses far larger and better than any that come from Venice." It was Evelyn who in 1671 discovered that "incomparable young man," Grinling Gibbon, and brought his carving to the notice of King Charles II and Sir Christopher Wren. In these rooms Wren appears to have given Gibbon a free hand, which in the ornamentation of this overpiece, Plate LXXX, has run riot, the circular band of carved flowers being quite out of scale with the mantel, a mere *tour de force*. It is singular that Wren, whose carved ornament, in doorheads and architraves, also by Gibbon as mentioned in the building accounts, is so strong in architectonic

FIG. 153. HAMPTON COURT PALACE: FIREPLACE IN THE KING'S GALLERY.

character, should have approved of the applied ornament which we see here, which is so lacking in this respect, although unsurpassed in delicacy of modelling and skill of execution.

Plate LXXXI shows the fireplace in the King's Dressing-Room, where advantage has been taken of its position in an angle to treat the chimney-piece in an original manner; a series of steps in the overpiece, receding to the angle of the room, provided shelves for Queen Mary's Delft-ware ornaments.

FIG. 154. KENSINGTON PALACE.

This plan of placing fireplaces in the corner of rooms had come into fashion; several of the fireplaces in the Queen's Palace at Greenwich had been built in this way. Evelyn criticized the custom after visiting the King's house at Newmarket, when he says: "Many of the rooms had the chimnies plac'd in the angles and corners, a mode now introduced by his Majesty which I do at no hand approve of. I predict that it will spoil many noble houses and rooms if followed. It does only well in very small and trifling rooms, but takes from the state of greater." This fireplace being in a small room would not have come under Evelyn's condemnation. The mirror, either by accident or design, is placed in such a position as to present to a person standing in front of it a vista of the whole range of southern state rooms through the doorways. A disadvantage of the corner position for a fireplace is that it reduces by half the space around the fire, from a semicircle to a quadrant.

Less characteristic of Wren's work, but with his usual architrave moulding, is the grey marble chimney-piece in the Queen's

Gallery (Plate LXXXII). A mirror in a brass frame is surmounted by a pair of turtle-doves billing and cooing beneath a bust of Venus, with garlands of flowers and Cupids of white marble. The same may be said also of that in the King's Gallery, where the heavy architrave mould is of breccia marble, and a white marble bas-relief representing Venus drawn in a car by amorini forms the frieze (Fig. 153). The outer jambs and shelf are of black marble, with metal mountings gilt. Replicas of this panel were made and cast in lead, one having recently come under the writer's notice.

That Wren was not averse to mirrors we see by his frequent use of them. He designed two chimney-pieces for Queen Mary's Gallery at Kensington Palace, where an imitation window is constructed with mirrors and curtains of wood carved and gilt (Fig. 154). Mr. Ernest Law, in his Guide to the Palace, calls special attention to these looking-glasses and gives the names of the executants by whom they were set up two hundred years ago: Gerard Johnson, cabinet-maker, and Robert Streeter, sergeant painter. They were in a very bad condition, but have now been carefully restored. The same writer refers also to the chimney-piece in the King's Gallery at Kensington Palace by Wren (Fig. 155). On the large circular dial is painted a map of the north-west of Europe, and a pointer actuated

FIG. 155. KENSINGTON PALACE.

by an iron rod connected with a vane above the roof registers the direction of the wind on this map. "It was the dial which so greatly interested Peter the Great, when he privately visited William III in this palace in 1698." Macaulay mentions that he was in raptures with this plate, but took no notice of the fine pictures with which the palace was adorned. The white marble chimney-piece is an uninteresting Georgian insertion.

At Belton House, Grantham, the design of which is attributed to Wren, the chimney-pieces in the dining and drawing-rooms are of marble, with a slight variation from his usual heavy architrave, but in this instance with frieze and mantel shelf (Fig. 156). A picture hangs above the shelf, and surrounding it *hang* also characteristic carved festoons by Grinling Gibbon, much of whose work is to be seen at Belton.

It is customary to attribute most of the carving of this post-Restoration period to Gibbon, but it is quite certain that he could with his own hands have executed but a small part of it. We know that at St. Paul's Cathedral he had a number of assistants, and doubtless a school was founded of men who worked in his style and whose work cannot now be differentiated from the master's.

It is clear from the numerous examples which remain of carving in the Gibbon style that his work had become the fashion and the chimney-piece of his day was designed specially for the display of this carving, the usual position for it being above and hanging in festoons down the sides of a picture over the mantel as in Plate LXXIX.

The south suite of rooms at Chatsworth House, Derbyshire, contains a series of superb chimney-pieces of this type. William Talman was the architect, and the building was going on at the same time as Hampton Court, where he was appointed comptroller of works to William III. This connects these designs with Wren, but whether he supplied drawings or Talman made use of those used at Hampton Court we do not know.

There appears to be no doubt about the names of the executants

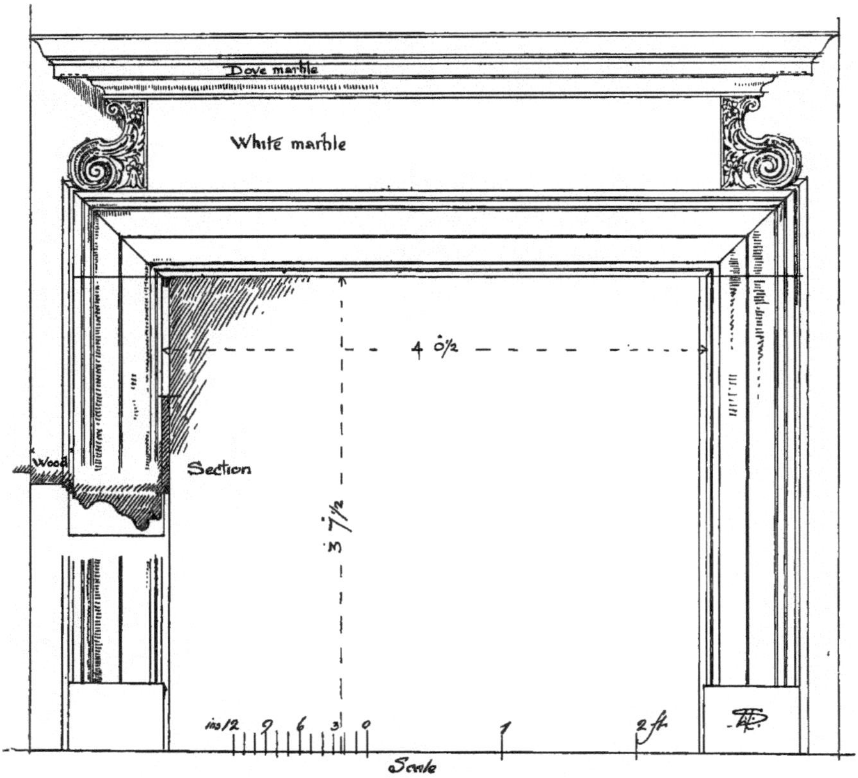

FIG. 156. A TYPICAL CHIMNEY-PIECE OF THE WREN TYPE.

of this carving, as a contract exists, dated September 9, 1692, in which "Joel Lobb, William Davis and Samuel Watson agreed with the Earl of Devonshire, to execute in lime-tree, the carving in the Great Chamber, to be done equal to anything of the kind before executed, for which they were to receive £400. This carving to consist of flowers, wreaths, fish, dead game, cherubs, etc." The work is in the most pronounced Gibbon's manner and could certainly not be carried out without full-sized drawings being made, and the presumption is that they were supplied by him. The close imitation of natural forms must have necessitated a long and careful study of the subjects selected, this imitation including at Chatsworth a pen hardly distinguishable from a real feather, a point cravat, a woodcock and all medal, a presented to the Duke by the carver. Horace Walpole, who assumed the work to be by Gibbon, says: "There is no instance of a man before Gibbon who gave to wood the loose and airy lightness of flowers and chained together the various productions of the elements with a free disorder natural to each species."

Some slight sketches of his for chimney-pieces at Hampton Court are preserved in the Soane Museum. The carvings, prominent in Plate LXXXIII, which shows a chimney-piece in the Central Library, Bristol, are said to have been purchased at the sale of his effects after his death in 1721, and given to the Library by Michael Beecher in 1739. The initials are taken to be those of Viscount Dursley, Earl of Berkeley. The lower part of this bold composition is of stone and apparently by a different hand.

A beautifully carved wooden mantel and overmantel at Stoke Hall, Derbyshire, shown in Plate CLXII of Messrs. Belcher and Macartney's *Later Renaissance*, is attributed to Grinling Gibbon, in which terminal figures almost life size support the wings of the mantel-shelf. A richly-carved marble architrave enframes the fireplace opening in which stands an original grate. Claim has been made to a Gibbon's authorship for carving in the city which on close comparison is hardly justified, such as is seen in the vestry of St. Lawrence Jewry, Plate LXXXV, and at the Tallow

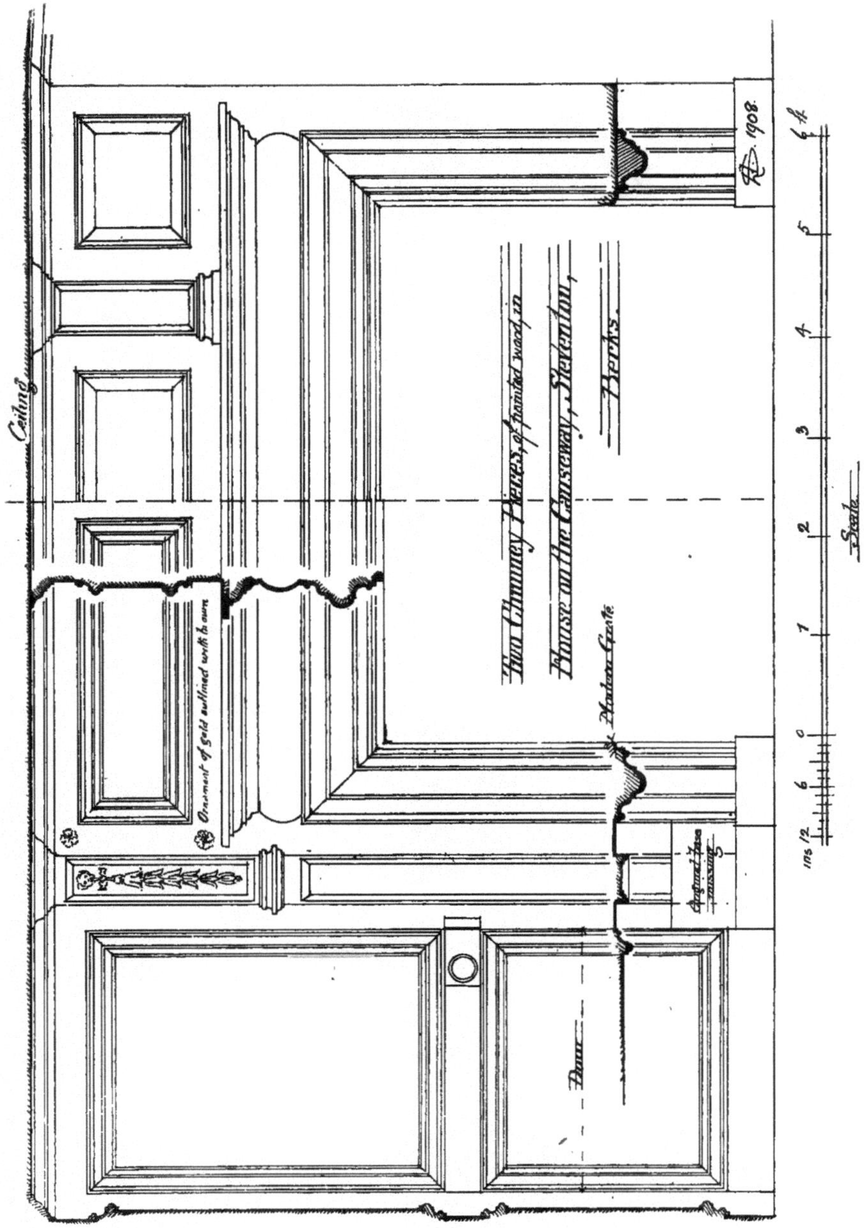

Two Chimney Pieces, of painted wood, in
House on the Causeway, Steventon,
Berks.
Ceiling
Ornament of gold outlined with brown
Modern Grate
Original Base missing
Door
1908
Scale
ins 12 6 0 1 2 3 4 5 6 ft

FIG. 157.

Chandlers' Hall, Plate LXXXVI. If by Gibbon, these were early works of his, as the softness and undercut seen in Plates LXXIX and LXXX are entirely absent. The court parlour of the Brewers' Hall was wainscoted at the expense of Lord Mayor Samuel Starling in 1870, as recorded on a tablet over the chimney-piece of this date, and this laudable example was followed in the parlour of the Tallow Chandlers' Hall, Dowgate Hill, where the inscription over the door runs : "This parlour was wainscotted at the expense of Sir Jno. Sheldon a member of this Company and Lord Mayor of the city A.D. 1675." Plate LXXXVI shows the chimney-piece, and it may be noticed that the style of the carving closely resembles that at St. Lawrence's Vestry, Plate LXXXV.

This broad panelled style of Wren and his contemporaries produced many dignified apartments, in which the chimney-piece was subordinated to the general design of the room. From more important buildings it spread to humbler, and an entirely panelled room may often be found in small manor or farm-houses, such as is seen in Fig. 157, from a house on the Causeway, Steventon, Berks, dated 1657, where heavy mouldings of wood frame the fireplace opening. Where stone was easily procurable it took the place of wood as in the chimney-piece at Lower Lypiatt, near Stroud, Plate LXXXVII.

Instead of being projected into the room examples may be found where the chimney-piece is thrown into a recess by columns being placed on either side, as in the drawing-room of the New River Company's Offices, Clerkenwell, where the arms of William III as an overmantel are surrounded by highly relieved carving consisting of birds, flowers, fish and nets, filling the intervening space between the columns.[1] A later example of this treatment

[1] Belcher and Macartney's *Later Renaissance Architecture*, Plate XIV.

THE KING'S DRAWING-ROOM, HAMPTON COURT.

THE KING'S PRIVATE DRESSING-ROOM, HAMPTON COURT.

THE KING'S DRESSING-ROOM, HAMPTON COURT.

Plate LXXXII.

THE QUEEN'S GALLERY, HAMPTON COURT.

AN OVERMANTEL, THE CENTRAL LIBRARY, BRISTOL.

WEALD HALL, BRENTWOOD, ESSEX.

OVERMANTEL IN THE VESTRY OF THE CHURCH OF
ST. LAWRENCE JEWRY, CITY OF LONDON.

THE COURT PARLOUR OF THE TALLOW CHANDLERS HALL,
DOWGATE HILL, LONDON.

IN LOWER LYPIATT HOUSE, STROUD, GLOUCESTERSHIRE.

CHIMNEY-PIECE REMOVED FROM 3 CLIFFORDS INN, LONDON.
Now in the Victoria and Albert Museum.

THE TAPESTRY-ROOM, HAM HOUSE, PETERSHAM, SURREY.

is in the Board Room of the Admiralty, Whitehall, by Ripley,[1] where nautical instruments figure in the carving and a wind register is placed over the shelf of a heavy marble mantel. Here fluted Corinthian pilasters bound the mantel on either side and the entablature of the room runs over them unbroken. As this building was erected after Grinling Gibbon's death he must have left some one capable of carrying on his work, although singularly enough we do not find any later examples in the same style.

To Wren's time belongs the chimney-piece, shown in Plate LXXXVIII, which is part of a panelled room removed from 3, Clifford's Inn to the Victoria and Albert Museum. This house was built in 1686 by John Penhallow, whose arms quartering Penwarin appear in the overmantel. The constructional parts are of oak and the laid on ornament of pearwood. This applied carving is lacking in contrast, insufficient prominence being given to its leading lines. The marble lining, with flattened arch and key block, is a characteristic form of the Restoration period, but the original firegrate is missing.

What may be regarded as an architectural freak is the chimney-piece in the Tapestry Room at Ham House, Surrey, where the Rococo style is met with unrestrained, Plate LXXXIX. The design of chimney-piece and its surroundings is apparently by the same hand as the Mortlake tapestry designs; the spiral column and clambering amorini both figure in the Charles I tapestries at Houghton Hall in combination with Rococo ornament by Artari. This composition, which in the actual work charms by its colour scheme, loses in the photograph, where its defects are emphasized. Underneath the basket grate is seen one of the silver-mounted firepans which preceded it in use at Ham House.

[1] Belcher and Macartney's *Later Renaissance Architecture*, Plate XX.

CHIMNEYS OF THE LATER RENAISSANCE

WHEN Inigo Jones introduced the formal plan of house after returning from his second visit to Italy this formality extended to the positions of the fireplaces and chimneys in connexion with them, and an effort was made to effect a symmetrical arrangement as seen from the front of the building. We find this in the Queen's House at Greenwich, Raynham Hall, Coleshill, and elsewhere. As previously mentioned with reference to this architect's work at Kirby Hall flues were massed by him in large rectangular stacks instead of in groups of separate shafts.

The stacks became very large, and at Raynham, to give scale their sides are broken up with vertical lines, formed by tall flat pilasters of brick with caps proportioned to their width (Fig. 158); but at Coleshill (Fig. 159), where the chimneys are of stone, about 5 ft. square, they are finished with a block cornice proportioned to the size of the shaft, the sides of which are disposed in one large panel surrounded by enriched mouldings. These form a perhaps too striking feature in the design, their great size tending to dwarf the main building. Inigo Jones' pupil, John Webb, following in his master's footsteps, has given us at Ashdown House, also planned symmetrically, very tall chimneys which bear close relationship to those at Coleshill but without the panelled sides.

At Thorpe Hall, near Peterborough, also by Webb, the vertical lines of the quoins, over which the cornice breaks, serve to improve the proportion of what would otherwise be a very stumpy chimney (Fig. 160).

FIG. 160. AT THORPE HALL, PETERBOROUGH.

FIG. 162. AT STAMFORD.

FIG. 158. AT RAINHAM HALL, NORFOLK.

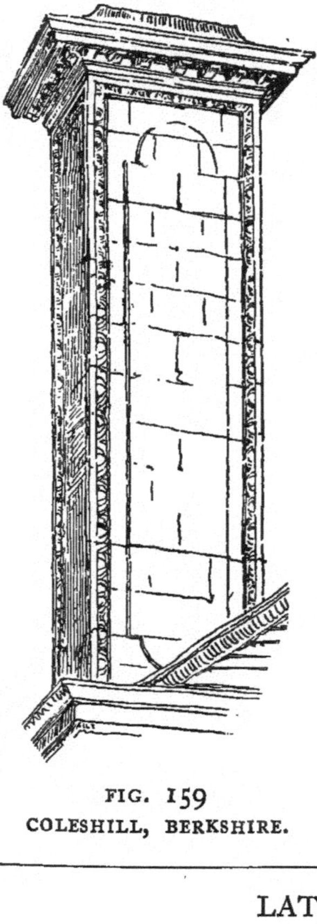

FIG. 159 COLESHILL, BERKSHIRE.

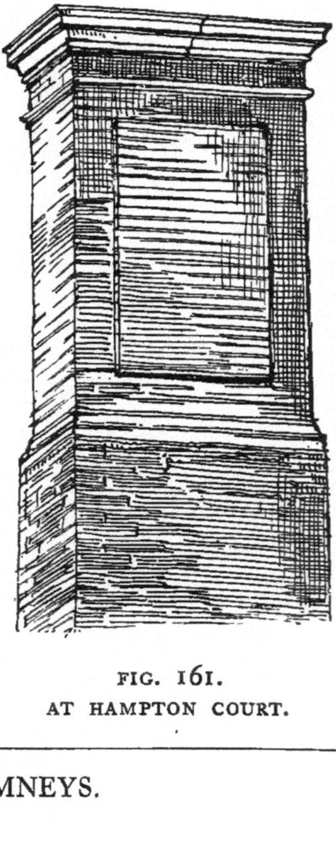

FIG. 161. AT HAMPTON COURT.

LATER RENAISSANCE CHIMNEYS.

Fig. 161 [1] shows a chimney at Hampton Court by Sir Christopher Wren which is of red brick with Portland stone cap and base, the side panels being raised instead of sunk as in previous examples. This plain rectangular stack with moulded plinth and cornice, as generally found in Wren's buildings, represents the type which was generally adopted during the succeeding century when parapets to a great extent superseded overhanging eaves cornices, and the chimney, becoming less in evidence, ceased to be regarded as an important feature in the design.

[1] Sir John Vanbrugh planned his chimneys to rise in a group and connected them by an arcade to form a tower-like composition, as at Blenheim Palace.

Fig. 162 is from a house at Stamford which shows a further development; pilasters are formed at the angles of the shaft with caps and bases, the recesses being finished at the top with arched heads and key stones. Similar chimneys are at Clare College, Cambridge.

Chimneys were made the subject of a tax in the reign of Charles I. On March 3, 1661, Samuel Pepys says: "I am told that this day the Parliament hath voted 2*s.* per annum for every chimney in England as a constant revenue for ever to the crowne." This lasted but a short time as we read that in 1666 "The business of buying off the chimney-money is passed in the house; and so the King to be satisfied some other way, and the King (was) supplied with money raised by this purchasing off the chimnies."

The rebuilding of London after the great fire in 1666 increased very largely the number of chimneys, each room being provided with a fireplace. Flues, although still larger than as now constructed, were reduced in size, and generally built in the party walls with projecting breasts; the chimney seen above the roofs was of brick finished with two or three oversailing courses or a course of paving tiles.

THE SMOKE NUISANCE

Coal which was then a staple fuel had, as we are told by Pepys, become in 1667 scarcer and dearer than it had ever been before; the price having gone up to £5 10*s.* per chaldron in consequence of the Dutch fleet lying off the mouth of the Thames and preventing our colliers from Newcastle landing their cargoes.

Jno. Evelyn tells us how he was commanded by his Majesty (Charles II) "to go with some others and search about the environs of the Citty, now exceedingly distressed for want of fuel, whether there could be any peate or turfe found fit for use." He continues, "The next day I went and discover'd enough, and made my report that there might be found a great deale; but nothing further was done in it." A few days after an artificial fuel called "houllies" from a receipt given in Evelyn's *Sylva* was tried with success at Gresham College for everybody to see. This is described by him as "very glowing and without smoke or ill smell." The object of producing a smokeless fuel which still exercises men's minds had commenced to do so in 1656, for he says: "Came home by Greenwich Ferry where I saw Sir John Winter's new project of charring sea-cole, to burn without sulphur and render it sweete. He did it by burning the coals in such earthen pots as the glassmen melt their mettall, so firing them without consuming them."

The smoke nuisance continued and appears to have excited the keenest interest in Evelyn who published a pamphlet called "Fumifugium" which was dedicated to his Majesty. He mentions that on October 1, 1661, when accompanying the latter in his yacht, "he was pleased to discourse with me about my book inveighing against the nuisance of the smoke of London and proposing expedients how by removing those particulars I mention'd it might be reformed; commanding me to prepare a bill against the next session of Parliament, being, as he said, resolved to have something done in it." On January 11, 1662, he further says, "I received of Sir Peter Ball the Queen's Attorney a draught of an act against the nuisance of the smoke of London, to be reformed by removing severall trades which are the cause of it and endanger the health of the king and his people. It was to have been offer'd to the Parliament as his Majesty commanded."

Evelyn's proposition was to remove the trades beyond Greenwich which produced this "fuliginous and filthy vapour" such as brewers, dyers, limeburners, salt and soap boilers; and to form plantations of shrubs which "yield the most fragrant and odoriferous flowers" such as sweetbriar, woodbine, white and yellow jessamine, lavender and rosemary. Nothing came of this beyond the planting of lime trees in St. James's Park.

It is probable that, when coal first took the place of wood as fuel for these trades, chimneys were not at first built high enough to carry the smoke away. In 1670 the tax on coal which had previously been 1*s*. per chaldron was raised to 2*s*., and the money was used for the rebuilding of the City churches after the fire.[1] Efforts were made about 1678 to improve the construction of domestic fireplaces. A bricklayer named Bingham built one in Prince Rupert's chamber, in which the smoke from an open grate was carried through an opening in the brick back the same width as the grate and 10 in. high, and had to descend under an iron baffle before rising up the chimney, thus to some extent being consumed by the fire. The baffle reduced the amount of air passing from the room up the chimney with its attendant draughts and was hinged so as to provide an ordinary exit for the smoke when the fire was first lighted.[2]

[1] *London Churches*, by G. H. Birch, F.S.A.

[2] Bernan's *History of Warming and Ventilation*, p. 208.

Later Renaissance Chimney-pieces

THE EIGHTEENTH CENTURY

MANY circumstances had combined to produce great diversity in the designs of chimney-pieces belonging to the first half of the eighteenth century. The intimate connexion of our Stuart sovereigns with the Court of France and the influx of French artificers following the Revocation of the Edict of Nantes, the advent of William of Orange with his Dutch artists,

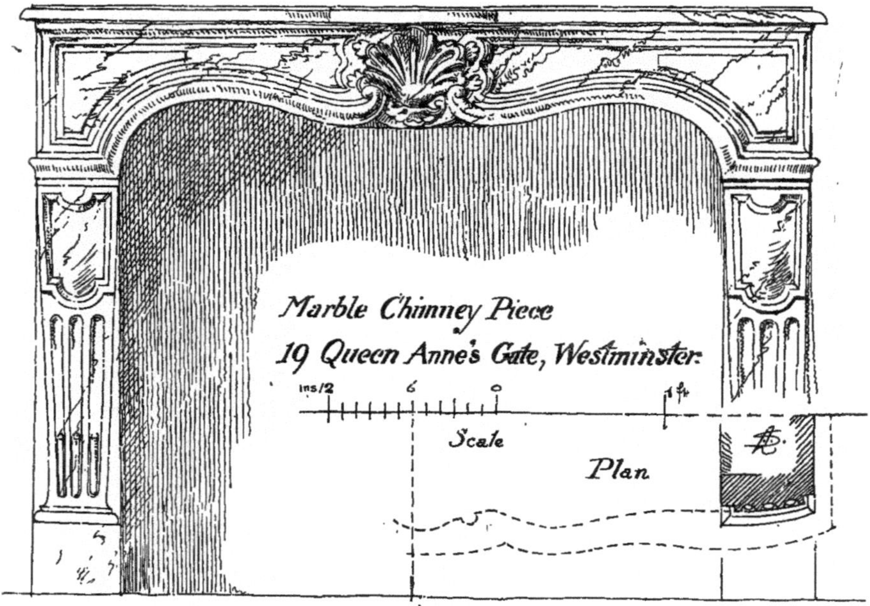

FIG. 163.

and later the Continental wars conducted by Marlborough, all served to increase our connexion with the art of the Continent. In addition to the foregoing, art patrons and architects continued to study Classic and Renaissance architecture in Italy.

FIG. 164.

Marble chimney-pieces had become a trade article; for in 1676 Evelyn tells us of the existence at that time of a rare magazine of marble in Lambeth whither he went to take an order for chimney-pieces for the house of his friend, Mrs. Godolphin. The owner was a Dutchman who had contracted with the Genoese for all their marble. He mentions also a visit to the Earl of Essex's new house at Cashioberie in Hertfordshire, where the "Chimney mantles are of Irish marble not inferior to Italian." French marble chimney-pieces were imported into England in Queen Anne's time. Fig. 163 shows one amongst others of rouge marble at 19, Queen Anne's Gate, which are thought to have been placed there when the house was built. Another, shown in Plate XCII, is from Carlisle House, Soho Square, where a rich effect is produced by inlaying the ground of the ornament with marble of a different colour. The example from Castle Howard (Fig. 164) shows the work of a French hand in both mouldings and ornament, as do others in Sir Jno. Vanbrugh's buildings. Original French marble chimney-pieces in the styles of both Louis XV and XVI may occasionally be met with in London houses, but not so frequently as within one's recollection; having passed through a long period when out of fashion many have been swept away.

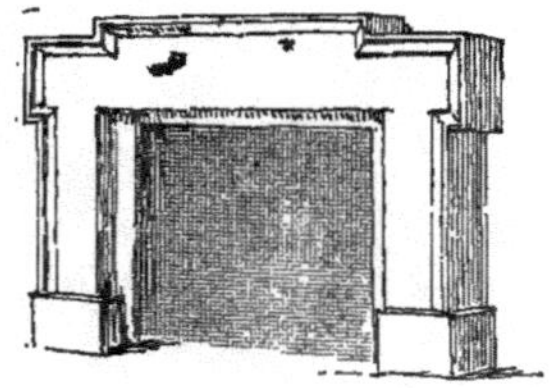

FIG. 165.

With the retirement of Wren we lose the genial wainscoted rooms with chimney-piece decorations by Gibbon, who died three years before his great patron. A more severely classical style was adopted in the great houses built by his successors for which the chimney-piece designs of Inigo Jones provided suitable models. Walls were plastered and painted, or covered with silk damask or wall paper which was then coming into use. Halls were lined with stone as at Blenheim and Houghton, others were decorated with stucco which extended to the overmantel as at Rushbrooke Hall, and as seen in Plate LXXXIV from Weald Hall, Essex. Sir John Vanbrugh's chimney-pieces at Blenheim are of the same ponderous character as his architecture, many of them consisting of a kneed architrave projected sufficiently from the wall to form a shelf or pedestal (Fig. 165).

FIG. 166. THE DINING-ROOM, EASTON NESTON, NORTHAMPTONSHIRE.

At Easton Neston, Hawksmoor has given us in the dining-room the same monumental character (Fig. 166).' Bellied trusses facing both front and sides are dressed up with key blocks and heavy rustications such as are used for outside work. These appear very unsuitable for chimney-pieces as providing a lodgment place for the dust which must necessarily accompany a fire.

James Gibbs, to whom we owe the churches of St. Martin in the Fields and St. Mary le Strand, was a skilful designer of chimney-pieces some of which figure in his published work; and Fig. 167 is a reproduction of an original drawing by him. He copied neither Inigo Jones nor Wren but built up compositions of his own on safe classical lines without any great originality. This design is well proportioned and the overpiece leads up pleasantly from the mantel with a good outline.

The more important marble mantels of this period were

FIG. 167. FROM AN ORIGINAL DRAWING BY JAS. GIBBS, ARCHITECT.

generally surmounted by elaborate overmantels made of wood and painted, the central panel being filled with a picture, as in Plate cv, where a portrait of Archbishop Laud is seen.

Often when both mantel and overmantel were of wood the designs partook of the same character as when of marble; no distinctive treatment being given to the material. The inner member nearest the fire was usually of marble as a protection from the fire, as in Plate xc from Norton Hall.

The chimney-piece shown in Plate xciii, which is of carved deal, would be equally suitable for execution in marble. It was originally in the studio of Romney the painter at the back of 30, Cavendish Square, and is now set up in the new house recently built on the site; having been thoroughly stripped of many coats of paint the delicate carving shows its original crispness. The weakness of design apparent in the centre of the frieze appears to be original.

Plate xciv shows a carved deal mantel from Great George Street, Westminster, which has been dealt with in a similar way and is now in one of the rooms of the Institute of Surveyors. The carving is in very high relief, the heads of reptiles standing out almost detached from the ground.

One of the most important of these wooden chimney-pieces is in the drawing-room at Brightling Park, Sussex (Plates xcv and xcvi). Consoles facing both front and sides support an entablature which breaks over them, and these are repeated in the overmantel with the addition of heads which rather uncomfortably support other consoles carrying the main cornice. The opened pediment, with a basket between overflowing with flowers, and the centre tablet with head and surrounding rays are characteristic details of this period; less so is the plain backing with enriched bead on the angles, tying together the whole composition, which in this instance would without it present a very weak outline.

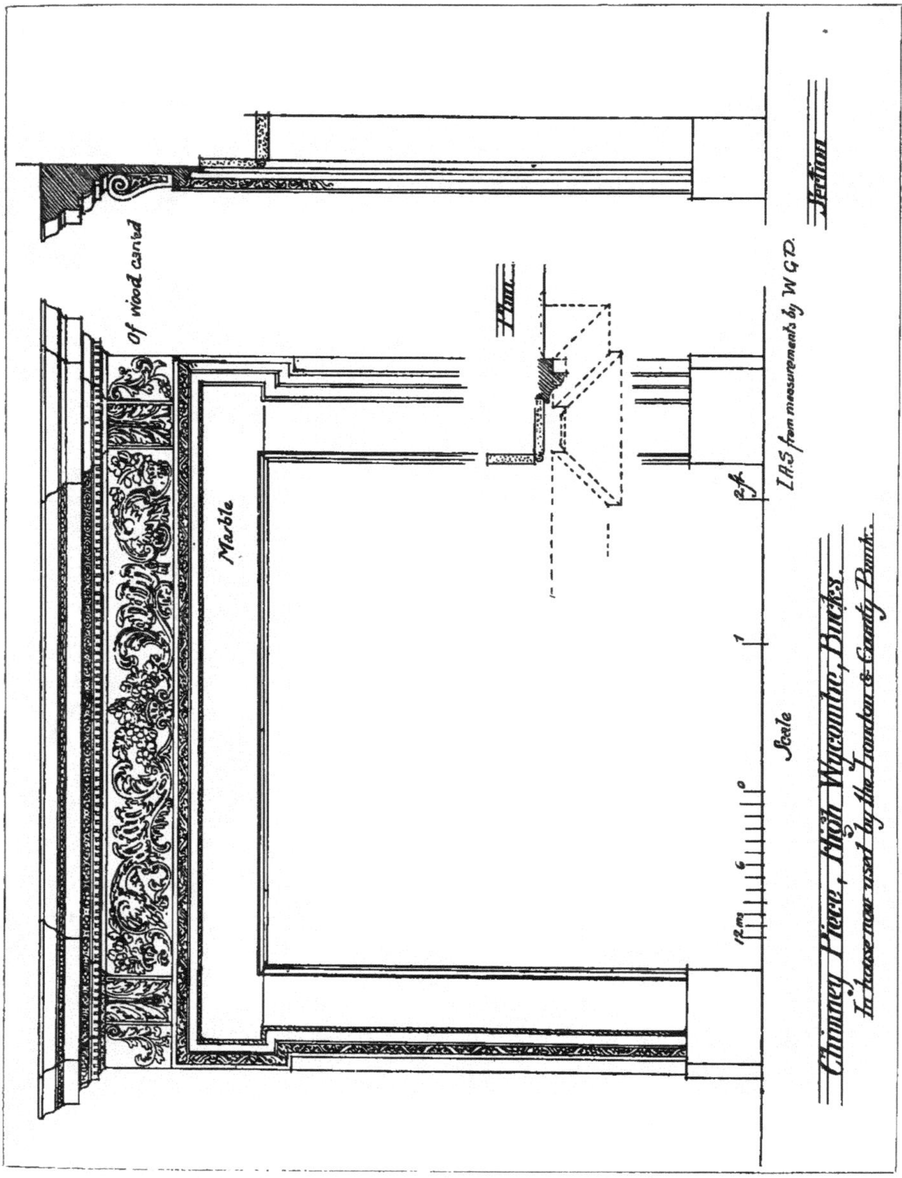

FIG. 168.

FIG. 169.

The carved ornament of this period was largely copied from the French of Louis XIV as in Fig. 168, which is a simple wooden design with facia and returns of marble. Many rooms in the city and elsewhere were lined with deal and had mantels which consisted of but little more than a narrow architrave with frieze and cornice laid on to the panelling, of which they formed a part, and marble lining with bases as in Plate xcviii from 2, Suffolk Place, E.C., which has rather elaborate side consoles. The frieze which here form a hollow curve often took an ogee form or had a plain segmental section. These simple wood mantels were a natural development from the requirements of their position and seldom fail to please.

Eighteenth-century marble chimney-pieces may be broadly divided into four kinds, which followed roughly this order: plain or elaborated architrave only, trussed pilaster, caryatid or terminal figure, and column supports to the mantel-shelf. Varieties of trussed pilaster chimney-pieces may be seen in Plates xcix–ciii. The Horsham Park example, Plate cii, differs from the others in having its trusses placed immediately under the cornice, thereby getting greater length in the pilasters. This chimney-piece is much disfigured by the coarseness of the carving in the frieze. In Plate c the details are too large for the size of the whole, particularly the projection of the central block, a fault not uncommonly met with in works of this period. The finest is seen, in Plate ciii, from 17, Hanover Square, which was for many years the home of the Arts Club and at one time previously of Mrs. Gordon, the actress. This combines good mouldings and ornament with good proportion, and the general effect is enhanced by contrasting the white statuary carving with a yellow background of Sienna marble.

Consoles as supports to mantel-shelves were frequently extended down to the hearth as at Ashburnham House, Sussex, by Dance.

Plate civ, from 60, Carey Street, Lincoln's Inn Fields, shows a masculine design, the centre of the frieze having a lion's head and fore-paws, and out of its mouth come wreaths of oak leaves, an ornament for which great preference was shown at the time. This plan of representing an animal's head with skin and paws was a favourite device; in a house in Queen Square, Bath, built for himself by the elder Wood, the architect, it is elaborately shown.

FIG. 170. CHIMNEY-PIECE WITH CARVED DRAPERY FROM HOLKHAM HALL.

The wreathing of drapery in and out the architrave, first seen in the design facing page 159 by Inigo Jones, was frequently copied, as in Fig. 170 from Holkham Hall.

Fine examples of marble chimney-pieces were made for the group of stately mansions erected in Norfolk during the first half of the eighteenth century; Wolterton Hall by Ripley, Houghton Hall designed by Colin Campbell, carried out under Ripley and decorated by Wm. Kent, and Holkham Hall by Kent. Figs. 171 and 172 show chimney-pieces from a book of drawings of Holkham by Matthew Brettingham, who was engaged upon its

FIG. 171. THE SCULPTURE GALLERY, HOLKHAM HALL.

completion after Kent's death, where they are described as designs by Inigo Jones. Fig. 171, that in the sculpture gallery which is now surmounted by a tall pedimented overpiece with niche for statue, is copied from one at Wilton where the mantel cornice has a broken pediment with central cartouche and swags. The drawing-room chimney-piece (Fig. 172) is of statuary marble and in the existing work has breaks in the cornice over the trusses which appear unduly wide for their position. Other chimney-pieces at Holkham have Kent's name attached to them as designer;

FIG. 172. THE DRAWING-ROOM, HOLKHAM HALL.

that in the Green State Bedroom consists of "Thermes with heads of the younger Empress Faustina" of statuary marble with basket capitals set anglewise on a Sienna ground made by the "late Mr. Carter." Holkham was built by Thomas Coke,

FIG. 173. THE SALOON, HOUGHTON HALL.

created Earl of Leicester, a virtuoso who had the assistance of Kent, and we are told by Brettingham, made use of Desgodetz's work on architecture; begun in 1734 it took thirty years to complete.

We look to Houghton Hall, Norfolk, erected regardless of expense by Sir Robert Walpole, 1722–35, for examples of important chimney - pieces and are not disappointed. A fine one of black and gold marble relieved with white in frieze caps and bases stands in the saloon (Plate CIV* and in Fig. 173). Well-proportioned Ionic columns with entablature are projected from the main wall in two planes, and over the front pair an opened pediment breaks. The central block bears the star and garter to which Sir Robert became entitled in 1726, and on it stands, in the executed work, a marble bust of Venus. The place of the overpiece seen in Fig. 173, which is taken from Ripley's book, is now occupied by a large framed portrait without the side caryatides there shown. In the hall both mantel and overmantel are of stone (Plate CIV **). Caryatides with fruit baskets on their heads form the side supports, over which the cornice breaks, and the lines of these are carried up as pilasters terminated with a broken pediment which crowns the overpiece. A bas-relief by Rysbrack occupies the central panel. In the Marble Parlour is another large chimney-piece, where the subject represented is a sacrifice to Bacchus also by Rysbrack, and festoons of the vine are used for the ornamentation of frieze and trusses.[1] With the exception of the saloon chimney-piece this work of Kent's at Houghton lacks any fine sense of proportion, the details are clumsy and mechanical and it is difficult to realize their size, that in the hall being about 18 ft. high. The saloon chimney-piece shown in Fig. 173 has the appearance of being by a different hand, possibly that of Isaac Ware who made the drawings of these chimney-pieces for the book on Houghton Hall. Kent's uncertainty in the matter of proportion is further exemplified in the piled up composition of cold veined white marble (Fig. 174) in the Cupola Room at Kensington Palace, where the height of the fireplace opening is that of an average man, although it entirely fails to give that impression. The skied bas-relief is a representation of a Roman marriage by Rysbrack.

The Caryatid support or terminal figure which we have seen so much used during the Early Renaissance period was revived in a more classical form for very general use, as in the Stone Hall at Houghton (Plate CIV **), and without the fruit baskets in the Vandyck Room at

[1] Belcher and Macartney's *Later Renaissance Architecture*, Plate CXL.

Wentworth Woodhouse, by Henry Flitcroft, Plate cv, where voluted trusses are terminated by female heads and shoulders, garlands of fruit and flowers hanging from the eyes of the volutes. This form of truss is seen again in Plate cvi in a statuary marble chimney-piece at 3, Tenterden Street, W. It is the subject of a plate in the *Complete Body of Architecture*, by Isaac Ware, who was employed on buildings in this street and the adjoining Hanover Square, about 1717, and is in what was the drawing-room on the first floor when these houses were occupied by persons of fashion ; French influence is observable in the plan and section of the somewhat meagre shelf, but the graceful line bounding the fireplace opening which became traditional in French chimney-pieces is absent and the side trusses appear stuck on instead of growing out of the jambs. The grate is of a kind in which air from the room is admitted through openings at the bottom, and when warmed by contact with the fire back and sides finds an exit through openings at the top. A register door is controlled by a key through a hole in the centre.

FIG. 174. IN KENSINGTON PALACE.

In the adjoining room is a chimney-piece of red granite with ormolu ornaments and enriched mouldings, Plate CVII. The cornucopia at the side discharging its contents on to the floor is a singular conceit, which violates one's sense of its fitness as ornament and makes an awkward finish between the mantel and base and surbase mouldings.

Isaac Ware was architect for Chesterfield House, Mayfair, which was built in 1749, and contains some excellent chimney-pieces. That in the drawing-room is shown in Plate CVIII. The lower stage of Sienna and statuary marble has detached Ionic columns supporting an entablature which forms the mantel-shelf. The ornament of the frieze of white marble is laid on to the coloured ground. The column type of chimney-piece, of which this is a rather early example, was made largely during the latter half of the eighteenth century, and when well proportioned, as it often was, and of fine material formed an object of great beauty. A fitting overpiece of wood completes this very handsome piece of work.

The grate, although apparently an old one, is too small for its position, which is emphasized by the darkness around. The marble hearths of this period were very large, and the pierced steel fenders without any return ends stood well within them and not around the edge as is our custom at the present day.

The dining-room chimney-piece, Plate CIX, is of equal importance, but less satisfactory in its general design, showing a want of harmony between the upper and lower stages, the free outline of the figures below calling for a less rigid one above. If Isaac Ware was responsible for this work it is singularly contrary to the views expressed in his book before mentioned, where speaking of the "Caryatick" order he says :—"The female figures of this order are to stand at seeming ease and it would be monstrous to load them with ornaments up to the ceiling. Themselves are sufficiently ornamental for the work and the less the eye is disturbed in contemplating them the better. A plain or simple chimney which terminates at the mantelpiece is the proper one for the Caryatick order."

FIG. 175. CHIMNEY-PIECE AT HORTON HALL.

As his book referred to was published in 1756, some years after the building of Chesterfield House, it may express his matured judgment on the subject. These designs probably had the benefit of Lord Chesterfield's criticism for whom they were prepared. The arrangement of carved drapery over the picture closely follows that of the overpiece in the "Double Cube Room" at Wilton.

NORTON HALL, BURY ST. EDMUNDS.

WEALD HALL, BRENTWOOD.

Plate XCII.

MARBLE CHIMNEY-PIECE AT 10 CARLISLE STREET, SOHO SQUARE, LONDON.

30 CAVENDISH SQUARE, LONDON.

IN THE SURVEYOR'S INSTITUTION, GREAT GEORGE STREET, LONDON.

THE DRAWING-ROOM, BRIGHTLING PARK, SUSSEX.

DETAIL OF DRAWING-ROOM CHIMNEY-PIECE,
BRIGHTLING PARK, SUSSEX.

Plate XCVII.

THE DINING-ROOM, HORSHAM PARK, SUSSEX.

2 SUFFOLK PLACE, LONDON, E.C.

Plate XCIX.

CHIMNEY-PIECE REMOVED FROM THE HALL OF THE EAST INDIA COMPANY LEADENHALL ST., TO THE INDIA OFFICES, WHITEHALL.

A BEDROOM, BRIGHTLING PARK, SUSSEX.

"ST. IVES," MAIDENHEAD, BERKSHIRE.

THE DRAWING-ROOM, HORSHAM PARK, SUSSEX.

MARBLE CHIMNEY-PIECE FORMERLY AT 17 HANOVER SQUARE, LONDON.

AT 60 CAREY STREET, LINCOLN'S INN FIELDS, LONDON.

THE SALOON, HOUGHTON HALL, NORFOLK.

THE STONE HALL, HOUGHTON HALL, NORFOLK.

THE VANDYKE-ROOM, WENTWORTH WOODHOUSE, YORKSHIRE.

3 TENTERDEN STREET, HANOVER SQUARE, LONDON.

CHIMNEY-PIECE OF GRANITE AND ORMOLU AT 3 TENTERDEN STREET,
HANOVER SQUARE, LONDON.

THE DRAWING-ROOM, CHESTERFIELD HOUSE, MAYFAIR.

THE DINING-ROOM, CHESTERFIELD HOUSE, MAYFAIR.

The "seeming ease" of the figures has been produced, but in profile they appear to lean against rather than support the mantel. The grate seen in the illustration is by the late Alfred Stevens.

The library at Blenheim Palace, which was not completed until after the death of its architect, Sir John Vanbrugh, contains two fine chimney-pieces in the style of Isaac Ware. These are of two stages, the Doric order of black and white marble being used for the lower and the Corinthian of wood above, finished with an opened pediment with bust in the intervening space, and have their original grates.

Important examples of the trussed pilaster marble chimney-piece may be seen at Stourhead, Dorset, by Colin Campbell, and at Chiswick by Lord Burlington; the type was continued by, amongst others, Sir Wm. Chambers, whose work on *Civil Architecture*, published in 1768, contains designs, and by Jas. Paine as shown in his two large folio vols. published in 1783.

The double column chimney-piece (Fig. 175), at Horton Hall Northamptonshire, shows the correct adhesion to the orders practised by Sir Wm. Chambers, and the form of grate hardly visible in the illustration points to its belonging to the latter half of the eighteenth century.

Referring to chimney-pieces, Sir Wm. Chambers writes:[1] "I believe we may justly consider Inigo Jones as the first who arrived at any degree of perfection in this material branch of the art," also that "Mr. Kent has furnished good inventions of his own," and as to the makers of these he continues: "England is at present possessed of many able sculptors whose chief employment being to execute magnificent chimney-pieces, now happily much in vogue, it may be said that in this particular we surpass all other nations." Joseph Wilton, R.A., was a friend of Chambers,

[1] Sir William Chambers' *Civil Architecture.*

and Allan Cunningham in his life of that sculptor[1] mentions that "although he resisted the interference of architects in his public monuments he did not refuse to embellish chimney-pieces for the mansions built by his intimate friend."

The chimney-piece now in the Council Room at Burlington House was the Diploma work deposited by Joseph Wilton. This originally at Somerset House, was transferred to the National Gallery in 1836, and in 1873 fixed in its present position.[2]

When the mansion at Ditchley Park, Oxon, was built from designs of Jas. Gibbs the most important chimney-pieces came from the studio of Sir William Cheere.

Matthew Brettingham gives the names of the makers of the Holkham chimney-pieces; that in the statue gallery of veined and statuary marble with Sienna tablet was made by Mr. Pickford and that in the dining-room by Thos. Carter.

A family of Carters had a sculptural business in Piccadilly, an establishment, we are told by Jno. Carter, architect and antiquary, the writer of a series of articles in the *Gentleman's Magazine*, traced back to the time of Henry VIII, and "many of the principal chimney-pieces and monuments of that day issued from his house." He was referring to his father, Benjamin Carter, a sculptor by profession. Roubiliac, who came to London in 1720, worked in the studios of Carter and Cheere.

Subjects in bas-relief by John Michael Rysbrack have been referred to at Houghton Hall and Kensington Palace. He came to England in 1720 and had workshops in Vere Street, where he had a great run of business, died in 1770 and was buried in Mary-le-bone Churchyard. An inscription "I. Devall fecit et donavit" is cut on the chimney-piece in the Court Room at the Foundling

[1] *The Lives of Painters, Sculptors and Architects*, by Allan Cunningham.
[2] "Burlington House," by R. Phené Spiers in the *Architectural Review*, vol. xvi.

Hospital, and the bas-relief over it by Rysbrack was presented by the sculptor.

This work, executed in a cold veined white marble, is suggestive of the sepulchral monument in its most uninteresting form, and with others of the middle of the eighteenth century gives the impression that the figure subject had first consideration and that the design for its architectural setting was left to less capable hands. In the Council Room of the India Office, Whitehall, is a monstrous marble chimney-piece originally in the Directors' Court Room of the East India House, Leadenhall Street. "Persians," as the male figures are called by Chambers, of white marble stand on either side of the fireplace, an animal's skin festooned over a man's head enriches the frieze and a subject panel above the shelf represents the Company's connexion with the East. The sculpture is good but its architectural setting is coarse and ugly. The marble chimney-pieces in the eastern wing of Hampton Court Palace have this repellent character, both in design and material; the side supports in that of the Queen's Guard Chamber represent Yeomen of the Guard about 10 ft. high. This was the style which gave place to the work of the brothers Adam.

DESIGNS IN PUBLISHED BOOKS

Many books on architecture, furniture and decoration were published during the eighteenth century by architects, decorative artists, carvers and cabinet makers, in which designs for chimney-pieces appear as frequently as illustrations of the five orders, without which they were considered by their authors incomplete. Amongst these many of merit may be found, others show a tendency towards overloading with ornament. This remark applies to the designs of Abraham Swan in a work published 1745 called *The British Architect, or the Builder's Treasury of Staircases.*

FIG. 176. IN THE CHIPPENDALE STYLE.

The proportions and mouldings of his chimney-pieces are excellent, but both these and the mirror frames over are bedizened with the wildest French Rococo carving.

The mirror had become an article of fashion, and is generally shown in a frame which presents a mixture of French and Chinese ornaments; the rectangular lines in Swan's designs quite disappear and their place is taken by a series of C and G scrolls intermixed with birds and Chinamen. Sir Wm. Chambers after a visit as a young man to China published a book of Chinese ornaments and the style became the rage, if we may judge by the published books, but fortunately many of the designs exist only on paper. Among the exponents of Chinese taste were Thos. Johnson, 1758, W. and I. Halfpenny, and Ince and Mayhew, 1760. A chimney-piece in this style of carved deal from a house at Putney is in the Victoria and Albert

Museum (Fig. 176). Acquired doubtless, as illustrating a phase of design historically, it is included here for the same reason. It

FIG. 177. CHIMNEY-PIECE FROM "THE GENTLEMAN AND CABINET-MAKERS' DIRECTOR," BY THOMAS CHIPPENDALE, 1742.

savours most of the style of W. and I. Halfpenny and is probably as pronounced a specimen of Rococo work as could be found.

Thomas Chippendale tried his hand at chimney-pieces and in Fig. 177 from *The Gentleman and Cabinet Makers' Director*, published in 1742, we see an example in which the cabriole leg is introduced. This shows more of the French and less of the Chinese style, but in others the reverse is the case. It is easy to understand that a designer, having acquired dexterity in this style, would hardly know on paper where to stop, and although in Fig. 176 we see that the wildest designs were sometimes carried out, they are somewhat rare, and it is not by work of this kind that Chippendale is best known.

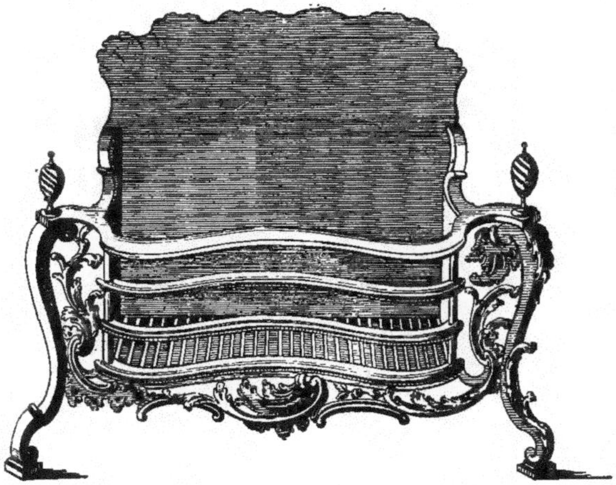

FIG. 178. A CHIPPENDALE GRATE.

The Stationers' Hall, Ludgate Hill, possesses an example which in its overpiece, Plate cx, exhibits this excessive use of scroll-work with birds in high relief as in Chippendale's design. The straight line which hardly finds a place in the overmantel is found in the mantel, which presents a good architectural character rather disfigured by the great size of the side scrolls.

FIREGRATES AND FENDERS

Chippendale gives a page of designs for firegrates in his book, from which Fig. 178 is taken. Other designs show an attempt at Gothic, such as is seen in some of his furniture.

Original grates of the first half of the eighteenth century

THE COURT ROOM, STATIONERS HALL, LONDON.

FIREGRATES, WILTON HOUSE, SALISBURY.

A. THE DINING ROOM. B. THE CORNER ROOM.

BASKET-GRATE, WILTON HOUSE, SALISBURY.

Plate CXIII.

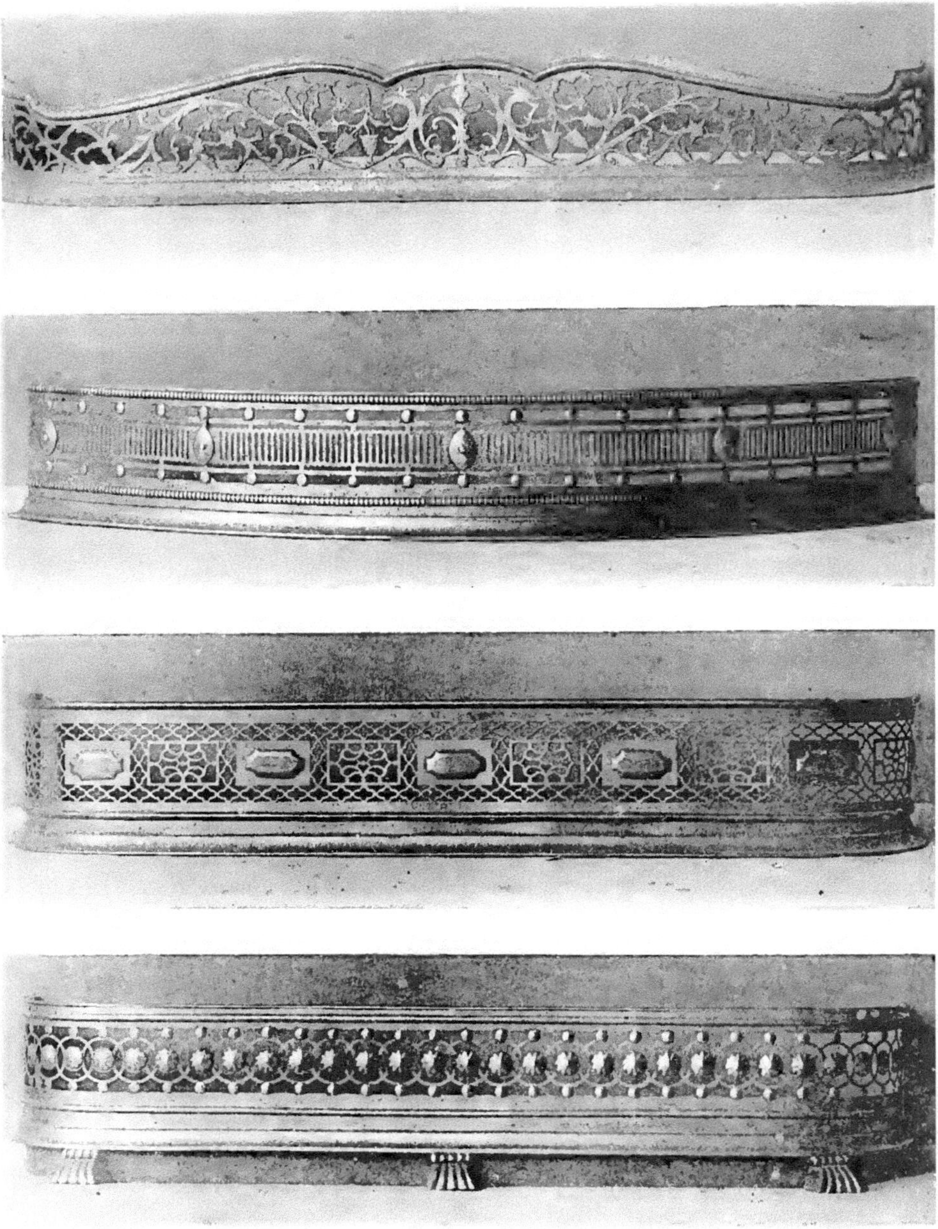

OLD STEEL FENDERS IN THE POSSESSION OF THE AUTHOR.

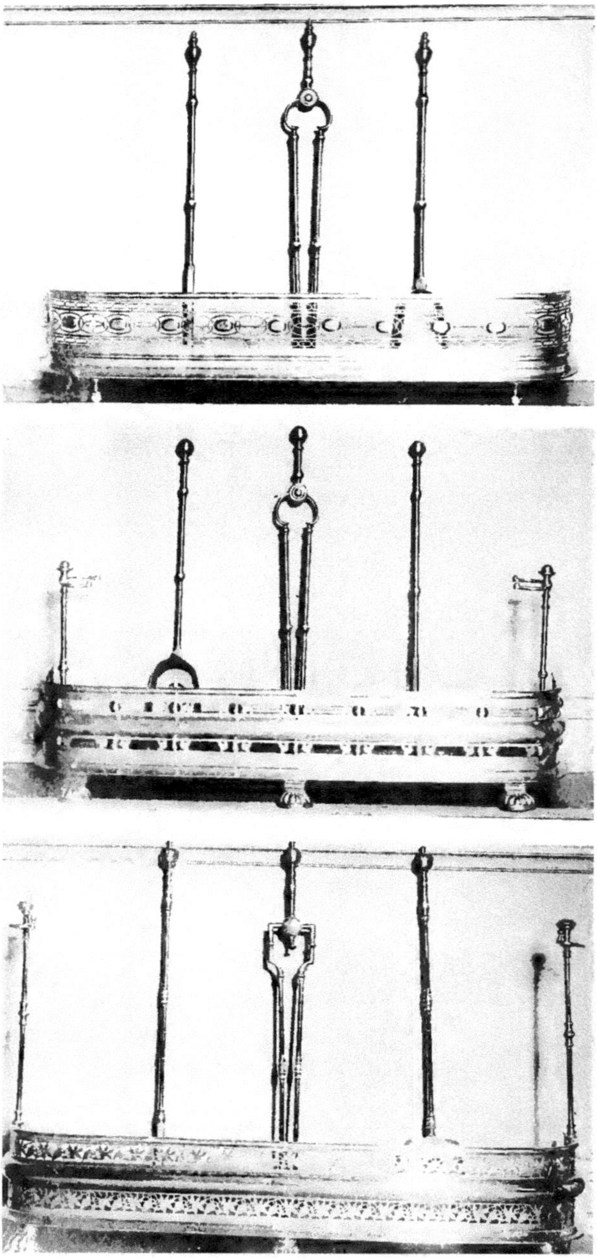

FENDERS AND FIRE IRONS IN THE POSSESSION OF THE AUTHOR.
A and B. OF STEEL. C. OF BRASS.

are comparatively rare, due doubtless to the fact that the use of andirons for burning logs had not been discontinued. The two from Houghton, shown on Plates CIV * and CIV * *, are probably original; others are at Wilton (Plate CXI). A quaint feature of the earlier grates is the quadrupled feet supporting the standards as in the upper of these, and a graceful one, the spreading scroll supports, set anglewise as in the lower. Spikes or balusters along the top fire-bars were for preventing logs of wood rolling off, and were abandoned when coal came into more general use. They were made of wrought iron and generally had pierced brass or steel aprons beneath the fire-bars.

FIG. 179. HOB-GRATE WITH ROCOCO ORNAMENT.

Fenders were made of both steel and brass. No. 1, Plate CXIII, is of steel saw pierced and engraved. With large marble hearths low pierced fenders without end were used, as in Plates CVIII and CIX. In others, taller ones of brass, with bands of stamped pierced ornament, bottom plates and feet. These usually had standards as rests for the fire brasses, shovel, tongs and poker, as in Plate CXIV. To strengthen the thin sheet brass large half round and other mouldings were devised with bead along the top and base moulding at the bottom, supported on cast feet, all suitable for hand cleaning, and presenting, with the helmet coal-scuttle, a very cheerful accompaniment to the fireside.

FIG. 180. AN ILLUSTRATION OF PIRANESI'S EXUBERANT FANCY.

THE ADAM PERIOD

Robert Adam, the son of a Scottish architect, after travelling in Italy for the purpose of studying classical architecture, returned to London, and commenced to practise in partnership with his brother James in 1758. When in Italy, he made the acquaintance of the Chevalier Piranesi, whose assistance he procured for supplying him with drawings of Greek ornament. Piranesi published a book of designs for chimney-pieces in Rome in 1769, one of which, described as for the Earl of Exeter, at Burleigh, is shown in Fig. 180. He appears to have possessed a most exuberant fancy, the subject given being one of the least fantastic, and although his influence may be found in Adam's work the latter made use of his designs with a wise discrimination. The talents of the brothers Adam were largely exercised in interior decoration and the chimney-piece with its accessories appears to have received their special attention, examples being found in the numerous buildings erected by them in the West End of London and in many country mansions. They also gave designs in their work published in 1773 and continued after, and left valuable folios of original drawings which are preserved in the Soane Museum. Two of these are reproduced in Figs. 181 and 182. By the admirers of the Anglo-Palladian style of the first half of the eighteenth century, Adams' work is spoken of disparagingly, from the small scale of the details of which it is composed; but what may be regarded as a demerit in external work, ceases to be so in chimney-pieces, which must necessarily be seen at close quarters.

Breadth of treatment and good proportion combined with delicacy of detail may be found in many Adams' designs, as in Fig. 181. They appear to have been uninfluenced by either the heavy marble designs of Kent or the vagaries of the Chippendale School which preceded them, and followed Greek rather than Roman work in the sections of their mouldings and selection of ornaments, making plentiful use of urns, vases, ram's heads and sphinxs.

Adams' chimney-pieces frequently ended with the shelf, the space above being treated with stucco ornament in keeping with the general decoration of the room. A medallion subject, either

FIG. 181. A DESIGN BY ROBERT ADAM IN THE SOANE MUSEUM.

painted or in relief, was used as a centre piece, in the production of which they had the assistance of Cipriani, Angelica Kauffman, or Antonio Zucchi, Joseph Rolfe doing the stucco work. In Fig. 182 we see the architectural lines carried up into the overpiece, but in many of the Adams' designs large mirrors are shown in gilt wood frames in the light style which is found in Pompeian wall decoration.

The beauty and refinement of the Adams' marble ornament is well seen in Plates cxv to cxix from 3, Stratford Place, W. In this they were assisted by Pergolesi, who, brought with others from Italy by Robert Adam, was an expert in Classical ornamentation as seen in his book of *Designs*.[1] The singular use of the ornamented discs at the base of the figures in Plate cxv is probably borrowed from Piranesi, and together with the incurving fluted base and the finish of the side tablets over the figures can hardly be commended.

The elongated vase in the pilasters of Plate cxvii which occurs in a lengthened form in Plate cxix is a characteristic Adams' feature. In the chimney-piece of the front drawing-room at 43, Portland Place, Plate cxx, they adopted the column treatment and beautified it with delicate carving and inlay, the detail of which may be seen in Plate cxxi to be of a very interesting character. The central tablet, with figure subject from the classics, is a typical feature, which was sometimes elongated to occupy almost the whole width, as in the ball-room at Stratford House, Fig. 188. This use of the order with detached columns for chimney-pieces, introduced and clumsily rendered during the Early Renaissance Period, and "according to the rules" by Isaac Ware at Chesterfield House, by Lord Burlington at Burlington House, and other early eighteenth century architects, produced in the hands of the brothers Adam works of great refinement and some originality, as seen in this example. Another, of which a drawing is in the Soane Museum, was made for the great chamber at Bowood, of statuary marble, in which the Corinthian order was used, and which well sustains their reputation as chimney-piece designers.

The grate seen in Plate cxx is of the sarcophagus type introduced towards the end of the eighteenth century, in which the

[1] *Designs*, by M. A. Pergolesi. Folio, London, 1777 *et seq.*

FIG. 182. A DESIGN BY ADAM.

THE FRONT DRAWING-ROOM, 3 STRATFORD PLACE, LONDON,

ENLARGED DETAIL OF THE DRAWING-ROOM CHIMNEY-PIECE
AT NO. 3 STRATFORD PLACE, LONDON.

WHITE MARBLE CHIMNEY-PIECE IN THE DINING-ROOM, 3 STRATFORD PLACE, LONDON.

DETAIL OF THE DINING-ROOM CHIMNEY-PIECE, 3 STRATFORD PLACE, LONDON.

Plate CXIX.

THE BACK DRAWING-ROOM, 3 STRATFORD PLACE, LONDON.

Plate CXX.

THE DRAWING-ROOM, 43 PORTLAND PLACE, LONDON.

DETAIL OF DRAWING-ROOM CHIMNEY-PIECE, 43 PORTLAND PLACE.

THE DRAWING-ROOM, 70 WIMPOLE STREET, LONDON.

THE DRAWING-ROOM, 77 HARLEY STREET, LONDON.

side supports of cast iron are enriched with brass claw feet and honeysuckle ornament.

In Plates CXXII from 70 Wimpole Street, and CXXIII from 77 Harley Street, we see examples of the Doric and Ionic orders respectively, with coloured marble backgrounds. The latter has its original firegrate or a contemporary one.

FIG. 183. AT HIGH WYCOMBE.

For chimney-pieces in less important rooms the brothers Adam used wood, ornamented with a composition composed of glue and whiting. The ornament was made by pressing the composition into moulds carved for the purpose in boxwood; and when both wood and composition were painted a rich effect was produced at much less expense than when of carved wood. Fig.

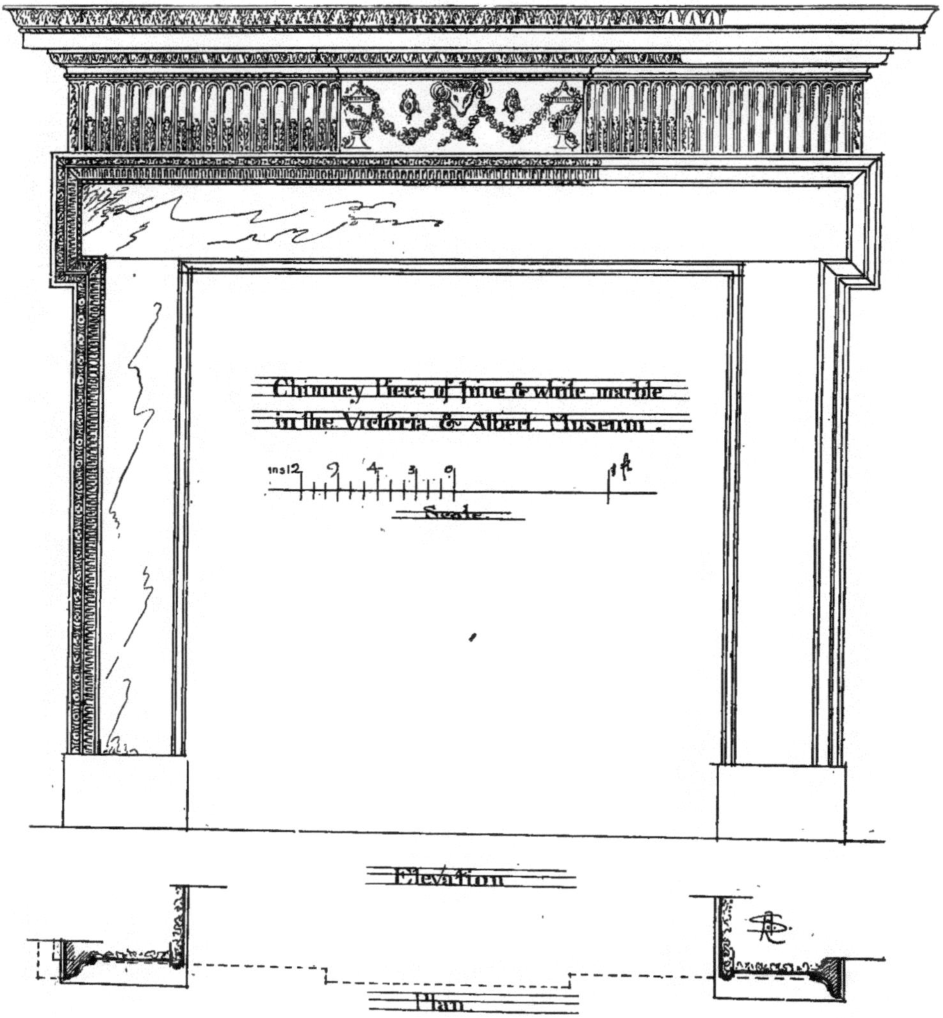

FIG. 184.

183, from a house at High Wycombe, Bucks, shows a typical example, the moulds of some of the ornaments still existing, with its original grate and marble lining.

This shows the thin mouldings so characteristic of the style,

THE MUSIC ROOM, COBHAM HALL, KENT.

AT HALTON HOUSE, HASTINGS. (Demolished).

and a distinct departure from anything which preceded it. Original examples show considerable refinement of detail, and are generally of pleasing proportion. The disadvantage of this material for enrichments is that they lose their sharpness by successive painting, and, unlike wood, cannot be stripped to their original form, as the solvent necessary for removing the paint softens the com-

FIG. 185. AN ADAM MANTELPIECE AT BUCKLEBURY VICARAGE, BERKS.

position also. Fig. 184 shows a mantel entirely of carved wood, with typical marble lining.

The Adam brothers had many followers; *A New Collection of Chimney-Pieces* by George Richardson, architect, published in 1781, follows their style very closely in "36 Designs Etched and Engraved in Aquatinta."

FIGS. 186, 187.
DESIGNS FOR GRATES BY THE BROTHERS ADAM.

Some of these designs are described as suitable for execution in "Scagliola," an imitation marble introduced during the Adam period by Italian artificers. These Italians are credited with introducing the art of inlaying marbles to Ireland, examples being found in Dublin. Coloured cements afterwards took the place of marble for the inlaid ornaments.

Fig. 185, from Bucklebury Vicarage, Berks, shows an original mantel and grate; the former, by comparison with his designs published in 1774, might be the work of I. Carter. His designs show the influence of Piranesi, and extend to grates as well as chimney-pieces, including the double semi-circle hob-grate.

Thos. Milton, John Crunden, Placido Columbani, and

FIG. 188. CHIMNEY-PIECE AND GRATE IN BALL ROOM AT STRATFORD HOUSE, STRATFORD PLACE, LONDON.

T. C. Overton, four working together, produced *The Chimney-Piece Maker's Daily Assistant* in 1766. Their designs cover much ground, but belong rather to the period preceding the Adams; Inigo Jones' and Wren's portraits figuring in the overmantels. They give a table showing "the true size that chimney-pieces ought to be" for the various sized rooms.

The Adams designed grates to accord with their chimney-pieces, as seen in Fig. 181, where the whole opening is enclosed. Very beautiful examples of their basket or detached grates remain at Drayton House, Northants, and designs for others in the Soane Museum, Figs. 186–7. That shown in Fig. 188 is in the Ball Room at Stratford House, London. The fronts of these were generally of bright steel with sometimes parts of brass, and both modelling and chasing were of a high order.

FIG. 189. LATE EIGHTEENTH-CENTURY GRATE OF SARCOPHAGUS FORM.

THE HOB GRATE.

The hob grate with double semi-circle, which was so largely used during the second half of the eighteenth century, figures amongst the Adams' drawings, but as it is found also in other books of design, we cannot necessarily attribute the invention of it to them. Many of these remain in bedrooms and the less important positions where they have had but little use. The fronts of them were of cast iron, and the bars of wrought. The designing of flat ornament for casting and blackleading was never better understood than at this period. Of the examples now met with many bear the name "Carron" on the front of the base mould, as may be seen indistinctly in Figs. 193 and 194.

The Carron Foundry in Scotland, founded in 1759, was one amongst others where these fire-grates were made, and designs for them were modelled by William and Henry Haworth, who

FIG. 190. A GRATE OF ADAM TYPE.

were students of the Royal Academy during the presidency of Sir Joshua Reynolds.

Three types are shown in Figs. 191–4: the double semi-circle, the double ogee, and rectangular cheeks; and another variety in Fig. 190.

These grates were usually placed in a square recess surrounded by a margin of stone or marble, composed of flat pieces set to

FIGS. 191, 192. HOB-GRATES OF THE SECOND HALF OF THE EIGHTEENTH CENTURY.

FIGS. 193, 194. HOB-GRATES OF THE SECOND HALF OF THE EIGHTEENTH CENTURY.

form a right angle or with astragal mould as in Fig. 184. In others a frame was cast with the front as in Fig. 195.

The recess above the hobs usually had a plastered back sloping up the chimney, and the sides were either plastered or lined with plates of fluted iron or Dutch tiles. No register door was used, and although found in modern practice liable to smoke, the short distance usually found between the fire-bars and the lintel to some extent prevented this. This tendency to smoke gave rise to the Bath grate, which was similar to these but the upper part was filled with an iron plate in which a semi-circular-headed aperture was made the same width as the bars. This, of course, did away with the use of the hobs, and by acting as a blower increased the draught and was a great waster of fuel. In some grates the semi-ellipse, as in the bars of Fig. 192, was reversed and completed above the fire.

The grate seen in Plate CXXIII was an advance in fireplace economy; a register door was provided, and as this was controlled by a pin and screw in the centre for raising or lowering the soot door the aperture could be adjusted to its position for regulating the amount of air passing from the room through it. The fronts of these grates were often of bright steel engraved, and had aprons of delicately pierced and engraved ornament with faceted rivets laid on, and fenders to accord with them as in Plate CXV.

Fig. 196 shows a form of pedestal stove in the Adam style, which was used for halls. The fire was lighted inside the door in the pedestal and the smoke, which ascended into the vase, was carried away by a circular flue pipe at the back.[1]

This and the accompanying illustration is a reproduction of a hand-drawing from what appears to be a contemporary book of designs used by the traveller for a foundry, in the possession of Mr. Fraser Walker.

[1] An existing one is shown in vol. xlvi, p. 19, of the Sussex Archæological Collections.

Plate CXXVI.

32 SOHO SQUARE, LONDON.

In the *Life of Josiah Wedgwood* by Eliza Meteyard we are told that Wedgwood and Bentley made panels for chimney-pieces, in which they were assisted by Flaxman and others. In January 1776, " Flaxman was at work upon large bas-reliefs for chimney-pieces." The tablets were made of their famous jasper body

FIG. 195. A HOB-GRATE.

FIG. 196. A PEDESTAL STOVE.

FROM OLD BOOK OF DESIGNS.

black basalt and unglazed terra-cotta, or ordinary biscuit. One of the first named forms the centre of a statuary marble chimney-piece in the mansion in Soho Square built for Sir Jos. Banks (Plate CXXVI). Their plan was to make the ornamental parts in these wares, and to frame them into wooden chimney-pieces. Wedgwood, who appears to have combined with his talents as a potter those of a business man, was desirous of selling these tablets in great numbers, and deplores the fact that the architects of his time would not take them up. Miss Meteyard says that Sir Wm. Chambers and others talked them down, "and persuaded the Queen that Wedgwood and Bentley's tablets were not fit for chimney-pieces." [1]

They were successful, however, in selling one to Sir Wm. Bagot of Blithefield, and he won the goodwill of Lord and Lady Gower and their architect, Brown, and was commissioned to execute a tablet and two friezes for their library, the subject of the frieze being Apollo and the nine muses.

Flaxman made designs for chimney-pieces, some of which form part of the Ionides collection in the Victoria and Albert Museum. Plate CXXVII is a reproduction of one of them, in which a rather commonplace design is enriched with delightful figure panels.

In 1762 Stuart and Revett published their book on Athenian Antiquities, which provided inspiration for buildings founded on Greek rather than Roman architecture. The chimney-piece came under consideration in the light of this new inspiration. That in the drawing-room of Litchfield House, No. 15, S. James's

[1] Well might Wedgwood write when he heard this:—"*Fashion* is infinitely superior to *merit* in many respects; it is plain from a thousand instances, that if you have a favourite child you wish the public to fondle and take notice of, you have only to make choice of proper sponsors. If you are lucky in them no matter what the brat is, black, brown, or fair, its fortune is made. We were really unfortunate in the introduction of our jaspers into public notice, that we could not prevail upon the architects to be godfathers to our child. Instead of taking it by the hand and giving it their benediction, they cursed the poor infant by bell, book and candle and it must have a hard struggle to support itself, and rise from under their maledictions." Letter from Wedgwood to Bentley, July 19, 1779.

Plate CXXVII.

DESIGN FOR CHIMNEY-PIÈCE AND FIREGRATE BY JOHN FLAXMAN, R.A.

IN SIR JOHN SOANE'S MUSEUM, LINCOLN'S INN FIELDS, LONDON.

Square, Stuart being the architect, has a frieze of figures attributed to Flaxman. This frieze instead of being in its usual position as part of the entablature is placed below it and immediately over the opening mould, and in line with the caps of the pilasters, thereby enabling greater length to be given to the latter without raising the shelf. One of the chief exponents of the style was Sir John Soane, and in Plate CXXVIII is shown a chimney-piece of white marble in his house in Lincoln's Inn Fields, now the Soane Museum, built in 1812. This and others by him show that he brought fresh ideas to bear upon chimney-piece design, treating it as a base or pedestal for other objects rather than as a complete composition. Its lowness may be considered due to the fashion of the day when mirrors were considered requisite for the dandies to see themselves in. This plate is interesting as showing with the chimney-piece a contemporary fire-grate, fender and fire-irons.

What little style is to be found in the marble chimney-pieces of the first half of the nineteenth century may be attributed to this Greek influence. During that time the fireplace reached its most degraded form; consisting of flat slabs of marble boxed together for jambs and lintel and another slab for the shelf, the refined mouldings occasionally met with were the only redeeming feature. This type watered down to its lowest dimensions, and made of foreign marbles became a trade article and continued in use until the architectural revivals of Queen Victoria's reign. In fire-grates the delicately modelled ornament of the Adams' work disappeared and coarse cast ornament took its place, as in Plates CIV and CXXV, culminating in the black ugliness of the semi-circular-headed register grate, which was in general use during the middle of the last century. For the best houses money was spent on finish rather than design; the fire basket was surrounded by ground and polished steel plates enframed with brass mouldings (Plate cx), in the production of which skill in manufacture was kept alive, and this to a great extent in the Sheffield district.

It will be noticed that a gradual contraction has taken place in the size of the chimney since the abandonment of wood in favour of coal as fuel, until we now find that a flue 14 by 9 inches or even less is sufficient to take away the smoke from a modern coal fire, and that the average fire area is not much greater; the problem is how to give architectural expression to this diminutive recess in the wall. Shall we construct it of stone or brick, as the wall goes up, like the Mediaeval builder, or rear in front of it a monument as was done in Queen Elizabeth's day? Shall we make the chimney-piece an enriched part of the wainscoting as in the reign of James I, or in the larger manner of Sir Christopher Wren which followed, or give it the form of a classical order whose entablature is the mantel-shelf, and construct it of materials of sufficient importance to stand alone? We may with propriety project the fireplace forward into the room as a chimney breast, for some thickening of the wall is necessary to take the flue, and thereby give it an importance which is increased by making the chimney-piece embrace the whole projection; but if we recess it into a chimney corner, we diminish its usefulness as a radiator of heat into the room generally and run the risk of producing an æsthetic sham, a fireplace within a fireplace.

We may employ for enclosing our fire space that erstwhile despised but most useful material, cast-iron, or discard it in favour of glazed bricks or tiles, which recommend themselves both for the ease with which they may be kept clean and for their valuable properties as retainers of heat.

There has been no lack of variety in fireplace treatment during the last fifty years, but rather too much haste to try all styles; too much eclecticism, and not sufficient time given to any to make real progress in any one. Although fireplace history tells us that this desire for change is not peculiar to modern times, certainly not since the Renaissance, we may learn from the past the benefit of greater continuity of effort in one direction. The Tattershall Castle fireplaces (Plates I and II) were the result of generations of masons improving little by little. The wood-workers of the Jacobean period produced a style, although not one of great refinement, as did also the carvers of Wren's day; and the beautiful fire-grates and fenders of the eighteenth century were the product of many years' work upon the same lines. Of the broken line of tradition, which only a heaven-born genius may ignore, we pick up the threads, but show no sign of binding them together again.

In the designing of a chimney-piece utility should be our guide, and in whatever style we work care should be taken to make the design proportionate in itself and in scale with the room in which it is placed.

As a subject for over-decoration in Mediaeval times a map or "history" was used, or "the chimney cloth set in a frayme of wood," to which the name chimney-piece was first applied; and Evelyn tells us that he bought "a very good chimney-piece of water colours by Breugel" for Sir Clepesby Crew.

For further choice we have the heraldic panel, the sculptured bas-relief, and lastly the mirror, which was not despised by the great architects of the past.

We have seen the over fondness of the Renaissance designer for the moral maxim, the portrayal of scriptural subjects and representations of the virtues and vices, the seasons and senses, and an occasional motto, but our modern works speak not at all. The continual presence of one's little joke in enduring stone, as when the late William Burges had a dropped H carved in the representation of the letters of the alphabet on his mantel-piece, must become trying at times; but a word fitly chosen and inscribed might add a note of interest to an otherwise dull work.

The increased interest shown of late in old examples has insured their preservation, which is so much to the good; but whilst it has improved the public taste, it has diverted the interest of patrons from modern works to the discouragement of those designers and craftsmen whom our schools of art have been fostered to produce. Sums far above the cost of production are often paid for old chimney-pieces, and sometimes for works of very doubtful merit. Surely this *réchauffé* of the works of our forefathers is a confession of weakness on the part of those who have to advise in these matters; either we have not suitable men to entrust with works of importance or, what is more probable, the necessary patronage is wanting. The splendid efforts of the late Alfred Stevens at Dorchester House remain, after a lapse of half a century, isolated examples of the work of an architect and sculptor combined in one man, in the treatment of the chimney-piece.

The fireplace is the natural focus of interest in the decoration of a room, and merits the greatest care and attention. How dull is a room without one! Other means of heating will produce the required temperature, but will not satisfy the artistic sense.

Mr. Rudyard Kipling has voiced the sentiment when he makes one of his characters when enchanted with an empty house exclaim, "That mantel—Orpheus and Eurydice—is the best of them all. Isn't it marvellous why the room seems furnished with nothing in it!"

Appendix

MECHANICAL INVENTIONS FOR THE IMPROVEMENT OF FIREPLACES

THE scarcity of coal experienced in the reign of Charles II, coupled with the smoke nuisance, set men thinking of remedies for both these evils; and from time to time various mechanical contrivances were brought out for economizing fuel by utilizing a greater proportion of the heat generated in an open fireplace, three-fourths of which it had been roughly estimated went up the chimney. On page 176 a fireplace constructed for Prince Rupert has been referred to, in which the smoke from an open fire was made to pass over the fire and to descend under an iron plate suspended in the flue before passing up the chimney at the back, thus being to some extent consumed. This is shown in Fig. 197. By means of a door the smoke was allowed to pass away when the fire was first lighted, and when burning clearly this was drawn forward and the aperture closed, when the smoke had to pass downwards under the iron plate. A hinged blower was used to assist the draught on first lighting the fire, and an opening was made in the under-back for the removal of soot.

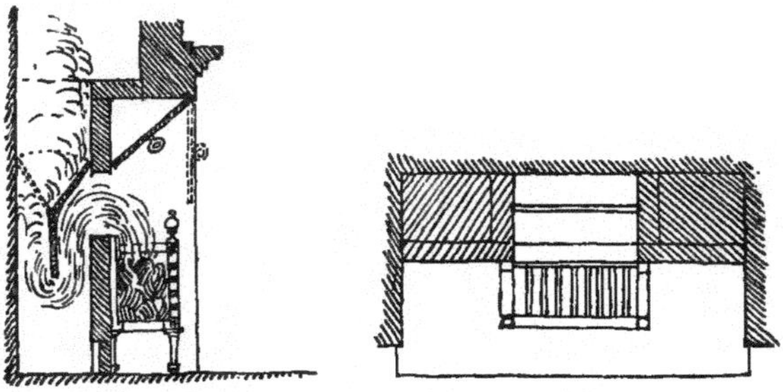

Section. *Plan.*

FIG. 197. PRINCE RUPERT'S FIREPLACE.

A treatise on this subject called *La Mecanique du Feu*, by Nicolas Gauger, was translated from the French and published in England by Dr. Desaguliers in 1716[1] who in conjunction with an architect named Du Bois started to manufacture the fireplace referred to in England; adapting it to the burning of coal as well as wood, for which it was first designed. The object aimed at was to utilize more of the reflected and conducted heat as well as the radiant heat given out by an ordinary fire on the hearth. On the principle that the rays proceeding from the focus of a parabola and striking its sides are reflected in a direction parallel to its axis, the fireplace recess was formed with parabolic curves, their vertices joined in the centre by a straight line which represented the ordinary length of a billet (Fig. 198). This parabolic back consisted of a hollow metal case to which fresh air from the exterior of the building was conducted. Entering low down on one side its too rapid passage was retarded by baffles, which diverted it from side to side until it made its exit from the opposite side near the top and passed into the room warmed. A cylinder with open section actuated by a spindle with a pointer to show its position enabled the passage of air to be closed or diverted. A "soufflet" or blower was placed in the hearth, consisting of a hinged flap through which air was brought for the double purpose of assisting combustion and reducing the draught from the room towards the chimney (*A*, Fig. 198).

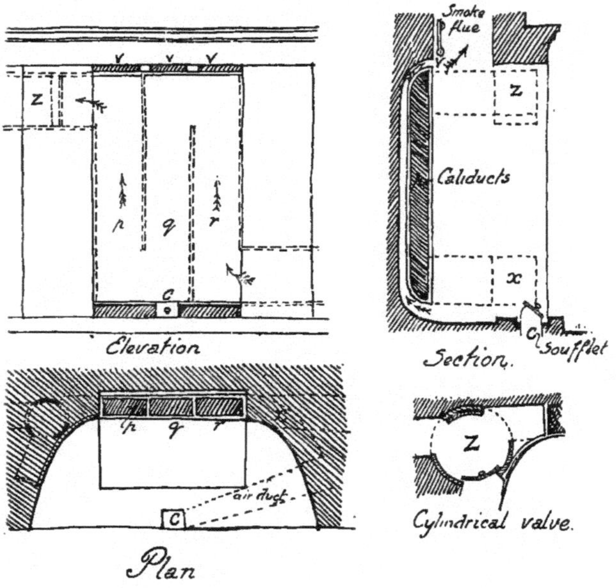

FIG. 198. THE "GAUGER" STOVE.

[1] *The Mechanism of Fire*, by Rev. J. T. Desaguliers.

This fireplace made enemies; a Mr. Wooster declared against it for "burning the air," and after the lapse of six and twenty years, when the indefatigable and ingenious Desaguliers looked back on this misfortune, he was touched with the sorrow of blighted hope, and said, "As I took so much pains and care, and was at some expense to make this management of air useful, I can't help complaining of those who endeavoured to defeat me in it." Bernan remarks: "This attempt to naturalize an improvement being bawled down, the English hearth fire was left in full possession of its ancient right of exhibiting an example of the manner of consuming the greatest quantity of fuel with the smallest possible return of comfort."

In 1742 Benjamin Franklin invented an open stove for the better warming of rooms, and at the same time saving fuel, as the fresh air admitted was warmed on entering, and this he called his "Pennsylvanian Fireplace." This stove combined the descending flue of Prince Rupert's fireplace (Fig. 197) with the caliducts of M. Gauger, and retained the soufflet or blower in the hearth (Fig. 199). The open fire burned on an iron hearth, and the smoke rose in front of a hollow metal back; passing over the top and down the other side it entered the flue by a curved channel at the level of the

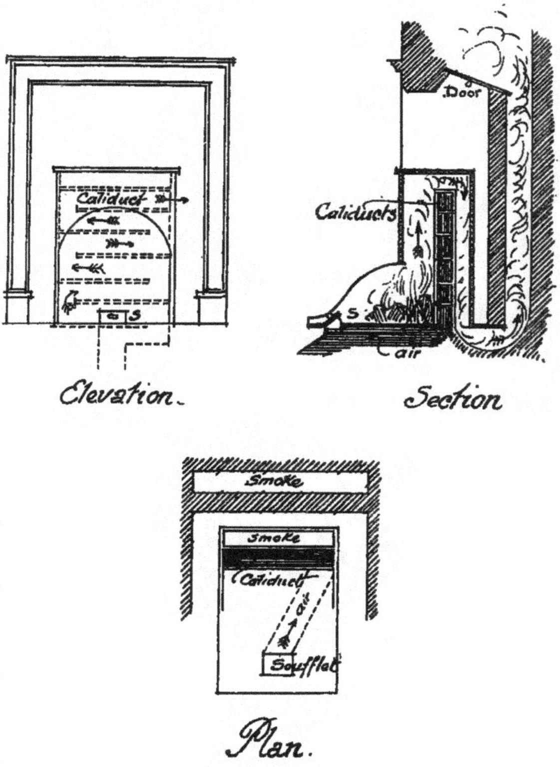

FIG. 199. DR. FRANKLIN'S PENNSYLVANIAN STOVE.

hearth. A register door was provided for the purpose of sweeping the flue and to enable any smoke to pass off which might escape on first lighting the fire. Fresh air was brought to the underside of the hearth and passed up through the caliducts, and meandering from side to side was warmed and discharged through a side opening near the top. The whole was encased in a metal frame which stood in the fireplace recess, insulated from the back and sides, and the surrounding air, warmed by contact, spread into the apartment. It was claimed for this stove that it effectually heated all parts of the room and that no draught was experienced by persons sitting round it; whereas in ordinary fireplaces they would often be burnt before and ready to freeze behind. Dr. Franklin writes [1]: "I made a present of the model to Mr. Robert Grace, one of my early friends, who having an iron furnace, found the casting of the plates for these stoves a profitable thing, as they were growing in demand. To promote that demand, I wrote and published a pamplet entitled *An Account of my New–invented Pennsylvania Fireplace*, etc." Dr. Franklin declined on philanthropic grounds to take out a patent for the stove, although offered one by Governor Thomas, and continues: "An ironmonger in London, however, assuming a good deal of my pamphlet, and working it up into his own, and making some small change in the machine, which rather hurt its operation, got a patent for it there, and made, as I was told, a little fortune by it." The ironmonger referred to was probably J. Durno, of Jermyn Street, Piccadilly, and the alteration made, in what he calls his "Machine Grate," was that he constructed his air chamber of brickwork, all covered over like an oven, except a narrow passage made of plate iron, with a register in it, and a handle into the room, so that it might be turned to such a degree as to either support or diminish the fire. He also adapted the stove for burning coal instead of wood. Durno's pamphlet was published in 1753, when he states that M. Gauger's fireplaces were entirely laid aside "on account of their expense." His own, which ranged from seven guineas for the smallest to thirteen guineas for the largest, appear far from cheap.[2]

These Pennsylvania Stoves are given in the *Stove-Grate-Maker's Assistant*, by W. Glossop, published about 1772.

[1] *Benjamin Franklin: Memoirs*, 1845.
[2] *A Description of a New Invented Stove Grate.* J. Durno.

It will be recognized that the objects aimed at by both Gauger and Franklin were sound, and were such as have since been worked out by many others in a more or less convenient form. The Pennsylvania Stove as seen in the diagrams presents difficulties of cleaning the smoke flues, which may, however, have been overcome in the stove itself, and being made apparently all of iron, including the fuel chamber, would soon wear out. The expense and inconvenience of providing a fresh air supply, especially to fireplaces in houses already built, has doubtless been a deterrent to the more general use of ventilating grates. This difficulty disappears in the case of a fireplace in an external wall, where it is possible by cutting a hole through and inserting a grating to bring air direct to the back of the fire. The benefits gained amply repay the extra labour incurred.

Rumford Fireplaces

It was towards the end of the century that the art of warming rooms by means of open fires received very valuable assistance at the hands of Count Rumford, who of all labourers to increase fireside comfort deservedly acquired the highest honour. The Count, a scientific man, devoted his talents to improving, by practical experiment, the form of the open fireplace, and to the preventing of "that greatest of all plagues, a smoky chimney." The diagrams on page 227 are made to show his recommendations applied to an ordinary modern brick fireplace of average size, 3 ft. wide by 14 in. deep, but any one interested in the subject is referred to the original Essays[1] and the diagrams accompanying them. By experiment he found that four inches was the best width from front to back for the mouth of the chimney or smoke passage, its length varying according to the width of the fire. The back was brought forward so as to be vertically in line with the back of the throat, or sloping inwards as shown—which was found to give the best results. For the purpose of breaking up the current of smoke in case of down blow, the back ended abruptly at *A*, and not sloping as shown by dotted line; and was carried up above the level of the soffite of the mantel or breast wall, which was rounded so as to present no angles to the ascending current. In setting out the plan the back of the fire space was made equal to the depth of the recess, and the cheeks built making an angle of 135° with the back,

[1] *Essays, Political, Economical, Philosophical*, by Benjamin Count of Rumford. 1798.

thereby dividing the width of the opening into three equal spaces. In the case of having to provide a larger fire without being able to extend the width of the opening, this angle might be reduced as shown by dotted line *B*; but in no case was it to be increased, as smoke would be liable to be wafted out into the room by any side draught if the cheeks were flatter. The side cheeks were carried up vertically to the same height as the back, and stopped off abruptly in the same way as the back. It will be noticed that the height of the opening shown is reduced to about 2 feet by extending the front breast downwards, at some inconvenience when the chimney arch is already built at a higher level, but to retain a greater height would be attended by a risk of the fireplace smoking.

For materials with which to diminish the size of the large openings prevalent in his day, the Count recommended the use of marble, fire-stone, or bricks and mortar covered with a thin coating of plaster, whitewashed, as white reflects more heat as well as more light than any colour.

He eschewed all metals for this purpose, pointing out that these being rapid conductors which readily absorb the radiant heat from the fire, less would be radiated into the room, and the air coming in contact with the hot metal would make its way quickly up the chimney. The use of metal was confined to the grate only. It may seem that the use of a register door, unless very carefully constructed to preserve the conditions laid down, would entirely upset the working of these fireplaces, and the Count would have none of them, considering them unnecessary. To get over any difficulty which might be experienced in sweeping the chimney, the 4 ins. shown being barely sufficient, a piece of stone about a foot wide, *C* in Fig. 200, was bedded dry on the brickwork, so that it could be removed easily by the sweep and replaced afterwards. An objection to this which might fairly be raised is that being out of sight it would be out of mind and its existence forgotten.

The Count remarks: "All twists, bends, prominences, excavations and other irregularities of form in the covings of a chimney never fail to produce eddies in the current of the air which is continually passing into and through an open fireplace in which a fire is burning; and all such eddies disturb, either the fire or the ascending current of smoke, or both; and not infrequently cause the smoke to be thrown back into the room." For this reason the parabolic curves of M. Gauger's fireplace must have met with his condemnation.

On the subject of smoky chimneys the Count says: "Those who will take the trouble to consider the nature and properties of elastic fluids, of air, smoke, and vapour, and to examine the laws of their motions, and the necessary consequences of their being rarefied with heat, will perceive

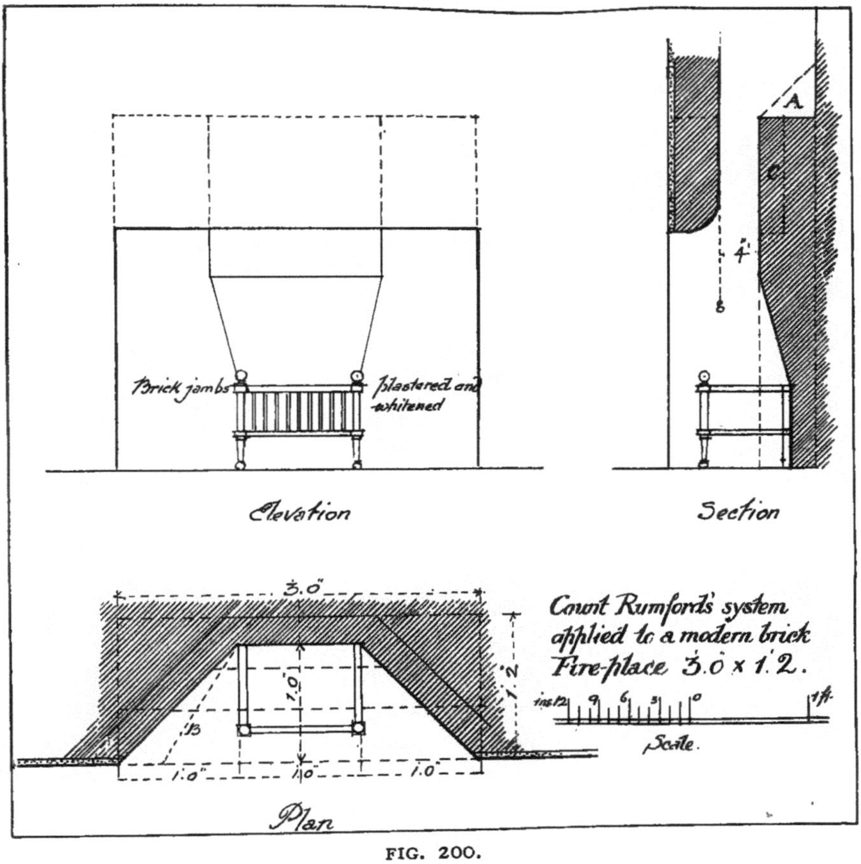

FIG. 200.

that it would be as much a miracle if smoke should not rise in a chimney (all hindrances to its ascent being removed), as that water should refuse to run in a siphon, or to descend in a river."

"The whole mystery, therefore, of curing smoking chimneys, is comprised in this simple direction—find out and remove those local hindrances which forcibly prevent the smoke following its natural tendency to go up the chimney; or rather, to speak more accurately, which prevent its being forced up the chimney by the pressure of the heavier air of the room." He continues: "In the course of all my experience and practice in curing smoky chimneys—and I have certainly not had less than five hundred under my hands, and among them many which were thought to be quite incurable —I have never been obliged, except in one single instance, to have recourse to any other method of cure than merely reducing the fireplace and the throat of the chimney, or that part of it which lies immediately above the fireplace, to a proper form and just dimensions."

The foregoing quotations from Count Rumford's essays show that his energies as a smoke doctor were almost entirely confined to the proper formation of the mouth of the flue, whereas at the present time this important part in fireplace construction is very frequently left to a bricklayer, who may or may not be experienced in stove setting. May not the presence of the variety of fearful and wonderful chimney-pots which disfigure the skyline of so many modern buildings be largely attributed to this cause?

Since the Count's day great improvement has undoubtedly been made in the form of the receptacle, stove or grate as it is called, in which the fuel burns, both as to the amount of heat given out and smoke consumed; the construction of flues is fairly well looked after, but the junction of the two for the successful working of the fireplace too often receives but little consideration.

The Count deplores "the enormous waste of fuel in London which may be estimated by the vast dark cloud which continually hangs over this great metropolis." We whose occupation ties us to London know that this is still with us, but speaking from experience, we may say that London is a much cleaner place that it was forty years ago; an improvement which may be attributed to progress in fireplace economy and the efforts which have been made up till now in the direction of smoke abatement.

INDEX TO THE TEXT

Note.—The References in Roman figures are to the pages in the Introduction. The Illustrations are fully indexed under Subjects and Places in the front of the book.

Butler & Tanner, The Selwood Printing Works, Frome, and London.

www.ingramcontent.com/pod-product-compliance
Ingram Content Group UK Ltd.
Pitfield, Milton Keynes, MK11 3LW, UK
UKHW041326280225
4809UKWH00035B/385

9 789389 525175